Frontier Stories

Frontier Stories

A New Mexico Federal Writers' Project Book

Compiled and Edited
by
Ann Lacy
and
Anne Valley-Fox

SUNSTONE
PRESS

SANTA FE

Sunstone books may be purchased for educational, business,
or sales promotional use. For information please write:
Special Markets Department, Sunstone Press,
P.O. Box 2321, Santa Fe, New Mexico 87504-2321.

Book and Cover design ~ Vicki Ahl
Body typeface ~ Palatino Linotype
Printed on acid free paper

Library of Congress Cataloging-in-Publication Data

Lacy, Ann, 1945-
  Frontier stories : a New Mexico Federal Writers' Project book / compiled and edited
by Ann Lacy and Anne Valley-Fox.
     p. cm.
  Includes bibliographical references.
  ISBN 978-0-86534-733-5 (softcover : alk. paper)
  1. Frontier and pioneer life--New Mexico--Anecdotes. 2. Pioneers--New Mexico-
-Biography--Anecdotes. 3. New Mexico--Social life and customs--Anecdotes. 4.
New Mexico--Biography--Anecdotes. 5. New Mexico--History, Local--Anecdotes.
I. Valley-Fox, Anne. II. Federal Writers' Project. New Mexico. III. Title.
  F801.L235 2011
  978.9--dc22

                         2009047707

WWW.SUNSTONEPRESS.COM
SUNSTONE PRESS / POST OFFICE BOX 2321 / SANTA FE, NM 87504-2321 /USA
(505) 988-4418 / ORDERS ONLY (800) 243-5644 / FAX (505) 988-1025

For Elise Rymer with deep appreciation.

Contents

District One: The Blizzard of 1889

District Two: Buster Degraftenreid as Buffalo Hunter / 111

District Three: The Snow Bride / 185

District Four: Stories of Old Time Happenings / 245

Acknowledgments

We wish to thank the New Mexico State Records Center and Archives, the Museum of New Mexico Palace of the Governors Photo Archives and the Fray Angélico Chávez History Library, Santa Fe, New Mexico for the use of their collections.

We are grateful to the Archivists at the NMSRCA for their able assistance with our research.

Special thanks to Estevan Rael-Gálvez, PhD, New Mexico State Historian.

Editors' Preface

Several years ago, while researching New Deal records at the New Mexico State Records Center and Archives in Santa Fe, New Mexico, we discovered a treasure trove of folders labeled "WPA 1936-1939." Inside were hundreds of manuscripts pecked out on old upright typewriters by New Mexico writers determined to make a buck by their wits while documenting some of the state's historical highlights. *Frontier Stories: A New Mexico Federal Writers' Project Book* is the second volume in a series featuring manuscripts culled from the Work Projects Administration files. The first book, *Outlaws & Desperados*, was published in 2008 to mark the 75th anniversary of the New Deal.

Between 1936 and 1940, the writers from the New Deal's New Mexico Federal Writers' Project collected stories throughout New Mexico describing a time that was beginning to fade into history. The experiences and exploits of settlers and earlier inhabitants of the New Mexico Territory during those territorial days after 1846 gave way to a less isolated and more modern era beginning with statehood in 1912. By the 1930s, NMFWP writers were recording the stories of old-timers who remembered New Mexico's vanishing past.

The stories in this volume offer many colorful first-hand accounts of life on the frontier. It is important to remember, however, that not all perspectives are represented in the WPA archives. For instance, as New Mexico State Historian Rael-Gálvez points out in his Foreword to this volume, the voices of Native Americans rarely show up in the New Mexico Writers' Project interviews. Given the limited representation of voices and perspectives included in the project, Rael-Gálvez wisely notes that readers should "be encouraged to read between the lines." Here we have accounts from Hispanos and Anglos who told their own stories or retold tales heard from earlier settlers in the Territory.

With a view towards authenticity, the writers of the New Mexico Federal Writers' Project attempted to capture each informant's particular way of speaking. As readers, we can sometimes hear in the language something of old New Mexico Territorial days as it may have been spoken at the time. As editors, we have tried to stay close to the original manuscripts and have changed punctuation and spelling only when necessary for readability and clarity. For the most part the manuscripts stand close to their original archival versions. We hope you enjoy them as an authentic expression of New Mexico's rich and colorful past.

About the New Mexico Federal Writers' Project

The Great Depression that came on the heels of the stock market crash of 1929 threw the country's financial institutions into chaos and put many people across the nation out of work. In 1933, President Franklin Delano Roosevelt inaugurated his New Deal administration, a comprehensive program designed to stimulate the country's economy while lending a hand to the unemployed. March, 2008, marked the seventy-fifth anniversary the New Deal.

At a time when many people were down on their luck during the Great Depression, the New Deal's New Mexico Federal Writers' Project (NMFWP) employed writers around the state to record the extraordinary history and lore of New Mexico. The Federal Writers' Project was one of a number of white-collar relief projects of the Work Projects Administration (WPA) that put Americans back to work. In addition to the Federal Writers' Project (FWP), the projects included the Federal Art Project, the Federal Music Project, the Federal Theater Project and the Historical Records Survey.

The New Mexico Federal Writers' Project was officially launched on August 2, 1935, under the direction of poet and writer Ina Sizer Cassidy. Between October, 1935, and August, 1939, a cadre of field writers wrote stories, collected articles, conducted interviews and transposed documents for the public record. Although each of the 48 states across the nation launched their own Federal Writers' Project, New Mexico was seen as geographically and culturally unique. From his office in Washington, DC, the national director of the Federal Writers' Project, Henry G. Alsberg, urged New Mexico project writers to emphasize the state's visual, scenic and human interest subjects in the project's guide, *New Mexico: A Guide to the Colorful State*: "Try to make the readers see the white midsummer haze, the dust that rises in unpaved New Mexican streets, the slithery red earth roads of winter, the purple shadows of later afternoon . . . ."

New Mexico field writers apparently felt a similar enthusiasm, as they created thousands of documents to preserve the state's vivid lore, scenic locale and colorful past for future generations. Their subjects ranged from the colonial New Mexico days of the 1600s and 1700s to the beginnings of the 1900s—from horse-drawn cart to car. Their many lively selections included firsthand oral accounts and remembrances by settlers and residents who lived to tell the story of New Mexico's Territorial days.

The NMFWP field writers plumbed the local resources in four prescribed areas of New Mexico, as follows: District One: Taos, Colfax, Union, Harding, Quay, Guadalupe, San Miguel, and Mora counties; District Two: Curry, Roosevelt, Lea, Eddy, Otero, Lincoln, De Baca, and Chaves counties; District Three: Santa Fe, Rio Arriba, San Juan, McKinley, Valencia, Bernalillo, Torrance and Sandoval counties; District Four: Socorro, Dona Ana, Luna, Hidalgo, Grant, Catron, and Sierra counties.

In 1939, under the WPA's reorganization, the New Mexico Federal Writers' Project became the Writers' Program. By that time, Aileen O'Bryan Nussbaum had replaced Ina Sizer Cassidy as project director. In Washington, DC, Charles Ethrige Minton supervised the New Mexico Writers Program until its closure in 1943. Through its tenure, the New Mexico program produced *Calendar of Events* written by project writers and illustrated by Federal New Mexico Art Project artists as well as *Over the Turquoise Trail* and *The Turquoise Trail*, two anthologies of New Mexican poems, stories, and folklore. A major achievement of the FWP was an American Guide Series publication entitled *New Mexico: A Guide to the Colorful State*, first published in 1940.

Project writers in New Mexico had a trove of sources to draw from and they mined them well. They collected tales from old-timers with a colorful heritage and culture—those who entered the territory as early explorers, diarists and journalists, poets and artists, miners, ranchers and cowboys, farmers and merchants, lawmen and outlaws, anthropologists and folklorists—the many travelers, *pasó por aquí,* who animate New Mexico history.

The efforts of the NMFWP field workers have left us a rich compilation of documents stored in various collections in New Mexico, including the New Mexico State Archives as well as museum and university collections. The Library of Congress in Washington, DC also holds copies of many of the manuscripts. Now, seventy-six years after FDR launched the New Deal, a substantial number of these readings have found their way out of archival folders and into print with the New Mexico Federal Writers' Project book series for the public's enjoyment.

Foreword

by Estevan Rael-Gálvez, PhD

New Mexico and its people are the heirs to a unique, complex and intricately woven past, the depth and breadth of which have only begun to be measured. Here, the past can reach through the layers as deep as time immemorial, to a moment when the rocks were still soft, imprints visible still of ancient migrations. The reach extends also to a time when legend itself motivated European movement across the ocean, a golden story that would make one Mexico into another, New Mexico. Indeed, in so many ways, the community we recognize today as "New Mexico" is one that has largely been imagined from the very beginning through to the present, a construction itself born from stories remembered, told and passed down from one generation to the next. What, when, where, how and who is remembered is a part of the imagining and, like the remembering and writing of histories generally, subject to power, position and even timing.

There are certain moments in time when oral stories are captured and indelibly inscribed on the pages of history. The stories compiled from the 1930s in this volume reveal how these stories about the past are often born from the delicacy and strength of memory. Indeed, the present tense of testimony is incredibly powerful, and the narratives of the 1930s oral history projects are particularly illustrative of this strength, delicately passing at an incredibly pivotal moment in time. In the face of the nation's economic depression of the 1930s, President Franklin Delano Roosevelt's New Deal Works Progress Administration (WPA) programs were established to implement work relief programs and affect a monumental government intervention which integrated a vast cultural infrastructure. One of several federal WPA programs, the Federal Writers Project (FWP) employed writers, teachers, photographers, reporters, editors, journalists, librarians and research workers. Thousands of writers were drawn from the relief rolls of every state, a project that placed bread on their table by having them listen to and record the creativity of expression of a nation.

Interpreted as both a play on the acronym and perhaps social critique of this intervention, in New Mexico the WPA became known as "El Diablo a Pie," the Devil on Foot. In New Mexico, under the Federal Writers Project, writers were instructed to interview older residents from various communities, identify cultural events that would be of interest to travelers, and catalogue the origin names of places. Focused on what was perceived as specific to New Mexico, a questionnaire was sent out to the writers to help shape their interview. The questions addressed the following topics: geographic features, costumes, language, customs relating to special family events (holidays, births, deaths and marriage, and dining), customs related to community events and gatherings (religious events, festivals, fairs), and stories and songs (including those about animals, witches, ghosts and tall tales). Very little is left of the process used to gather these firsthand accounts of the past; no record exists pointing to why certain people were chosen to be interviewed and why others were not chosen. We are left with questions and the stories.

But all history is subject to power relations, and these stories gathered in the interwar years are no exception. Indeed, the premise of "frontier" in the title of this volume is perhaps an entirely accurate portrayal of the Federal Writers Project as a whole. While "frontier" is a term literally meaning extreme boundary or limit and demarcating a settled and so-called civilized region from its opposite, it nonetheless inevitably premises a hegemonic expansionist perspective and implies an ethnocentrism. While it is true that the experience of Hispana/o New Mexicans are included both in this volume and in the project as a whole, the portrayal of this community is notably romanticized and contains singular perspectives rather than more inclusive and nuanced perspectives driven by gender, race and class. The marginalized, including indigenous peoples, are largely denied both voice and visibility in these stories and are indeed *frontiered*, due probably to the process

20

of the project as a whole. The voices of Pueblo Indian people are virtually silent. This is hardly surprising, since it was a moment when political participation was still being denied to indigenous peoples nationally and certainly within the state of New Mexico. Yet, while most of the stories are replete with the "threat and terror" of American Indians, the testimony of Louis Goforth is noteworthy: "The Indians were never as bad as they were pictured." These tellings reveal that storytelling is always about perspective. Lew Wallace, a New Mexico governor and storyteller/author, once wrote, "Every calculation based on experience elsewhere, fails in New Mexico." True though this often quoted phrase may be for some, it simply and erroneously presumes that one's experience is not based on being born and raised in New Mexico.

It is true that while an imagined and constructed New Mexican community emerges from the concerted efforts of boosters and others, the willing reader should be encouraged to read between the lines and recognize the more complicated narrative that actually contextualized these events, stories, places and people. The tricultural mythology that has so profoundly (and inaccurately) shaped New Mexico into a static portrayal of three cultures is revealed, if not fully deconstructed in these pages. In the stories that follow, a more nuanced picture emerges of New Mexico, where homesteaders arrive from everywhere in the nation, including Arkansas, Oklahoma, Tennessee and Mississippi. New Mexico is a global community, as is clear from stories drawn from migrations and the presence of individuals from Germany, Canada, Mexico and China. Wisdom may sit in the places that we settle and become a part of, but it is also infused with the places we leave behind.

One cannot grow wise by simply looking at the surface; one gains wisdom by uncovering the layers, which in essence reveal history to be deeply and profoundly contested and interconnected. It means thinking about what connects one site to the next as part of a complex and intricate network. Here, everything holds meaning: the flow of the *acequia*; the profundity of language; music and traditions that linger long after a note has been played; the dust rising ever so slightly from a dance danced for ages. Each act holds the memory of place, people and spirit. While the stories of the past may certainly be concealed within official documents, maps, census records, they are also intricately woven within place names, songs, prayers and carried in those seemingly fleeting moments, when someone who knows exactly where to cross a river though they have never crossed it looks at a ruin and sees a home full of laughter and tears; it is in the rise of the grito, *¡Tierra o muerte!* and the sentiment of the chorus, *volver, volver y volver*, and it is in the subtlety of silent stares, returning the gaze, turning the story around. I think of place names, of how some communities create the world in which they live simply by speaking about it, naming it.

As with all stories, there are gaps, and yet this compilation has something for everyone. Where there is context lacking, let this serve as an invitation for scholars, genealogists and students of every age to fill in the blanks. *Frontier Stories*, a compilation of ninety of the stories remembered and collected during this important time in history, provides openings, windows through which the reader can glimpse the past. While every story invites the reader to imagine the past, the stories sometimes also reveal the actual "story-telling occasions," including the excitement of Mr. Maes becoming an attentive listener, or the nearly one-hundred-year-old Mrs. Tafoya, who, when asked to remember, "her old face lighted . . . glad to have an audience for the thoughts that ordinarily surge through her mind." Remembering the past is subject to nostalgia and romance, but sometimes tragedy and pain as well, a reality revealed poignantly in an old-timer's remark to Mrs. W. C. Totty, "We who were alive don't like to think and talk of those days." These were stories collected and meant to be passed on, and the editors hope the reader will enter these stories and emerge with their own to tell.

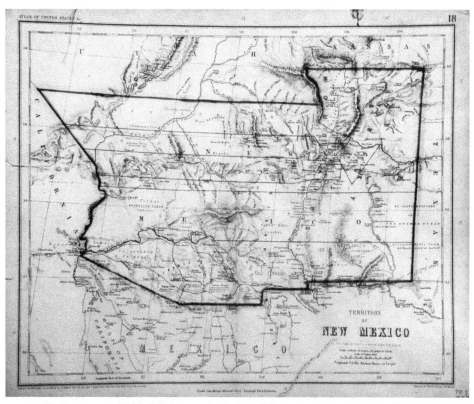

A. D. Rogers, A. Keith Johnston, *Territory of New Mexico,* Fray Angélico
Chávez History Library, Map Collection (78.9) ca. 1857

District One: The Blizzard of 1889

"That storm lasted for thirteen days.
When it was over there wasn't a cow to be seen.
They had all drifted with the storm."

From "The Blizzard of 1889" by W. M. Emery

Old Bank Building—Raton

by Manville Chapman

Located at the corner of Clark Avenue and North First Street in Raton still stands a small white frame, pitched roof building that was the first bank in the town called the Raton Bank and started sometime in the first two years of the town's existence, about 1880. On the sign of this bank, which stretched out over the sidewalk, a man was hung on the morning of June 27th, 1882 following a lurid night of murders and terror. The man's name was Gus Menser, a diminutive man who had been a gambler and had become drunk and troublesome. In an attempt to arrest him he was chased over the town and when cornered, wounded two men fatally. He was then jailed in the back end of the saloon until he could be taken to the county seat of Springer in the morning. However, friends of the wounded men planned to take Menser from Deputy Sheriff Bergen and hang him and in so doing a gun battle ensued in which Bergen and a locomotive engineer named Harvey Moulton shot each other to death. Menser escaped, was taken into custody by another deputy, and in turn was taken from the officer by an infuriated mob, which hung the little man from the bank sign without further delay. His body hung there until 8 o'clock the next morning, being cut down shortly before the arrival of a passenger train.

Source: *A Brief Community History of Raton* by Jay Conway, "Local Crimes and Tragedies" section.

Pioneer Story: Mrs. Mary E. Burleson

by Edith L. Crawford

The Government train we came to New Mexico in had about one hundred prairie schooners in it. Of this number four belonged to my family: My grandfather and grandmother Searcy, with six girls and one boy and my father, O. K. Chittenden, with my mother, brother Tom and myself. I was five years old and my brother was about one year old. My grandfather and my father sold their farms in West Port, Missouri. We brought all of our supplies along with us. We had our flour in barrels, our own meat, lard and sugar. We were not allowed to stop and hunt buffalo on the way out here on account of the Indians. The women made the bread out of sour dough and used soda. There was no such thing as baking powder in those days. The men baked the bread in Dutch ovens over the camp fires. When we stopped at night the schooners with families were put in a circle and the Government schooners would form a circle around the family wagons. In between the two circles they put the oxen and horses, to keep the Indians from getting them. Every night the men took turns standing guard. All the soldiers rode horses. Every few days the train would stop and everybody would get rested. The feet of the oxen would get so sore that they could not go without resting them every few days. When the train stopped it was nearly always at water and the women would do their washing. The train used cow and buffalo chips and anything they could find to burn. The men did all this as the women and children were never allowed far from the schooners on account of Indians. We did not milk our cow as she had to be worked along with the oxen. Our schooners had cow hides fastened underneath and our cooking utensils were packed in them. Our drinking water was carried in barrels and tied to the sides of the schooners.

We had no trouble of any kind on our trip but we were always in fear of the Indians as other trains had been attacked by them. Mr. Tom Boggs, the foreman of the Government train, told us that there was a band of Indians just ahead of our train. The Indians had attacked a train not long before we came along and had killed the people, stolen the horses and cattle and burned the wagons. We saw what was left of the wagons as we passed by.

We left the wagon train on Raton Pass. Enoch Tipton who was a relative of my grandmother and who had persuaded my grandfather and father to come out to this country, met us on Raton Pass. We stopped at his place in Tiptonville, New Mexico. Enoch Tipton had come out here some time before from West Port, Missouri. I do not remember just when he came or how he happened to settle here. Tiptonville is the same place as Mora, New Mexico is now. My father and grandfather farmed a year at Tiptonville. When we found our new home had dirt floors and a dirt roof my mother was so very homesick to go back to Missouri where we had a nice farm home. My mother had brought her spinning wheel with her. She spun all the yarn for our clothes and knitted all our socks and stockings. My father and grandfather made a loom for her and she made us two carpets for our floors to keep the baby from getting so awful dirty on the floor. We had brought some seed cane with us and my father and grandfather made a homemade syrup mill and made syrup, the first ever made in that country. The mill was a crude affair made of logs and drawn by a horse. The juice was pressed out with the logs and put in a vat and cooked into syrup. People came from miles around to see this mill.

We always saved all our beef and mutton tallow to make our candles. We brought our moulds from Missouri with us. We made our wicks out of cotton strings. We tied a large knot in the end of the wick, slipped the mould over the wick and poured the hot tallow into the mould. When the tallow got cold we cut the knot off and slipped the candle out of the mould. Our candle moulds were the first ones brought into that part of the country, and all the neighbors borrowed them to mould their candles.

My father moved to Ute Creek, New Mexico, in 1867, when they struck placer gold there, and he put in a country store to supply the needs of the miners and the people who were rushing to the gold strike.

A man by the name of Stevens, I can't remember any other name as everyone called him "Steve," wheeled a wheelbarrow all the way from the State of Maine to Colorado. In this wheelbarrow he had his bed, his clothes and his provisions. He did not stay long in Colorado. He came on to Tiptonville and put in a toll road to Ute Creek and my father took care of the toll gate for him. They charged $1.00 for a wagon, 50¢ for a horse and rider and 25¢ for a person on foot. Mr. Stevens made a lot of money as there were lots of miners rushing to Ute Creek looking for gold.

When my brother and I were old enough to go to school we had to walk three miles. My mother was always so afraid of wild animals and Indians. We had a big bull dog who used to go with us to school. When he got tired waiting for us he would go home and when it was time for us to get home he would come to meet us. We lived down in a valley and had to go over a big hill and he would wait for us on top of this hill. We went to school at Ute Creek. The Indians were not so hostile as when we first came to New Mexico. It was the Apache and Ute Indians who gave so much trouble and sometimes the Kiowas and Cheyennes would slip in and make raids on settlers.

My father was from Connecticut originally and came to West Port, Mo. and married my mother there. She was Elizabeth Searcy. I am the last one left of the Searcy and Chittenden families. By brother Tom died in Lincoln, New Mexico, in 1900. My brother Jap who was born after we came to New Mexico died in Gallup New Mexico, in 1926.

Source: Mrs. Mary E. Burleson, aged 78 years. Carrizozo, New Mexico.

The Blizzard of 1889

by W. M. Emery

"The worse blizzard I was ever in? Well, I'll tell you about it. It happened in 1889. I was working for the New England Livestock Company. This was a big outfit down by Ft. Sumner. When the government had moved the Indians away from Ft. Sumner and abandoned the Fort in 1868, they sold the improvements to Pete Maxwell. Then in 1882 they divided the land in forty acre plots and put it up for sale. Through a man by the name of Lon Horn, who handled the deal, the New England Livestock Company purchased a large tract of the land, and started one of the largest ranches in New Mexico.

"I had come to Fort Sumner in 1883 as a messenger, and in 1884 I returned to the Fort and went to work for this company as their foreman.

"I had made several trips up the Trail with cattle before this trip in 1889.

"It was in October of that year that we started to the new town of Clayton, with 2000 head of cattle, to put them on cars. Everything went fine until we reached the mouth of the Muerto. We made camp there for the night on October 30; the next morning, October 31, the storm hit just after daylight. We got the herd and started to the IL ranch, about seven miles up the Tramperos from our camp.

"Everyone has always laughed at me about my old lead steer saving our lives in this storm, but he sure did. We were traveling up a ridge between two canyons and not sure of the location of the IL ranch. We came to a trail leading down into the canyon to our left. I tried to turn the cattle down the ridge as it looked like it was a used trail. Of course we couldn't see very far in that storm. Well, this old steer—we called him John Chisum—just refused to go that way; every time I tried to turn him he started right up the ridge in the same direction we had been going.

"Finally I said, 'Well if you know so blamed much about where you're going we'll just follow you.'

"It wasn't ten minutes until the ranch buildings of the IL ranch appeared in sight. Old John sure knew where he was going. We would have frozen to death if we had gone the way I wanted to go. We were all dressed in our summer clothes; we hadn't expected a blizzard this time of year.

"There were ten of us slept in the bunkhouse at the IL's that night. We burned pine knots for fuel. It was forty hours before we were again on our way.

"We hadn't gone far when the storm started again; this time worse than before, with snow falling every minute. This was November 2nd. We finally made it to Clayton, and corralled our cattle in a pasture just north of town in Apache Canyon, near old Apache Springs. This pasture was owned by a man named McCullum.

"We went back to town to find a place where we could stay until the storm was over and our cars came. Here we found Jim Wiggins, who had a herd of three thousand head of cattle near Clayton. He had been waiting twenty days for his cars. The Carlisle Brothers from Moab, Utah, had trailed their cattle from Moab and were waiting for their cars. There were a number of other outfits there too; all together there were thirteen large herds of cattle waiting for shipment around Clayton.

"That storm lasted for thirteen days. When it was over there wasn't a cow to be seen. They had all drifted with the storm. There were 20,000 head of cattle left their herders and went south. Two hundred of the Carlisle cattle had drifted over the edge of the Carrizo mesa and died, but the rest went on to scatter over the plains from Clayton to the Canadian river.

"The snow drifted higher than the fences and froze solid, so my cattle just walked right out of the pasture and drifted down the canyon until they hit the MIT fence. They followed around the fence, and we found them the next year around Adobe Walls, and Cold Water, Texas.

"We were snow bound, but the C & S railroad got a snow plow from the Union Pacific railroad—paying $500.00 a day for the use of it—and cleared the drifts off of their tracks. The stockyards were so full of snow that it would have been impossible to have corralled the cattle even if they had been there.

"Reports began coming in from around the country; five men belonging to the Dick Head outfit, who were waiting with their herd for cars, south of Grenville—were frozen to death. A prominent rancher south of Clayton had been caught in the storm several miles from home, and had stopped at an isolated cabin for the night. After eating supper he started to go to bed, but as he threw back the tarpaulin he found a dead Mexican in the bunk. This man had evidently been out with sheep and had been so cold when he reached the cabin that he had gotten into bed rather than build a fire, and had frozen to death. This was too much for the rancher, who got on the horse and braved the storm until he reached home. Numerous other reports on the same order came in.

"When the round-up wagons went out the next fall—a year later—all of these cattle were gathered and were again brought into Clayton, this time to be put on the cars and shipped."

Source of Information: Potter, Colonel Jack. Story as told to the writer by Mr. Potter of his experiences in this historical storm.

His First Bear

by W. M. Emery

Ever since his fifteenth birthday, which had been in June, Bud had looked forward to the time when Juan would take him bear hunting, for the promise of this wonderful experience had been Juan's birthday gift to the boy.

It was a clear cool morning in late fall when, armed with an old cap-and-ball rifle, the boy and man started out on their hunt. Bud was riding his own little grey pony, and Juan was mounted on a big rangy bay horse.

They had ridden for several hours and were far from home when a huge dark object lumbered across their path, several yards ahead.

"A bear! A bear!" cried the excited boy, and started his horse on a run after the animal.

The Mexican's horse scented the bear, and it was all the man could do to ride him. When he had quieted the animal he turned to look for Bud, but the boy was nowhere to be seen.

When the bear saw the boy and horse coming toward him he tried to run away. With surprising swiftness he headed towards the canyons. Bud shouldered his rifle and fired; the bear stumbled, regained his feet and increased his speed. Bud thought he had hit him and was assured of it when he discovered blood on the trail. The bear had disappeared among the trees and shrubbery which grew along the rim of the canyon, but the trail of fresh blood was easily followed.

Without thought of danger to himself, or the whereabouts of Juan, Bud urged his frightened horse over rocks and through trees. As he came in sight of the canyon's edge he again caught sight of "Bruno" as he started down the canyon trail over the rim. Bud fired at him again, but had no way of knowing whether or not the bullet hit its mark. It was a down hill shot, and the sun had already set over the high hills across the canyon, leaving the lower slopes in a shadow.

Bud kicked his horse to a faster gait, but as he started down the steep slope his saddle turned. Bud jumped off from his horse and discovered that somewhere in the race he had lost his saddle blanket. He jerked the saddle off and mounted bareback. He sent his horse down the steep rocky slope as fast as possible, fearing every minute that the wounded bear had gotten away, and would maybe crawl off into a cave and die, then no one would believe he had ever shot a bear. And that would never do. He had to find that bear and take his hide home for proof.

When the trail became too rough to ride his pony over, Bud jumped off and tied his horse to a tree, then scrambled over the rocks to the edge of the cliff.

Far down below with his head hanging over a bank near a deep pool of water, lay Mr. Bear. At first Bud thought he was trying to get a drink, but the animal lay so quiet Bud decided he might be dead; still he could be playing possum. Bud debated for several minutes what would be the wisest move for him to make. He knew that if the bear was just resting, and he should go near him the bear could very easily tear him to pieces with one swipe of his huge paws. Then, too, if the animal was dying a very little movement might cause him to slide over the edge of the pool, and be lost forever. Bud crept cautiously down the trail, until he was again near enough for another shot. He took deliberate aim, and pulled the trigger. The bullet struck the bear in the head but the animal never moved. Satisfied that he was really dead, Bud hurried back to his horse and took one of his bridle reins from his bridle. He partly ran and partly slid down the trail to the bear. He fastened one end of the bridle rein around the animal's neck and the other securely around a nearby tree, to prevent the animal slipping into the pool.

Scrambling back up the hill he ran to his horse, and raced back across the mesa to find Juan. He could hardly wait to tell him about the bear.

The sun had set now, and the early twilight covered the top

of the mesa. On the top of a round knoll and silhouetted against the evening sky was Juan, searching in all directions for sight of the missing boy. As soon as Bud saw him he began yelling and calling and kicking his horse to a faster pace, until Juan saw him and rode to meet him.

"I got him, I got him!" yelled the excited boy, as Juan drew nearer.

"Oh, my God, boy, where have you been!" cried the frightened Mexican in his own language.

Words fairly tumbled out of Bud's mouth as he told of his wild race with the bear, and how he had at last killed him and tied him to the tree to keep him from falling into the pool of water until he—Bud—could get back. Like most people who have been under a nervous strain and find that there has been no ground for their fears, Juan became angry.

"You damn little fool," he scolded, "don't you know that bear could have killed you and your horse, too, if he had turned on you. Why did you run away from Juan? What would your mamma have said if anything happened to you when you were with me?"

Part of the reproof was in English and part in Spanish. Although Bud understood both languages he was too thrilled over his bear to be depressed by a scolding or frightened over what-might-have-been.

When Juan saw the enormous size of the bear he was as excited and proud as the boy.

At the back of the ledge on which the dead bear lay, was a large cave. Juan and Bud pulled and rolled the big animal into this cave. They gathered dry wood and soon had a good fire started at the entrance of the cave. This furnished them with sufficient light to skin the bear.

They had eaten their lunch at noon, and had nothing left for supper. It was ten o'clock before the bear was skinned. Juan sliced off several steaks from the carcass and fried them over the camp fire. Nothing he had ever eaten had tasted so good to the hungry boy as the greasy meat from the first bear he had ever killed, even though he did have to eat it without salt or bread.

After eating their fill the man and boy lay down near the fire to sleep. About two o'clock Bud woke up, deathly sick. He called Juan and told him he thought he was going to die, but wise Juan knew it was only too much bear meat without salt. Juan worked with him and finally got him comfortable, and he again dropped off to sleep.

When Bud awoke he was feeling better. The sun was shining into the canyon and Juan had the horse saddled and ready for the journey home. Across Bud's pony was thrown the greasy bear skin. The pony had put up a valiant fight to keep from carrying the hide of his hated enemy, but Juan had finally conquered it and thrown the dirty, smelly thing across its back. He had then put Bud's saddle on, and the pony was quietly waiting for his young rider.

The journey home was uneventful, but as the two came in sight of the house they could see Bud's mother and other members of the family anxiously waiting for them. They had worried all night as they had expected the bear hunters back for supper. But Bud was too proud and elated over his recent success to notice how worried his mother had been.

With arms waving, and the black bear skin flapping over the back and legs of the white pony, he made a grotesque picture as he ran his horse toward the astonished group in the yard.

For days the story of the bear was related over and over again. The tanned hide held a place of honor in the home for years.

Source of Information: Old Timers Story told by the late W. F. Sumpter, of his experiences in killing his first bear.

Old Timers Stories:
Indians, Firewater, A Night of Terror

by W. M. Emery

𝖂as there ever a more feared, hated, or terrorizing word in the English language than the word "Indian" was to the early settler of the United States? Almost from the time the Pilgrims landed on the rocky coasts of New England, to the final conquering of the Western States when the Indians were put on the Reservations, the cry of "Indians" was dreaded and feared by one and all.

The early pioneers of northeastern New Mexico were not to be exempt from trouble with the First Americans, in their last attempts to retain the soil which had belonged to their race since the beginning of time. For this country was the Indians' hunting grounds. From early fall until spring countless numbers of Indians made their camps under the protection of the friendly hills along the Dry Cimarron river; along the Corrumpa Creek; at the foot of the Rabbit Ears Mountains, on the Seneca Creek; and along the banks of the Tramperos.

Game was plentiful in those days; buffalo, deer, antelope, and wild turkeys covered the wide rolling prairies and deep, rocky hills of the canyons; there was water in abundance. Every creek was lined with such delicious wild fruits as grapes, cherries, plums, and currants. This was a veritable paradise for the Indian.

Occasionally bitter battles were fought between the Mountain Indians and the Plains Indians, over the rights to the hunting grounds, but all tribes continued to hunt there and make this country their winter home.

In 1824 the first wagon trains—those forerunners of civilization—crossed what is now Union County, searching for a shorter route to Santa Fe than the one then in use, which led up the Arkansas river, over the mountains near the present town of Raton, through Taos and on to Santa Fe.

The Indians were inclined to be friendly to these first trespassers on their land, but it is not to be said that the traders were entirely innocent of the trouble that soon arose between them and the Indians.

It was not long before the caravans were being attacked or a band of Indians would follow a caravan for miles stealing from them at every opportunity.

On one trip when the traders were returning home from Santa Fe, two young men rode ahead of the caravan and upon reaching the banks of a creek, lay down to rest until the rest of the party could catch up with them. When the caravan arrived one of the young men, whose name was McNees, had been brutally murdered by the Indians, and the other young man—"Monroe"— had been seriously wounded. They buried McNees on the bank of the creek, which afterwards bore his name; Monroe was taken on to Cold Springs, but died on the way and was buried there.

It was not until 1864 that the white men came into Union County and established permanent settlements. The first of these settlements was made about eight miles northeast of the present town of Folsom, and was named Madison, after its founder Madison Emery; a short time later a Spanish settlement was located about eleven miles west of there; this was called Los Alamos, or the Cottonwoods.

In 1865 the men who had founded Madison, went back to Cimarron—Maxwell—as the early settlers called the country around Cimarron—for their families. On the return trip two hundred Ute Indians followed the caravan and stayed with them nearly to the Dry Cimarron. Although they were not unfriendly, they were very annoying, especially to the women. When meals were being prepared they would come into camp and, lifting the lids off the cooking utensils, would grab out anything that they wanted with their dirty, black hands; especially if it was bread or meat that was cooking, they would eat it raw or cooked. Finally the women were compelled to get up at night and do their cooking after the Indians were asleep. One night the white families, under the leadership of Madison Emery, caught their mules and horses and slipped away from the Indians while the Indians slept. They traveled all night and all the next day. As they were nearing their destination they met a band of Arapahoes, who were looking for their old enemy, the Utes.

The Arapahoes were a Plains Indian, they were tall and slender and used a long bow and arrow, while the Ute Indian was from the Mountains. He was short and stout, and used a short bow and arrow.

Upon being told that a band of two hundred Utes were following the wagon train, the Arapahoes hastened on. They came upon the Utes not far from the Capulin Mountain, and after a big battle, succeeded in driving the Utes back to Cimarron-Maxwell.

An Indian's Revenge

About four miles below Madison lived a family of Mexicans. One day a party of Ute Indians rode up to the house and demanded bread, but were refused by the women of the house. A short time later a war party belonging to the same tribe came upon their family as they were gathering corn in the field. At sight of the Indians the family fled to the hills and escaped, with the exception of the woman who had refused the Indians bread; she was caught and stabbed in the shoulder. The Indians then went on their way without molesting any of the other settlers.

"Firewater" and Indians

The Indians often camped not far from Madison and their frequent visits in the village kept the inhabitants on constant vigil, for they had little confidence in their Red neighbors.

One day the village was visited by traders, and before nightfall drunk Indians were to be seen everywhere. That evening as Bud Sumpter—Madison Emery's step-son—started to the corrals to do the chores, he found an Indian on the ground behind the store, apparently asleep. Bud rolled him over with his foot and discovered he was dead; he had drunk himself to death on the white man's "firewater." Bud ran back to tell his step-father of his discovery. Mr. Emery knew that it would take a good deal of diplomacy to keep the Indians from going on the war-path, and massacring the whole village.

That night he called a meeting with the Chief and the headmen of the tribe. This nearly resulted in a catastrophe. As the Chief stepped quickly inside the door of the store (an Indian would never stand in a lighted doorway any longer than possible, for fear of being shot from the dark) a shell, which had accidentally been thrown into the stove with a pile of trash, exploded. The Chief thought someone was shooting at him, and it took a great deal of explaining on the part of Mr. Emery to persuade him that this was not a ruse to get him killed. They finally compromised by Emery giving the tribe the fattest beef he owned.

That night the Indians took their dead man into one of the rooms of the store building, and, laying him before the fireplace, worked with him all night to bring him back to life. They kept the body so close to the fire that the flesh was cooked from the shoulder and arms. The next morning the wife and mother of the dead man took his remains, and horse, and all of his property up the canyon, just east of the present Toll Gate Canyon, and building a scaffold, placed the blanket-clad body on top; the cooking utensils and all other property was hung on the scaffold, and the horse was lead underneath and shot, so that the dead Indian would not be without his horse and other necessary possessions in the Happy Hunting Grounds.

A Night of Terror

The men were all away from home on the round-up, and the women and children had gathered together at the home of W. P. Duncan. Shortly before sundown a cowboy rode up the canyon of the Dry Cimarron river, with the warning that the Indians were coming up that way. The women hastily finished the outside chores, and barricaded themselves inside of the rock house. Doors and windows were locked, and a pillow stuffed into a broken window; trunks and other heavy furniture were piled against them for added protection. Guns were loaded and placed in convenient places; fire and lights were extinguished and everything settled down to a night of watchful waiting.

The children were put to bed, but their sleep was often broken by a cry, as though even in sleep they sensed some unknown danger lurking near. The night wore on; stories of other Indian scares and attacks were told by the older women thus increasing the fear of the younger women and older children who were allowed to stay up.

The dogs began barking in the middle of the night, and nearby a coyote howled, but no moving object could be detected in the inky blackness of the night.

At last a faint golden glow appeared in the east; the chickens began to crow, a cow mooed in the corral; the barking of the dogs was quieted with the coming of a new day. In the early morning sunlight the brave little women, who had so valiantly guarded their loved ones through that horrible night, made coffee, and prepared breakfast. The chores had to be done and the work of another day started.

Under the windows were found the footprints of moccasined feet, but the main band of Indians had left the Cimarron Canyon by way of Cow Canyon, about five miles below and had left the scattered ranches up the river in peace.

That day the men returned home with the news that the Indians were only fighting among themselves. A Ute Chief, with his wife and daughter, had gone to Washington to visit the "Great White Father," and to sign certain Treaties of Peace with the Government. The other Indians had felt as though they had been betrayed, and had determined to kill the traitor. They had met the Chief and his small party of warriors, not far from the New Mexico-Oklahoma line and had annihilated the whole party. They had then traveled up the Dry Cimarron as far as Cow Canyon, and had left the Cimarron at this point.

1. Gregg, Josiah, *Commerce of the Prairies*, Published by Southwest Press.
2. Owens, T. E., Clayton, New Mexico. The story of the Emery's trip from Cimarron-Maxwell to Madison was told to Mr. Owens, years ago by Mrs. Susan Emery, grandmother of the writer, who was one of the women in

the wagon train. Gleason, Sarah Jane, Folsom, New Mexico.

3. Mrs. Gleason is the oldest resident of Union County, and was a neighbor to the Mexican woman who was stabbed by the Indians. She was also one of the women who stayed at the Duncan home when they thought the Indians were coming; she had been married just over a year at the time and had her tiny baby daughter with her.

4. Sumpter, W. F. Mr. Sumpter was the Bud of the story "'Firewater' and Indians." He was a brother to Mrs. Sarah Jane Gleason. Mr. Sumpter passed away March 21, 1935, at his home ranch near Folsom.

Early Settlements in Northeastern New Mexico

by W. M. Emery

The earliest settlement in Northeastern New Mexico was made in what is now Guadalupe County. This was made on what was known as the Anton Chico Grant, in the year 1822. This grant comprised 268,537 acres of land in Guadalupe County and 110,000 acres in San Miguel County. It was given for the purpose of encouraging settlement in the country.

The first petition which was filed with the "Tribunal of Independence"—presumably the ayuntamiento of San Miguel del Bado—was that filed by Don Salvador Tapia "for himself and sixteen others" for a tract of land on the Pecos known as Anton Chico, on the 24th of January, 1822. These people came into possession of the land May 2nd of the same year, the land having been granted to Manuel Rivera and thirty-six men.

These original petitioners and settlers were: Savador Tapia, Francisco Baca, Rafael Duran, Juan Sebastian Duran, Diego Antonio Tapia, Bernardo Ullibarri, Felipe Valencia, Luis Gonzales, Juan Cristobal Garcia, Tomas Martin, Juan Jose Martin, Miguel Martin, Jose Medina, Simon Estrada, Lorenzo Tapia, Mariano Aragon, and Jose Duran.

Another document dated March 3, 1834, which purports to be a distribution of lands at Anton Chico, by Don Juan Cabeza de Baca, states that the original settlers were driven off by Indians.

The name Anton Chico was a slang term, the place being properly known as "Sangre de Christo."

The boundaries of this land was as follows: "On the north, the boundary of Don Antonio Ortiz; on the south the ridge of the Piedra Pintada and the table-land of Guadalupe; on the east, the Sabino Spring, with Alto de Los Esteros, where the men were killed, and on the west, the Cuesta and the Little Bernal Hill, which is the boundary of El Bado."

The possession of this land was given in the presence of "thirty-six" settlers and that of two "aldermen"; Don Ventura

Truilla, second alderman. "The conditions were, among others, that the place selected should be common, not only for themselves, but for others who in the future should remove there; and also that the settlers be equipped 'with fire-arms and arrows and they shall pass muster upon entering the land and whenever the justice sent to them shall deem proper.' They cried, 'long life to the Independence' and took possession of the lands."

It was near this place that the Texas-Santa Fe expedition under McLeod came in 1841; at that time Anton Chico had a population of 600.

In the southeastern part of this district there were no very early settlements.

A man by the name of E. Bullard built a store between Fort Bascom and the site of the present Tucumcari, in the late sixties. This was called the Liberty Trading Post. Bullard lived near the store with his family. He built a seven room adobe house and put a shingled roof on it. This was a very outstanding residence at that time as most of the buildings could boast of nothing better than a dirt roof. The shingles were freighted from Las Vegas, a distance of over one hundred and twenty miles. Bullard later sold this store to a Mr. McCrone, who sold to Levi and Maurice Herzstein.

In the fall of 1894, the notorious "Black Jack" Ketchum entered the store and held up Levi Herzstein and robbed the store. Herzstein, with two Mexicans, attempted to follow Black Jack and capture him. Black Jack trapped them several miles from the store and killed—or thought he had killed—all three of them. One of the Mexicans, however, was only wounded and managed to get back to the settlement and tell what had happened. This man died only a few years ago.

With the exception of this store and a few Mexican Plazas, the only other settlers in what is now Quay county, in this early day, were the cattle ranchers. The first large cattle company to locate in this section was the Red River Cattle Company, which was called the S-Ts. Another company was the "Circle S" which was owned by Levi Straus. A man by the name of Austin and his partner owned the Quarter Circle Double A, which was located where the town of

Tucumcari now stands, in 1883. Farther east near the Texas-New Mexico line was the Howry Land and Cattle Company, whose brand was the H C W. They were located on Rana Creek. On the Canadian river just east of the present town of Logan, William Lackey had his ranch. He was one of the first to settle in this county. In 1882, Cristobal Garcia and some of his friends established a Mexican Plaza, called Cow Springs Plaza, between Rana Creek and the Canadian River.

A number of military posts were built in New Mexico in the early '60s, for the protection of the State. Among these was Fort Bascom, on the Canadian river. This fort was built in 1863 to protect settlers against the Comanche. It had accommodations for three companies. General Carleton was then in charge of the military forces in New Mexico. In 1865 there were three hundred and twenty-five men stationed at Fort Bascom. This fort was discontinued in 1871.

In the extreme northeastern part of the state another settlement was established, in 1868, by Benito and Jose Baca. This was located where Road Canyon Creek enters the Carrizozo, about four miles south of the Dry Cimarron river. These men came from Las Vegas with their cattle and sheep. On the ranch now known as the Carter Gillispie Ranch, the ruins of the rock corrals which were used by these people to hide their cattle and sheep when the Indians came through the country, can still be seen. These people lived here for ten years, selling their ranch in 1878, to Sam Doss, who was the owner of the original 101 Ranch, with headquarters on the Tequesquite four miles east of the present town of Kenton, Oklahoma. This ranch later became the Western Land and Cattle Company.

Bibliography:
1) Twitchell, *The Spanish Archives of New Mexico*. Vol. 1, p. 267, published by the Torch Press, Cedar Rapids, Iowa. New Edition published by Sunstone Press, 2008.
2) Potter, Colonel Jack. Interview to Mr. Emery, March 26, 1936.
3) Coan, Charles F. *A History of New Mexico*, published by the American Historical Society, Inc., Chicago and New York. Vol. 1, p. 378.

Raines, Lester   5/13/36 cl 215

THE OLD WINDMILL, LAS VEGAS PLAZA

At one time an old windmill stood in the plaza of Old Las Vegas which was used for other purposes than pumping water. In the 70's the windmill was erected to supply people and horses with water. In the then flourishing little cattle town of Las Vegas robberies and killings became so frequently a daily occurrence that a Vigilante Committee was formed. On March 24, 1882 they placarded the town with the following notice:

NOTICE!

To Thieves, Thugs, Fakirs and Bunko-Steerers,

Among Whom Are

J. J. Harlin, alias "Off Wheeler;" Saw Dust Charlie,
Wm. Hedges, Billy the Kid, Billy Mullin, Little Jack,
The Cuter, Pock-Marked Kit, and about Twenty Others:
If found within the Limits of this City after Ten O'Clock
P.M., this Night, you will be Invited to attend a Grand
Neck-Tie Party,

The Expense of which will be borne by

100 SUBSTANTIAL CITIZENS.

The Vigilante activity for a time bore daily fruit, and the inhabitants woke in the morning to find men hanging on the old windmill. The hangings became so numerous and the sight so ghastly that the owner of the windmill decided it was no longer serving its intended purpose and had it removed.

The frequent picture of forms dangling at rope's end from the old windmill had served one purpose, however; the raids and murders rapidly decreased.

SOURCE OF INFORMATION

Information supplied by John Murphy, whose grandfather was a veteran railroad engineer who settled in Las Vegas in the 70's.

"The Old Windmill," Las Vegas Plaza, Lester Raines, May 13, 1936,
NMFWP, WPA #227, NMSRCA

A Good Bluffer at the Toll Road

by W. M. Emery

"When Metcalfs had their Toll Road in Toll Gate Canyon, Bill Metcalf would throw the money he collected from the travelers on the road into a barrel behind the door. Every so often he would make a trip to Trinidad and stay until he had gambled and drank it all up before returning home.

"One time, when their oldest child was a tiny baby, he went on one of those trips and his wife asked me to stay with her. I was only about twelve years old, but I guess I was some company for her. She didn't like to stay alone. There were all kinds of people traveling on that road—Indians, traders, cowboys, outlaws; you never knew who was coming through.

"There was a big gate across the road that was padlocked to a post. The post was set a little way from the corner of the house, with enough room between that a person on horseback could pass through without any trouble.

"Early one morning a cowboy rode past the house and started through this opening. Martha saw him and went out to the gate to collect the toll. The cowboy refused to pay.

"'But you can't pass through here without paying,' she said.

"'Sure I can,' was the reply, 'I can go anywhere I want to over this country without paying.'

"'But this is a Toll Road,' explained Martha, 'and anyone passing through the gate has to pay.'

"'Not me,' laughed the cowboy, as he again started through the opening.

"I was standing in the door watching them, and Martha called me, 'Get me that six shooter, Cora!'

"The gun was lying on the dining room table. I ran out with it—although I was scared to death of it—and handed it to Martha. When the cowboy saw the gun he paid in a hurry, and, glancing back every few seconds he raced his horse down the canyon.

"After he was out of sight Martha and I had a good laugh.

"'I would never have the nerve to have shot him,' laughed Martha, 'but I sure did bluff him into thinking I would, didn't I?'"

Told to writer by Mrs. Cora Starr, Folsom, New Mexico.

Old Timers Stories: Captured

by W. M. Emery

Weary and hot after a long day in the saddle hunting horses, George Thompson lay down in the cool shade of the trees on the banks of the dry Cimarron river, to rest before returning to camp. Suddenly he was awakened with a start; as he sat up he found two big Indians standing over him. They quietly motioned him to mount his horse and go with them.

In a short time they rode into an Indian camp and the prisoner was taken before the chief. As he could not understand their language, he believed that they were preparing to kill him. After the chief had given his instructions to Thompson's two captors, they led Thompson to one of their tepees. He was given comfortable lodgings and a good supper, but was carefully guarded during the night.

The next morning he was allowed to enjoy a good breakfast before his captives again appeared, and motioned him to go with them. He was sure that this would be his last ride, but try as he would he could not conceive just what fate the Indians had planned for him. When he emerged from the tent he was surprised to find his own horse—saddled and bridled—waiting for him.

The three rode along in silence and Thompson soon recognized the trail as that which they had traveled the afternoon before, when he was being taken to the Indian Village. As they neared the spot where he had slept the day before, the Indians halted and told him—by sign language—to go on. Thompson rode on expecting every minute to be shot in the back; never daring to look back. When he had rounded a turn in the trail, and knew he was out of sight of the Indians, he kicked his horse into a run and returned to his own camp as fast as possible.

As long as George Thompson lived (and he lived to be nearly 97) he could never understand just why those Indians never killed him.

Indians and Sheepmen

The early settlements located in what is now the southern part of Union County and the northeastern part of Harding County were not troubled by the Indians as those along the dry Cimarron river or in the northern sections, although the Apache and the Ute Indians often came through the country on hunting expeditions, and frequently stole livestock from the settlers.

They often camped near the Georgia Plaza, a Spanish settlement located, in 1873, by the Garcia Brothers, and their families. The Indians often demanded mutton from the Garcias and their demands were complied with, but the Garcia finally told them they could not give them any more sheep. The Indians then began picking out the best lambs from the herds, and butchering them. They were warned by Stillus Gonzales—a brother-in-law of the Garcias—to quit stealing the sheep or he would kill them.

One day Gonzales was riding when he came across three Indians butchering one of their fat lambs. He fired at the Indians and one of them dropped down, the other two ran towards their camp. Gonzales found he had killed the one man; knowing the other Indian would try to get revenge, he immediately caught another horse and left the country.

The Indians followed him as far as the Rio Colorado, but they were thrown off the track. Gonzalez had entered the stream and had traveled about four miles up the middle of it before going ashore; a big rainstorm also came up and aided him in covering up his tracks. The Indians were forced to give up the chase. Gonzales stayed away from home for several months before the Indians left the country and he felt that it was safe to return.

The Last Indian Raid

On July 4, 1874 the Indians made their last raid in northeastern New Mexico. A band of Ute Indians broke away from their reservation and came across the northern part of the present Union County.

Three sheepherders were killed and several horses stolen near Los Alamos—or the Cottonwoods—about three miles above the present town of Folsom. Word of their coming was sent to the scattered settlers around Madison, and all banded together for protection, but the Indians never went down the river. They cut across to the Corrumpa creek and came to a cow-camp belonging to the Cross-Ell ranch. Here they killed two men, and stole their horses.

One of the men killed was Jim Roberts, an Englishman. Roberts had taken up a claim on the Dry Cimarron and later sold to the Hall Brothers, from Texas; this was 1871. This was the beginning of the famous Cross-Ell ranch. Roberts stayed with the Hall brothers and worked as a cowboy until his death.

In the spring of 1874, the Hall Brothers had trailed a herd of cattle to Denver. It lay between Jim Roberts and W. F. Sumpter as to who should go with the cattle and who should go to the cow camp on the Corrumpa. It was finally decided that Sumpter should go with the cattle, providing he would leave his pet saddle horse—a very fine animal—with Roberts. When the Indians killed Roberts they also stole this horse. Sumpter searched for the horse for a long time but could never get any trace of it.

Roberts and his partner both lie buried on the banks of the Corrumpa creek, near the spot where they were killed. This is now the site of one of the noted ranches and fishing resorts of this section, the Weatherby Ranch and Dam—formerly known as the James Ranch and Dam. Few who visit this resort know the story of the tragedy which took place here a little more than fifty years ago, or of the two isolated graves within sight of their fishing grounds.

1. Emery, Mrs. Roxie, Clayton, New Mexico. Mr. George Thompson was Mr. Emery's father and one of the early pioneers of the country, having freighted over the Cimarron cut-off of the Santa Fe trail, for the government. He passed away in Las Animas, Colorado, February 8, 1934, at the age of 97.

2. Garcia, Vicente, Clayton, New Mexico. Mr. Garcia is a descendant of the Garcias who located Garcia Plaza, now known as Miera.
3. Sumpter, W. F., late of Folsom, New Mexico.

Rumaldo Martinez: Indians on the Martinez Ranch

by Kenneth Fordyce

Along the abandoned and dismantled right-of-way of the Santa Fe Railroad between Capulin and Des Moines, there is a little station house with the name "Rumaldo" on it. The point on the railroad was named Rumaldo for Mr. Rumaldo Martinez, a prosperous rancher in the neighborhood.

Rumaldo Martinez left Mora, in Mora County, New Mexico about the middle of the nineteenth century and came into northern New Mexico to settle and make a home. The spot he chose was Ojo Pina Bete (Pine Springs) for there was an abundance of good water there, and water is necessary to make a good home especially in the flatlands.

The springs were just north of the Sierra Grande Mountain, the mountain with the largest base of any individual mountain in the world; no other mountain standing away from all others covers as great an area as does Sierra Grande.

There were many who envied Mr. Martinez the land with its springs for it was the choice spot of the section. There being no land office nearer than Santa Fe, Rumaldo Martinez had to make the trip to the capital city to file on his land. As was often done in those times, the size of the ranch was increased by having the young Spaniards who worked for Rumaldo each file on an additional one hundred and sixty acres, adjoining his land. Later he bought these properties and thereby acquired a sizeable ranch in a choice spot. It was a fine ranch with good water and was located on the Dry Cimarron branch of the Santa Fe Trail. Rumaldo had his own Catholic Church at the ranch. He ran his cattle on his own ranch land and his sheep grazed on the slopes of the Sierra Grande which was government grazing land. The ranch is still operated today by Rumaldo's son, Juan Martinez.

Rumaldo's grandson, J. Frank Trujillo, who has given this bit of history about the Martinez Ranch also tells of his grand-father's difficulties with the Indians.

Shortly after the arrival on Ojo Pina Bete, Rumaldo was grieved by the slaying of his brother by Indians, who continuously harassed the Spanish settlers to dissuade them from settling so far north in the Territory. Later, on a buffalo hunt, Rumaldo and his party routed a group of Navajos and captured a Navajo woman and her son, who were left behind by the rapidly retreating Indians. The two Indians were taken back to the Martinez Ranch and the woman was put to work for her new master. According to our informant this was the usual procedure in those first days of occupation and before slavery was abolished. Many ranches had captured Indians working on them.

It was just a little later that the Ute Indians who were warring with the Navajos at the time found out that there was a Navajo woman at the Martinez Ranch. They went directly to Mr. Martinez and demanded the woman. To save his own people from the Ute Indians, Rumaldo ordered the Navajo woman brought out. The Utes took her and killed her before the eyes of all present at the ranch. The Utes evidently did not know about the Navajo boy at the ranch. He had been hidden as the Utes approached and they did not learn of his presence and he was saved.

Rumaldo Martinez raised the Navajo boy as his own. The Indian youth grew up to be a fine, tall, manly fellow. He lives today in another state with his wife and sons. He was a Navajo but liked to be known as a Spaniard; he took as his name "Martinez."

It is interesting to note that when this Navajo boy was almost grown he took part in the Indian warring long enough to kill one Ute chieftain. Perhaps he figured that was in retaliation for the slaying of his mother by the savage Utes a few years before.

Informant: Mr. J. Frank Trujillo, Raton, New Mexico. Note: Mr. J. Frank Trujillo is a grandson of Mr. Rumaldo Martinez. Frank's mother was a daughter of Mr. Rumaldo. Frank was born, raised, and educated in northern New Mexico. He holds a position in the County Clerk's office in Raton at this time (1938).

Excerpts from Kenneth Fordyce letter of September 8, 1938: "Rumaldo Martinez" — The Indian lad who was raised by Rumaldo was called Callentano Martinez. He lived near La Junta but died about five or six years ago. He was a plasterer. His two sons live out in northeastern New Mexico new Des Moines. This additional information was secured by J. Frank Trujillo from some relative with whom he has recently been talking. He could not give me this when I talked to him before but referred me to his Uncle who lived 45 miles from here, too far for me to contact. However, he visited them and brought this bit to me.

"Sierra Grande Mountain" — I stated that the mountain had the largest base of any individual mountain in the world. Mr. W. J. Haggard who owns a ranch near the base of the Sierra Grande recently told me that about the mountain. I have visited in Des Moines on a dozen occasions and each time some old-time resident or even newer residents proudly tell of this distinguishing feature of their mountain. I called Miss Shuler at the Library today to see if I could get book verification on the point and she says that she has heard that point made about Sierra Grande many times but as yet has not found it in any book for me. It is an accepted fact in the neighborhood of the Sierra Grande and I had heard it so long that I never doubted but what it was a fact. I think it must be a fact and shall continue to search for verification and report when I have it. I am sure that I saw it stated in some book but cannot think just where now.

The Magician

by Kenneth Fordyce

"Chuck" Carsen lived with the Ute Indians in Northern New Mexico for over two months. Not by choice either, for the Indians had captured him and he had at least postponed a horrible death at their hands by resorting to his ingenuity. "Chuck" was quick-witted and a very quick thinker. He had come from Missouri in the early 1800's to locate a trail through the southwest to southern California. This was before the gold rush. In an Indian raid he had become lost from his companions and had been captured. He was a man of thirty or forty years at the time and very often his fast thinking had saved his life.

"Chuck's" magnifying glass, his hunting knife with a disappearing blade, and his fire-water in a bottle enabled him to show the Indians tricks which caused them to consider him a magician or super-medicine man.

"Chuck's" luck was not to last. The fire-water ran out and the other tricks became common-place after awhile, and the Indians began to wonder if they had been tricked. "Chuck" realized his disadvantage and at great risk and in an unguarded moment succeeded in making his escape. His capturers and guards were soon on his trail. He made his way down out of the canyon and followed along the fringe of the mountains where he could get water and where the wind was not so cold and headed for the Raton mountains hoping to make it safely to the Kansas country and on to safety.

Even as fast as he traveled, the Indians were a little faster and along in the evening he realized that the Indians were soon going to overtake him. "Chuck" traveled as rapidly as possible but his horse needed rest as he also did. It was difficult riding without a saddle! He finally decided that both must have rest and he dismounted and threw himself upon the ground.

He was numb with the cold and he decided to risk a very

small fire over which he could cook some meat, which he had brought with him. A fire was greatly needed to warm over before continuing into the night. To his great surprise his camp fire burned exceedingly bright and did not burn out as the fuel diminished, and as he watched, it got brighter and larger until he became alarmed for fear that its brightness would attract the Indians whom he knew were not very far behind him. He took his hunting knife and quickly cut some branches from the nearby evergreens and beat the fire out; as he worked he planned, for he was recognizing his great opportunity.

The fire extinguished, he sat down to wait the coming of the Indians and he did not have long to wait. The five big bucks rode late into the clearing and drew to a halt, surprised to see "Chuck" apparently waiting for them. He addressed them, and told them that they had doubted his ability of late and to prove that he really had great powers, like they had not yet seen, he would produce ever-burning flames, powerful enough to consume them at his command. Their silence spoke the doubts within their minds. So he proceeded to light the fire again. By digging around in the ground for a little it blazed twice as high as his head with no apparent source of fuel. The Indians were amazed and soon were begging that he refrain from harming them. They believed that escape was the best thing when a man had power like that, so they backed out of the clearing and galloped away southward and homeward, glad to be out of the clearing, and out of the clutches of the magician. This left "Chuck" free to warm by the fire which was too large now to extinguish, and to proceed on to safety and freedom.

For over 100 years the fire, fed by an underground supply of natural gas, has been burning, about a mile from the present site of Van Houten, New Mexico—a coal camp. Neither wind nor snow affect its burning, and at night it can be seen for miles, especially on nights when some new underground passage gives up a new supply of gas.

The ever-burning spot is about ten feet square. For thirty feet in any direction a few scratches on the ground bring forth the flames. Picnics are common to the spot. Individuals take delight in using a stick to write their names on the surface of the ground, watching the flames burn up through the ground, and continue for several minutes to spell out the letters in the fire.

Source: Alice Wade Bullock, relater.

Buffalo Hides

by Kenneth Fordyce

In those early days of the 1870's, they called him Martinez. In late years—after 1910—he was called Mr. Martinez, because he was getting so old. He signed his name N. Martinez. He was a respected and admired man by his many friends in Raton, New Mexico. The last years before his death, in 1931, he frequently related some of the most interesting stories of those early days with the Santa Fe Railroad.

You see, Martinez was about the first man to work for the Santa Fe in New Mexico. His job was to hunt buffaloes and get their skins for the company.

As the railroad built across Kansas and the south-east corner of Colorado, it employed men to bring in the skins of buffaloes which it made profit on, to help finance the extension of the railroad westward.

Long before they approached the Raton Mountains, they foresaw difficulties in making a crossing on that range. It would take time to figure out a way to surmount this obstacle. But the company sent Martinez on over the Raton Mountains with a crew of Spanish-American huntsmen to bring in buffalo hides.

Martinez and his men dropped down over the Raton Mountains with their wagons, horses and supplies. They found something which today is hard to imagine; over the flat lands of Northern New Mexico, and extending for miles south and east, there was an abundance of tall, thick grass. Of course, with feed like that growing on the New Mexico prairies, there would be herds of buffaloes.

(The droughts of the last twenty years, and the pasturing of stock on lands which were already nearly depleted of feed, has made these same fields almost barren today. But it has been a case of necessity and has been a condition which was beyond the control of men.) But as was pointed out there was at one time grass twenty-four inches tall, and it furnished abundance of feed for livestock and buffaloes in great numbers.

The work of the men was to ride into a herd and shoot down as many of the buffaloes as they could, all the while driving the herd in a circle so that the kill would accumulate in a more centralized spot. After they had slaughtered a great number of the buffaloes and the rest had galloped off, out of range, the next job was to skin the fallen animals. The skins were what they were after, of course, although they used the meat as food.

The skinning process, with so many animals involved, was a difficult proposition. This was overcome by a method of staking the carcasses to the ground and doing the first bit of the skinning by hand; then they fastened several hooks to the loose hide and fastened a team of horses to the ropes tied to the hooks. By driving the team away from the animal, the hide was pulled off very satisfactorily. In this way they could skin a great number of the buffaloes in a short time, which was what they were after.

These hunting operations took these men all over Northern New Mexico; they went as far east as Clayton, and as far south as Tucumcari, that is, where these towns are located today. Their next job was to deliver the hides to the Railroad. At first, they had to haul them into Colorado, to load them aboard trains for the east. Later, they only had to take them to Trinidad, Colorado.

In 1879, the Santa Fe extended its line into New Mexico. Their tracks across the Raton Mountains were built using the switch-back method because the ascent and the descent made more of a grade than their engines could handle. They would ascend to a certain point, then by means of a switch they would reverse and gain a higher point, switch again and once more proceeding forward, would rise that much nearer to the top of the mountain. This procedure would continue to the top, and be reversed for the descent on the other side. The tracks were extended through Willow Springs, and several miles farther on to Otero which was then the end of the line.

Mr. Martinez, and his men, could then deliver their hides to the railroad at Otero. This eliminated the hauling of the heavy loads across the Raton Pass, but the herds were scattering to the south, and to the east, as the hunters persisted in killing the animals.

In that same year the town of Raton sprang up near Willow Springs, when the railroad felt the need of shops and helping-engines at the south foot of the Raton Mountains. Thereafter, the hunters delivered the hides, which they secured in north-eastern New Mexico, to the railroad-headquarters in Raton.

Soon after, the scarcity of buffaloes caused Mr. Martinez to abandon the hunting of the animals over the grassy plains of Northern New Mexico, to take other work with the Santa Fe, and to make his home in Raton where he lived until his death.

Source: Robert Tomlinson—Raton, December 1936.

Pursued by Wolves

by Kenneth Fordyce

One winter evening back in the early days 'Old John' Fanning sat having a very friendly chat with his neighbor Tony Meloche at the T O Ranchhouse. The shadows had begun to lengthen and John decided that he had allowed enough of the afternoon to idle by, and that he had better take his quarter of beef and go home.

John had come down from his ranch in Johnson Park, which is on the south slope of Johnson Mesa in northern New Mexico, to the T O to get some meat. The T O Ranch is sixteen miles east of the present site of Raton. 'Old John' mounted his horse and the quarter of beef was tied on behind him. John Fanning started homeward. The evening wind was cold and a crust of snow lay all over the mountainsides. John had scarcely left the ranch property when the howls of a band of wolves told him that a pack was on the trail.

John spurred his horse to a faster pace but with the passing of every minute the howls showed that the wolves were getting nearer and nearer to their prey. Finally at the end of each straight section of the trail 'Old John' could look back and see the wolves gradually getting closer.

John Fanning still had several miles to go and those hungry wolves meant to have something to eat. This race kept up for some time.

The evening shadows had thickened until darkness was sinking down over the world. 'Old John,' hurrying ahead at top speed through the darkness, could hear the wolves closing in on his trail; he could hear not only their howls but their little yaps of excitement which they give when anticipating a kill. It was too much for John. He unstrapped the quarter of beef, let it fall to the ground where the wolves were upon it in a few seconds. This gave John Fanning time in which to put distance between the wolves and himself, and it enabled him to reach the safety of his home before the wolves again took up his trail.

Told by Ed Popejoy, Raton, New Mexico, February 11, 1937.

"Cump" Reed—On the Vermejo

by Kenneth Fordyce

The beautiful valley along the Vermejo River in northern New Mexico from Colfax through Dawson to the Colorado state line at one time promised to become the center of population in the northern part of the territory. Many families came and settled on those lands which promised so much; they worked, suffered, and sacrificed to make homes and establish a community. But it was not to be, it seemed. This is the opinion expressed by Mrs. Wills. She was a Reed and gave the information for this article.

There were the Dawsons, the Youngs, the Bracketts, the Meloches, the Reeds and dozens of others (all early settlers). They did their part but today the Vermejo Valley is remote from busy places; no railroad passes through that valley, no paved highways run across its fertile fields. The magnificent estate of the Bartletts, early residents, at Vermejo Park stands little used and the homes that have not succumbed already are now falling into ruins.

The Reeds held high hopes and dreamed of a home for their future generations when they settled there in July 1872. "Cump" Reed, as Mortimer Columbus Reed was familiarly known in the seventies and later in northern New Mexico and southern Colorado, came from near Otterville, Missouri. His wife, a native of Culpepper, Virginia was Julia Ann Frances Brannin. They were married in the late sixties (probably 1868) in Missouri. They had one son and one daughter. In 1870, Oliver Lee Reed was born in Missouri. In 1871, Lucy Reed was born there. Lucy was just sixteen months old when "Cump" Reed and a group (names not obtainable) came from Missouri to make their homes on the Vermejo River. "Cump" had served in the Confederate Army during the Civil War. He had four brothers who did not serve, but two of them had driven freighting teams back and forth to Fort Union in New Mexico from Missouri and they had come home with complimentary descriptions of southern Colorado and northern New Mexico on their tongues and finally persuaded "Cump" to come out and see for himself. The group had come to the Vermejo Valley. They were poor as they had lost almost everything during the war years. Pioneering was hard and discouraging. After a few weeks some returned but the Reeds and a few others stuck it out. A Mr. Dick Taylor stayed; Miss Ezilda Brannin stayed. (Miss Ezilda finally married Mr. Will Templeton and their home was in Cimarron where Mrs. Templeton is now buried.)

Two years after the Reeds came, the Jeff Young family from Otterville, Missouri came, arriving on August 25, 1875. Others came through in wagons and the Vermejo River valley took on an air of settlement. Crops and cattle were raised and the next few years saw times get easier for the Vermejo folk. They worked hard for what they had; they had earned their way. They firmly believed that in settling the land and making proper registration at the land office it would give them clear title to it.

Then after those first years of toll and hardship when a home had been established and some property and material assets had been gotten together, that notice from the Land Grant Office was sent out and posted everywhere from the Maxwell Land Grant with its many "Don'ts" and its warning to pay for the land or get off. Here again we see the results of that conflict between the Maxwell Land Grant Company and the settlers who firmly believed that they had a perfect right to their lands. The notices gave them just so many days to purchase their lands or sell out to the company at a price set by the company for all cattle and improvements on their places after which they could look for new homes. The "Don'ts" were posted conspicuously over the valley; it was "Don't use the water, Don't let your cattle graze company lands, Don't cut the timber for timber or firewood on company lands, etc. etc."

It was sickening and most discouraging. It meant that many homes must be broken up, many dreams forgotten, many lives crushed with disappointment.

Elkins P.O. and the other little villages which were beginning to spring up died away. The many homes and ranches, the nucleuses of what was to be the Eden of the northern New

Mexico district, were necessarily abandoned. The trouble lasted for months but finally terminated with the battle of Stonewall. Again we find a Reed, Oliver, the son of "Cump" taking an active part. He is a cripple but living today in California. He was only sixteen years of age at the time but relates very vividly the incidents of the battle of Stonewall, Mrs. Wills says. She has a letter, recently received, from her brother which tells all of these things which follow.

The squatters as they were known had gathered at Stonewall to discuss the situation and decided on a definite line of procedure. The officials of the company sent six armed deputies from Trinidad to Stonewall to serve papers and to suppress any action or uprising of the squatters. The deputies arrived at the hotel in Stonewall. The squatters became alarmed and overly excited over the invasion of company men—even if only six of them. They enlisted all of the squatters who could be summoned on short notice and started up in the street in a body to inquire the purpose of the invasion of deputies. The deputies became alarmed at the approach of such a large and apparently angry and determined group. One of them fired from a window of the hotel and shot and killed the leader, a Mr. Russell; that was the start of the battle of Stonewall. The firing continued all day; one other of the squatters was wounded seriously but not mortally. None of the deputies were killed. At the fall of night the squatters fired the hotel building in an effort to get the deputies out into the open, but the deputies escaped in the shadows of the building and fled down the river, back to Trinidad.

Oliver Lee Reed was in the group of squatters and took part in the battle in the street at Stonewall. He was not wounded but a bullet did strike the pommel of his horse's saddle and run down the leather to the stirrup and drop off onto the ground.

The decision of the Supreme Court of the United States finding for the Grant company left no hope for the people in Vermejo valley. It was pay or get out. Many had to go. The Reeds went back to Trinidad, Colorado to start over to make a home and eventually became well to do.

On February 13, 1896, Miss Lucy Reed married Mr. William Loren Wills whose family was from Peoria, Illinois, before it went to St. Louis, Missouri where Mr. Wills, the father, engaged in the steamboating business. Later he became a banker in the state of Kansas. It was from there that W. L. Wills came to Colorado where he met and married Lucy Reed. Mrs. Lucy Wills lives in Trinidad, Colorado today (1938). She has been pronounced incurable by many physicians who claimed that she had cancer, but that same fighting spirit of her father and mother which carried the Reeds through those first trying years in the Vermejo valley has enabled her to partially overcome her physical difficulties. Although she must use crutches she gets around very well and enjoys life and lives a life of hope and optimism.

Informant: Mrs. Lucy Reed Wills, Columbian Hotel, Trinidad, Colorado. This entire story was secured from Mrs. Wills including the information and the opinions expressed.

Foster's Log House

by Kenneth Fordyce

An old weather-beaten log house stands on the corner of Savage avenue and North Forth street in Raton, New Mexico; it is an interesting log house because of its age and construction, and also because of the story connected with the name of the man who built it.

Buck Foster built the house in 1880, out of logs which he cut, and he plastered the cracks with adobe mud. It originally had two rooms and Foster and his wife lived there for a time—about a year. Although today it is considered almost centrally located, at that time it was far out in the bushes which reached down from the wooded slopes of the hill where the goats grazed. Buck Foster had come from Texas and after the house was built seemed to live without working although he was constantly seen around the gambling halls of First street at night. He was said to be a "bad one," and a gun-man, who found New Mexico a safer place in which to live than his former home. For some reason or other, he was thoroughly disliked and had no friends in the little city of Raton, and that may have been why it was told that the woman with him was not his legal wife.

The reason why the Fosters lived in the log house only a few months was because Buck Foster met his death and Mrs. Foster disappeared.

A Mr. Blackwell, who managed the Captain George W. Cook Ranch five miles east of Raton, came to town with fresh vegetables during the garden season and peddled them, and it was on one of these visits to Raton that he encountered Buck Foster in the 200 block of North Second street. An argument over money—believed to be a gambling debt—took place in the middle of the block and continued as the men walked north to the corner of Second street and Savage avenue. At that point, Buck Foster who was very quick-tempered made an attempt to draw his six-shooter, and Blackwell, being quicker on the draw jerked out his pistol and shot Buck, killing him instantly.

A crowd of men gathered on First street at the sound of the shots and saw Blackwell fleeing to'rd the wooded slopes which now constitute the North side of Raton; they pursued the fleeing man without even finding out whom he had shot. After a search of an hour or so over the mountain slopes the men returned to Raton without capturing their man—Blackwell.

When it was discovered that it was Foster that Blackwell, who was well liked, had killed, the attitude of the crowd changed completely. The men agreed that it was a job well done and were inclined to send Blackwell a vote of thanks, but the man, thoroughly frightened by the crowd that had chased him out of town, had started out of the country. The crowd on the corner where the body still lay waited for someone to carry dead Foster to his home. No one volunteered. Finally two young Mexicans were hired to see that the man was taken home, adequately boxed, and buried.

Two years slipped by and a sheriff in northern Colorado sent word to Raton that he had captured a man by the name of Blackwell whom he understood had murdered a man in Raton. Local citizens sent word back that Blackwell was not wanted for any crime and was welcome to return to Raton whenever he wished.

The log house which stood on Maxwell Land Grant property was turned into a school house and Miss Ann McArthur taught school in it for some time. It was later used for a residence again when it was sold to private individuals. An addition had been made to the log house, but some day before too long it may be restored to its original size—two rooms—and turned into a museum or show place, for it is old and picturesque, and its 1880 appearance as it nestles there in its modern surroundings gives rise to memories of those early days when men gambled, built of logs, killed, and took the law into their own hands very often.

On the Vermejo in '74

by Kenneth Fordyce

Today at the age of ninety-two "Granny" Brackett, as she is lovingly called, lives in Raton, New Mexico with her daughters. Mrs. Brackett first came into New Mexico on June 10, 1874 and she, with her husband and their family, settled on the Vermejo ten miles above the present site of Dawson, New Mexico.

It is a pleasure to hear Mrs. Brackett tell of those early days, and of the many experiences which they had, that were so different from the way that they were used to living in North Carolina and Tennessee from whence they came.

That first house in which the Bracketts lived on the Vermejo was made of logs, and it had a dirt floor and dirt roof. There were many disadvantages to the dirt above and below. When it rained the water soaked the sod above and the dirt fell all over the house. The home-made beds sat right on the dirt floor—that is until one day when Mrs. Brackett was cleaning out the house and found young rattlesnakes under the provision box. The snakes would frequently crawl in through the log joints and enjoy a nap in the warm cabin. Very often this cost them their lives, though—when they were discovered.

When the Bracketts first settled in New Mexico, the Indians informed them that they could not stay as this was their land. "Go!" was the brief command from the Indian band whose home camp was only a few miles above the Brackett homestead. The Bracketts explained to the Indians that the Government wanted them out here to work for the Indians and to make bread for them. The Indians informed the Bracketts that they ate the meat that they killed and the hard-tack that their squaws made. However, they let the Bracketts stay and soon became friendly with them. During the first summer in New Mexico, three of the Indians came one rainy evening and stayed over night at the Bracketts'. During the evening they became very friendly and taught the children to count in Spanish. The Indians spoke Spanish for the most part; their own Indian language consisted of grunts and signs. At bedtime the braves rolled up in their blankets, curled up on the floor, and slept during the night.

The Indians were almost more of a problem after they became friendly. They would walk in unannounced and ask for something to eat; they usually asked for "bisc" (biscuit), and coffee. They were extremely fond of coffee. The Indians would bring Mrs. Brackett bags of pinions, and she was expected to serve them coffee and something to eat. She invariably did.

With Mr. Bracket gone often, it left Mrs. Bracket to cope with the Indians. Another reason that the Indians were unwelcome was because they invariably had several dogs with them and their dogs would run after the chickens and kill some of them. An old-time friend made a suggestion to Mrs. Brackett which she tried out with no little amount of success. When Mrs. Brackett saw the Indians coming soon after that, she tied up the heads of the children and put one of them to bed. The Indians entered without knocking as usual and soon inquired about the children and their bandaged heads. Mrs. Brackett mumbled something about, "virvuela" (Spanish— smallpox). The Indians were terrified, for they had a great fear of smallpox. They made a rapid exit. They did not return for quite some time either.

After the Bracketts had been on the Vermejo for a few years, the Government removed the Indians. These Utes and Apaches were given land in the Blue Mountains in Colorado. The Indians had been gone for months when one Sunday morning when Mr. Brackett was away on a hunting trip, Mrs. Brackett saw three of the braves coming across the stream to'rd the house. Dinner was cooked and she was putting it on the table when they came. They had come to confiscate Mr. Brackett's gun. When told that the gun was in use, they did not believe Mrs. Brackett and proceeded to pull the beds apart and ransack the house, looking for the gun. Failing to find it they decided that she had told them the truth and as they were in no particular hurry they sat down to the dinner on the table.

They scooped up the food with their dirty hands, eating their fill of the corn, beans, sour cream and soda bread, and drank cups of the delicious coffee. They stayed about an hour and then departed, taking their dogs with them. The food left on the table had had many hands in it and it was necessary to cook more food for the children and their mother. The Indians were not seen often after that day.

When the Bracketts came to New Mexico they brought school-books with them for their children. The first winter they taught their children from these books, one of which was the very familiar McGruffey's Reader. By 1875, a school was built on the Vermejo and very good teachers were kept at that school from then on to teach the children.

One of the Brackett boys, Will, decided that he wanted to learn to speak Spanish. He was allowed to go to live with a fine Spanish-American family for five months during which time he acquired a thorough knowledge of the language. This was when he was about ten years of age. In later life he was frequently employed as an interpreter.

Wild game and wild animals were thick in Northern New Mexico in those early years. On one occasion Mrs. Brackett found herself about one hundred yards from her door with her small daughter. Looking toward the house she saw between her and the door a catamount (wild cat). Its presence was particularly terrifying because of the fact that only a short time before that one of these animals had attacked a Mrs. Chase who lived on a ranch two dozen miles south of the Bracket home. She died from the effects of the mauling later. Mrs. Brackett instinctively grabbed up her baby daughter, clutched her to her breast, and backed to'rd the house, screaming all the while at the top of her voice. The animal was hungry, that is why it had come down so close to the house, but at the surprise attack of the screaming woman, the animal gave way and it caused him to delay just long enough for her to gain the safety of her cabin. The animal was tracked down and killed by Mr. Brackett and a neighbor within that week.

Frequently bandits going through the country stopped and

demanded food when they found the housewife alone. The bad-men had to be handled carefully. Mr. Brackett was on a buying trip in Trinidad, Colorado (fifty miles away) when one came in the late afternoon. After he had eaten his supper he made no move to leave. He evidently meant to stay all night. Mrs. Brackett was alone; she was scared. It was a delicate situation for the pioneer mother. Shortly before sundown, the arrival of a Mr. Robertson, a neighbor, saved the situation. He put his horse up, as though he were to stay all night, and suggested to the bad-man that if he intended getting far by nightfall, he had better be on his way. Not caring to enter into an argument which might mean more trouble, the man left.

Food was a problem in the early days. It was difficult to keep meat. There was an abundance of wild game and a good hunter could provide his table with plenty of meat. Keeping the unused portion of a deer was difficult. This was often accomplished by leaving the hide on the animal and cutting it back as the meat was used. It was not unusual for a hunter to come in home with five or six nice turkey hens, which were cleaned, and cut up and used until the supply was exhausted. The younger birds were often fried. In the flat lands there were quail too. Later the pioneers raised hogs and of course there were the cattle. When a cow or hog was killed and dressed it was the custom to give the neighbors a quarter, which was hung up in a tree until it was all used. This was a good way to keep meat especially in the winter time. Strangers and travelers would often come along and buy meat, venison, beef, or pork.

Another source of income for the pioneer housewife was the sale of butter, which sold for seventy-five cents per pound. In the summer time when the cows were producing, butter was put up in jars and milk was stored in a barrel. This could be used later in making sour milk and soda bread.

Potatoes were grown in abundance in the Red River Valley and other vegetables were produced in the district. There were some orchards. A few apples and peaches were grown but the plum crops were remarkable. Everyone had plums to eat and put up, and every table had a jar of plum-butter or plum-preserves.

After the Bracketts had lived above Dawson for about fourteen years, the Maxwell Land Grant Company claimed the land and the Bracketts had to move out. They secured a place twelve miles below Dawson from the company and there built their new home. This was fine land and they had a fine home. At the new place they had large orchards which produced delicious, select fruits.

Mrs. Brackett cannot understand why people do not visit more today. She relates how in those early years they were delighted to have town people or any friends (including neighbors who were left alone) come in and stay with them for a day, a week, or two weeks. They were always welcome at the western pioneer home.

Perhaps the phonograph, the radio, and the movies have taken something away from our lives as well as to add much to them. But there are few of us modern people who would trade that life of the pioneer with its glamour, its romance, and all the adventure of it, for the much easier, faster moving, and convenience-filled life of today.

Source: "Granny Brackett," c/o C. E. Donnelly, Raton, New Mexico, February, 1937.

AUG 1 4 1936
W. M. Emery
8/7/36 ol 156 words

A CHURCH AS A STABLE

It was in 1862 that a party of freighters returning east from
Santa Fe, made camp one night at the little village of Pecos. Some time
during the night a band of Apache Indians stole nearly every horse in the
outfit - about seventy-five head in all.

The next morning one of the freighters, Thomas Holland, insisted
that the men go after the Indians and try to get back their horses, but the
men, being strange in the country, thought it would be useless to try to
follow the Indians through that mountainous region. So Holland undertook
the task by himself. He trailed the Indians until night fell and they
camped. When all were asleep he slipped quietly into their camp, got all
the horses - and probably a few more - and returned to Pecos with them.

That night the horses were hidden in the Old Pecos Church. The
next morning the freighters resumed their journey unmolested.

SOURCES OF INFORMATION

Knox, Mrs. John , Interview to W. M. Emery, July 31.
Thomas Holland, in this story, was the grandfather of Mrs. Knox.
he was an old freighter on the Santa Fe Trail for a number of years.

"A Church as a Stable," W. M. Emery, August 14, 1936,
NMFWP, WPA #227, NMSRCA

In the Year 1893

by Rosario O. Hinjos

In the year 1893—I don't recollect the exact date—Tomas Martinez, a brother of Pablo Martinez, a merchant of Abiquiu, lived on his ranch, not very far from this town. He was herding his cattle and sheep, with him was his big yellow dog. About dusk one evening a man came to ask for a bite to eat; Tomas killed a lamb, roasted part of it, made some coffee, and gave him of the best he had there.

On the following day, a man living on a ranch a few miles distant saw a large yellow dog coming towards him, panting and tired. On seeing the man, he began to bark and howl, and taking hold of his trousers, would pull at them, then run a little distance towards the same direction from whence he came and seeing the man did not follow he would come back, and go through the same performance, until the man recognized the dog and realized that the dog was trying the best way he could to tell him something. So he followed the dog, who kept running ahead and looking back to see if the man was following until they arrived at Tomas's ranch. Then the dog led him to a pile of embers and ashes; and there sticking out from the coals and ashes was a human foot, and the charred remains of what he thought was Tomas.

He went to his ranch, saddled his horse, as Tomas's horse had been taken, and came into town to notify his relatives and friends. Relatives and friends went there and recognized the boot and sock as belonging to Tomas; after two men, Jesus Villalpando and Donaciano Chavez, cattle thieves, on whom the deceased had come upon as they were killing and roasting one of his steers and on the ashes—they found the remains of Tomas. The real murderers were apprehended, tried, convicted and hung on a little hill on the north side of town, and the man whom he had fed and whom all suspected as the culprit, although they never knew who he was, was cleared.

Biographies of Mr. and Mrs. Thomas O. Boggs

by Carrie L. Hodges

"Among those prominent and useful personages of frontier days in New Mexico, at the time of the American occupation, when the providence of New Mexico stretched its long, slow-moving arm from the Rio Grande to the Arkansas rivers, were Mr. and Mrs. Thomas O. Boggs.

"Mrs. Boggs, before her marriage in Taos, was Rumalda Luna, daughter of the wife of Governor Charles Bent by a former marriage. She was also a niece of Mrs. Kit Carson. It was Mrs. Boggs who held (a mere slip of a girl she then was, though possessing undaunted courage) the dying Governor of New Mexico, her stepfather, Charles Bent, the first chief executive of the territory after its capitulation to General Kearny in 1846, the night he was slain. I knew 'Uncle Tom' and 'Grandma Boggs,' as we affectionately called them in Clayton, intimately, in the 1890's, and have listened to the latter's story, not once but many times, of the uprising in Taos in January, 1847, of Governor Bent's murder, and the shocking details incidental to it. Mrs. Boggs' vivid relation of this cruel orgy is vividly recalled as I write, and her animation as the story progressed is repainted to the scene where 'Tomasito,' the Indian murderer, struck the final blow to the already wounded chief executive.

"Mrs. Boggs was seated on the floor of the room into which she, her mother Mrs. Bent, Mrs. Kit Carson and others had drawn her wounded stepfather after an opening had been made through an adobe wall, by the women aided by a peon, with no other tools than a spoon and a poker. The Governor had been wounded by arrows and scalped a short time prior to his removal to the new quarters, into which members of the family had dragged him. In his anguish, according to Mrs. Boggs, Governor Bent raised his hand occasionally to his bleeding, mutilated head and moaned, though made no outcry nor registered complaint against his assailants. Presently 'Tomasito' and others of the mob broke in the doors of the room in which the defenseless women and the stricken Governor Bent crouched in terror, and despite the prayers and petitions of Mrs. Bent and Mrs. Carson, approached Mrs. Boggs who was holding Governor Bent's head in her lap, and killed him. The plucky woman did not desert her charge. As she reached this stage of the drama Mrs. Boggs, who after fifty years brought again to life the painful incidents of the early morning of January 19, 1847, shaded her eyes with her hand and murmured, 'por Dios.' Then followed the recollections of the arrival of General Price's soldiers from Santa Fe, a trip made through deep snow and cold, of the bombardment of the church, Taos Pueblo, the surrender of the insurgents, and of their execution in Taos.

"Thomas O. Boggs, frontiersman and plainsman, who lies buried near his wife in Clayton, was no less illustrious in family and fortune than his wife. He was born August 22, 1824, on the Neosho river, Indian Territory, among the Osage Indians. His father was an Indian trader, and early governor of Missouri. Governor Boggs was twice married, first to Julia Ann Bent, sister of the Fort's Bent brothers, and second, to Panthea Boon, granddaughter of the redoubtable Daniel Boone. Thomas O. Boggs, great grandson of Daniel Boone, was her first child.

"Tom Boggs spent his boyhood years with his uncle near Independence, Missouri, whose business brought the young man into contact with the Indians from whom he learned their language and customs. By the native tribes he was known as 'Wank-po-hun,' or White Horse. Joining a Santa Fe wagon train in the 1840's, he reached Bent's Fort on the Arkansas river, where he was set to work. A boon friend of Maxwell's of Land Grant fame, and of Kit Carson, he joined these and other noted scouts in many active campaigns against the plains Indians. In 1844 Boggs visited Taos, and the next year with George Bent, made a trip into Mexico, returning to Bent's fort with a goodly number of mules, which the two had purchased. In 1846 Boggs was married in Taos to Miss Luna, and that same year, was at Bent's Fort again. In 1847 at the time of the uprising in Taos, Boggs was on his way from Santa Fe to Ft. Leavenworth, bearing dispatches relative to the Mexican war.

"In 1876 Boggs left Boggsville, near Las Animas, Colorado, driving overland to New Mexico, several thousand sheep. He located on the Tramperos. His ranches included those of the present Donald Carter and Jack Zurick. Later, he moved to Clayton, where a married daughter, the wife of a George A. Bushnell, resided. Here he died in 1894."

All data for this manuscript taken from *The Story of Early Clayton, New Mexico* by Albert Thompson, 1933, pages 61 and 62.

Turley's Mill

A Frontier Barony

by B. W. Kenny

Simeon Turley was a character unique even in a land and time of unique characters. An ex-trapper, he had found his way into New Mexico by way of the fur trade, met there a bright eyed senorita, married her and settled down.

On the banks of the Arroyo Hondo (north of Taos) he built a grist mill and a distillery, where he produced more than his share of the famous "Taos Lighting," a fiery whisky made from native wheat, much in demand among the trappers, traders, and Indians because of its potency.

The years passed and prosperity came to Turley. His rancho, in 1847, included numerous substantial buildings such as granaries, stables, and offices, as well as the mill, distillery, and his home, all arranged in a hollow square with a large front gate and a small postern gate leading to the corral enclosed within. Here Turley lived in feudal happiness. His door was always open to the wayfarer; his table groaned with the luxuries of the country and guests were ever welcomed to it. He was never known to refuse a request for financial or other assistance. Well did he merit the esteem in which his neighbors held him.

The morning of January 10, 1847, Simeon Turley, at peace with the world and entertaining a half dozen or more of his friends who had "dropped in" for a meal or two and copious draughts of the fiery "Taos Lightning," received ominous information. A rider sped by, halting just long enough to drop word that the Taos Indians had broken out, had raged through the Taos Village killing every American they met, and had murdered and scalped the Governor of New Mexico, Charles Bent.

Turley's face was grave as he heard this news, but so friendly were his relations with the natives that it did not occur to him that he himself might be in danger. But there was with him eight men who never took anything for granted. Not for nothing had those trappers fought Indians and grizzlies through the Rockies and shared a thousand adventures.

"Better bar them gates," was their laconic recommendation. To please his guests, Turley did so. The trappers lounged about, loose jointed and deliberate. One took his hickory cleaning rod and ran an oiled rag down the polished barrel of his rifle. Another whetted his hunting knife to razor keenness on the sole of his moccasin. They did not appear apprehensive but they seemed watchful, as men who expect momentous events.

Loud yells down the valley sent the men to the windows. Armed with guns, bows, and lances, a mob of Pueblo Indians and Mexicans could be seen coming toward the mill. It was the same crowed who had murdered Bent and other Americans at Taos that morning.

A white flag broke out at the head of the on-marching Indians. Shortly a small group came forward to negotiate with Turley.

"Have you anybody in there yourself?" they demanded.

"Yes," said Turley. "There are eight Americans here."

"Senor Turley, you are a friend of the Indians and of the Nuevo Mejicanos," was the next remark. "We do not wish to shed your blood. But every other American in the valley must die. Surrender these men with you, and you will be spared."

That was a hard choice which Turley faced. If he surrendered the trappers, he and his family and property would be safe. He did not hesitate.

"I will never surrender my house or my men," he growled. "If you want them you'll have to come and get them."

Events moved rapidly after that. At Turley's refusal, the Indians with wild yells, scattered and took to cover in the cedar and pinion brush and rocks which covered the hills on each side of the narrow valley. White smoke wreaths began to curl up from the shrubbery. Like a rattle of hail the first volley of bullets thudded into the sides and roofs of the buildings. From that moment to the end of the bloody episode there was scarcely a second when the leaden balls were not smacking into the house, seeking every cranny and crack and loophole as constant danger to the men inside.

The defendants knew exactly what they were about. No green-horns, these. Every man had been through a "scrimmage." Shifting their quids in their jaws, they moved deliberately to points of vantage. The windows were blocked with sacks of grain and chunks of wood, leaving only narrow apertures through which the trappers aimed their long rifles. Whenever a gun spoke from Turley's Mill, it generally carried death to an enemy.

Through the whole day the fight continued—tumultuous, noisy, and harmless on one side; slow and deadly on the other. Now and then a besieging Indian or Mexican fell among the bushes or rocks. By night several had been killed or wounded, while Turley's men had not yet suffered a scratch. The trappers knew they were scoring by the sight of the Mexicans down the valley carrying away the wounded.

Darkness came and with it a new peril—the enemy might attack under the cover of night. Sentinels watched, but the veteran mountain men wasted no lead in the gloom. Inside Turley's house they discussed the chances of escape, ran bullets, or cut patches. With Turley were Albert Tarbush, William Hatfield, Louis Tolque, Peter Roberts, Joseph Marshall, John Albert, and one other whose name is not recorded. All knew their chances of escape were almost nonexistent. But there was no sign of fear as they prepared in the morning to resume the fight.

During the night, the attacking party, which had originally numbered about five hundred, had grown greatly. They spent the dark hours shooting at the Turley house. And some time that night a few of them sneaked through the flume and reached the stables in the square. One of these adjoined the main building in which Turley and his men were barricaded. Here the Indians tried their best to break through the wall of adobe reinforced with logs. However, it resisted them so well that they gave up the effort.

All at once it seemed very desirable to the Indians in the shed that they get back to their friends. To do so they had to cross a wide stretch of open ground in order to reach the far side of the enclosure. Several had already dashed to safety when the trappers noticed them. The very next man who made the dash was a Taos chief. A rifle rang from one of the loopholes and the chief "drilled plumb center," dropped dead in almost the exact middle of the area.

It was an instinct with most Indian tribes to try to rescue the bodies of the fallen. As the chief dropped, one of his braves ran out and tried to drag the corpse to shelter. Again the rifle spoke. Surely the fate of these two should have warned the others. With heroic but futile resolution, the Pueblos tried and tried to get that body. A second rescuer, followed by a third, added their bleeding forms to the gory heap in the corral. And now three Indians worthy of the highest admiration, rushed out together. One took the chief's legs, another his head, and the third his body. Lifting together, they had started toward safety when three puffs of blue smoke sprang out from Turley's house and all three collapsed in a pile.

As the bloody wreck fell, a single, concerted yell of rage rose from the attackers, an instant later the heaviest volley they had so far discharged, blazed at the house. For the first time two of the trappers were hit. One, shot through the loins, suffered excruciating agony. He was carried to the still-house and laid on the grain in one of the bins, the softest bed which could be found for him. Both wounded men died soon.

The shooting lulled. Only seven defenders were left and their ammunition was running low. The Indians and Mexicans had lost heavily. Both sides rested.

Shortly after noon the attack began again. The Americans, unruffled and calm, watched with keen eyes for any exposure of their enemies and made every shot tell. In spite of this the besiegers succeeded in setting fire to the mill. It blazed up in a shower of sparks and smoke. This new danger was met only by the greatest effort by Turley and his men, but they succeeded in quenching the flames before they spread to the rest of the structure.

While the trappers were busy with the blaze, the Indians occupied all the out buildings on the other side of the corral. There they vented their anger in typical Indian fashion by slaughtering Turley's hogs and sheep. Fires kept breaking out in different parts of the defenses. It was increasingly apparent that the place could not be held another twelve hours.

Turley called a council of war. The trappers voted to wait until night. Then each was to make his escape as he could. Darkness fell at last. Suddenly the wild trapper yell rang out. Together they charged forth, long rifles cracking. John Albert and a companion rushed through the litter postern gate, firing their guns right into the faces of the enemy, then leaped forward with clubbed rifles. As his comrade was beaten down, Albert threw himself under the fence. There he lay in the darkness, listening to the other trapper's screams as they clubbed and stabbed him to death. The Indians thought Albert had escaped and made no search for him. Later he found a chance to get away, reached the mountains, and eventually a rendezvous of his friends near the present site of Pueblo, Colorado. Two others also escaped and got to Santa Fe.

The crowning tragedy befell Simeon Turley himself. Having risked and lost for his friends, he broke through the cordon. He reached the mountains and was hiding when he saw approaching Mexicans he had known for years. Turley stepped out from his hiding place and asked for help. He offered his valuable watch for the use of the Mexican's horse, although the animal was not worth half as much. The Mexican refused, pretended pity and rode away, promising to bring help. As fast as his horse could carry him, he galloped to the mill and told the Indians where Turley hid. A little later they found him and mercilessly killed him.

A Pioneer Horse Race

by J. Aveguel Maes

Whenever I see a group of older people relating stories of early life, I hurry over and become an attentive listener. To me they are always interesting, exciting, and sometimes humorous. On one of these story-telling occasions I was glad to hear a true story of a member of my family, my grandfather.

My grandfather, as the story goes, had a good deal of Indian blood in his veins. His personal appearance easily convinced anyone of his Indian qualities. His hair hung down over his shoulders; in his ears he wore large, round earrings; his clothes were buckskin.

On one of his customary roamings he met a man who owned a very famous racehorse. My grandfather and this man became very intimate friends. Being a skilled rider, my grandfather offered his services as jockey, and the horse owner quickly accepted.

The locality where the horse owner lived no longer offered any competition. He was virtually king in his realm. His fame had spread so far that it was nearly impossible to match him in a race.

My grandfather and Mr. Sandoval, the horse owner, formulated a plan to race the horse in a far away village whose residents boasted of an equally famous racehorse. They prepared for the journey and started out, accompanied by many friends who wished to bet on the horse from their village.

When the party made camp on the last night, Mr. Sandoval and my grandfather proceeded to alter the appearance of the horse. They shaved its shoulder and cut its mane in an uneven, jagged line. They clipped its tail until it appeared like a caricature of a horse.

The next morning the cavalcade approached the little village which was to be the scene of the race. Groups of people surged from the village to meet the newcomers. News of the coming of the racehorse had aroused them to high excitement. Betting on horses was one way of becoming rich overnight and such an opportunity was now at hand. The villagers were overjoyed to see such a horse arrive to race with their prized racer and began to count the wealth they would win. Sandoval's horse was indeed a sorry sight. Its head drooped; its tail—what was left of it—hung like an old broom; its feet dragged along the dusty road. One look at it was enough: people scurried to their homes and prepared for the next day's gambling.

The day of the big race dawned. To the scene of the race came a crowd of people carrying goods on their backs, urging on heavily laden donkeys, driving before them whatever stock they possessed. Sandoval and my grandfather busied themselves preparing their horse for the race, while others from their village bustled about in the crowd, accepting bets of every nature.

As he was leading the horse to the racing ground, my grandfather purposely allowed it to run away. It ran over the countryside, and by the time it was apprehended by my grandfather it was apparently exhausted. By this time the villagers were so certain of victory that they were ready to lay hands on the goods Sandoval's friends had put up.

But the race was not yet to begin. The strangers contended that their horse was tired; that it could not do justice to its racing ability; that it was not receiving an equal chance; that, in short, the race should be postponed until the following day.

Their suggestion met scant favor. Insistent on having the race immediately, the villagers threatened the little party. Those who had withheld their bets now hurriedly bet all they possessed, feeling assured that the exhausted horse would fail miserably.

The moment arrived. The horses were led to the starting line, amid wild shouting. The horses started. The cries gave way to profound silence as my grandfather leaned forward on his mount. He spurred his horse, galloped to the finish line, and won the race.

Surprise gave way to menacing looks, as the villagers realized they had been tricked. Many of them were left with nothing but the clothing they wore. Mr. Sandoval and his party needed no urging. Gleefully collecting all that they had won, they started on their triumphant way homeward.

The Death Sentence

by Reyes N. Martinez

Believed to have been the first sentence of death imposed by a Judge in Taos county, the case of Jose Maria Martin presents one of those rare court episodes wherein judicial exercise of authority is expressed in such a dramatic manner that it becomes, with the passing of the years, truly a literary gem of jurisprudence. The judge presiding in this case was Judge Kirby Benedict, associate Justice of the Supreme Court, about the year 1860.

"Jose Maria Martin, stand up! Jose Maria Martin, you have been indicted, tried and convicted by a jury of your countrymen of the crime of murder, and the court is now about to pass upon you the dread sentence of the law. As a usual thing, Jose Maria Martin, it is a painful duty for a judge of a court of justice to pronounce upon a human being the sentence of death. There is something horrible in it, and the mind of the court naturally revolts from the performance of such a duty. Happily, however, your case is relieved of all such unpleasant features and the court takes positive delight in sentencing you to death!

"You are a young man, Jose Maria Martin, apparently in good physical condition and robust health. Ordinarily you might have looked forward to many years of life, and the court has no doubt you have, and have expected to die at a ripe old age; but you are about to be cut off in consequence of your own act. Jose Maria Martin, it is now spring-time; in a little while the grass will be blooming; birds will be singing their sweet carols, and nature will be putting on her most gorgeous and most attractive robes, and life will be pleasant and men will want to stay; but none of this for you, Jose Maria Martin, the flowers will not bloom for you, Jose Maria Martin: the birds will not carol for you, Jose Maria Martin: when these things come to gladden the senses of men, you will be occupying a space about six feet by two beneath the sod, and green grass and those beautiful flowers will be growing above your lovely head.

"The sentence of the court is, that you be taken from this place to the county jail; that you be kept there safely and securely confined, in the custody of the sheriff, until the day appointed for your execution. (Be very careful, Mr. Sheriff, that he have no opportunity to escape and that you have him at the appointed place at the appointed time.) That you be so kept, Jose Maria Martin, until — (Mr. Clerk, on what day of the month does Friday, about two weeks from this time, come? 'March twenty-second, your Honor.') Very well — until Friday, the twenty-second of March, when you will be taken by the sheriff from your place of confinement to some safe and convenient spot within the county (that is in your discretion, Mr. Sheriff; you are only confined to the limits of this county), and that you be hanged by the neck until you are dead, and the court was about to add, Jose Maria Martin, 'May God have mercy on your soul' but the court will not assume the responsibility of asking an all wise Providence to do that which a jury of your peers has refused to do. The Lord could not have mercy on your soul, Jose Maria Martin! However, if you affect any religious belief, or are connected with any religious organization, it might be well for you to send for your priest or your minister and get from him — well — such consolation as you can: but the court advises you to place no reliance upon anything of that kind! Mr. Sheriff, remove the prisoner."

Some say that Jose Maria Martin broke away from the county jail and escaped; however, there are those who believe that Spring flowers in the breezes were not for Jose Maria Martin.

Source: Knowledge of Reyes Martinez of original document among the files of the District Court. Actual wording of sentence copied from *When Old Trails Were New* by Blanche C. Grant.

Societies—Severity Corruption

by Reyes Martinez

During the early nineties of the nineteenth century, there sprung up in the village of Arroyo Seco, in Taos County, a number of societies. Some of these were political organizations, such as "Los Caballeros de Labor" (The Gentleman of Labor) and "Les Gorras Blancas" (The White Caps), by means of which Don Cesario Gracia established himself as political boss of Taos County during that era and up to the end of the century. There was another, however, that was wholly different in purpose from the first two names. This was "La Sociedad de Proteccion y Justicia" (The Society of Protection and Justice), a cooperative and mutual benefit organization.

The members drew up a constitution and registered it according to law with the Secretary of the Territory at Santa Fe, and drew up by-laws for the guidance of the members. Within the first year it drew up a large membership from Arroyo Seco and the surrounding villages. It was well founded and operated under competent management for a number of years. Its members were respected and prospered. Its rules were vigorously enforced. No offense, big or small, was let pass. Punishment for infraction of the rules was severe. One form of punishment was "Sepo de Campana." This was applied to the culprit by forcing him to sit with his knees drawn up, then tying his wrists together with strong twine and forcing his knees between his forearms, so that his wrists rested over his shins. A broomstick was then forced through the bend of his elbows, under his knees, from one side to the other. This secured him tightly and rendered him almost immovable. A lash was then applied to his back as many times as the gravity of the offense deserved. Other forms of punishment were applied by hanging a culprit by his two thumbs, by means of a light rope, from the ceiling of the room; or by suspending him several feet off the floor, by clasping his fingers together over a horizontal rod or pole. The lash was then applied several times to his back. It is impossible to unclasp the fingers when suspended from a horizontal bar; and the pain resulting from hanging by the thumbs is really excruciating.

Help was given sick members in raising and harvesting their crops. Flour and other provisions were furnished them by society, when they had no means of buying them.

This society brought quite a big change in the relations of the residents of the village with one another. Previous to its organization, two bandit gangs, the Vigils and the Maeres, carried on their nefarious operations in the Desmontes region nearby. Upon the organization of this society, the members of these gangs, finding their activities more risky, dispersed and left the district.

Finally, with the passing of the years, as old members died or dropped out and new ones joined, corruption crept in. Undue privileges were extended to some members. Many of the older members feigned sickness and claimed to be destitute for long periods of time. The funds of the society were used up in supplying them with food and other necessities. The younger and more inexperienced members were made to raise and harvest their crops and haul wood for them. In the end, differences and heated controversies broke out among them and the functions of the society came to a standstill, and have remained so till the present time. Many still claim membership in it, but no cooperative organization exists any longer. Their lodge, a two-story adobe building, remained standing many years after the society ceased functioning, a mute monument to the frailty of human endeavor, and finally fell down.

Source of Information: Personal knowledge of writer.

The Fulfillment of a Longed for Wish

by Reyes Martinez

At his home in the Desmontes District, ten miles north of Taos, Jose Rafael Vigil, eccentric farmer and extensive landowner, lay on his deathbed. Although illiterate, he was considered an astute business man; and yet there were some persons who had fleeced him in business transactions during his lifetime. Among these were his two compadres, Manuel Navarro and Juan de Jesus Herrera (both names fictitious).

Now, for obvious reason, in his last hours, reminiscences of many of these occurrences occupied his thoughts; and the ones that cut most deeply into his feelings were those recalling the occasion when his two dear compadres (godfathers of two of his children) had taken advantage of his trust in them and had carried away from his farm two fat steers and butchered them, agreeing to pay him for them by working for him on the farm and never having complied with the obligation. His spirit was not at ease. Finally he summoned his wife to his bedside and asked her to send for his two compadres; he wished to see them before he died. He ordered her to place a chair at each side of his bed. In due time they arrived. Motioning weakly towards each chair, he requested them to be seated.

The compadres eagerly waited for the dying man to express himself. Perhaps he was about to bequeath to them part of his savings, notwithstanding the fact that their accounts for the steers still remained unpaid. He was known to be of a very charitable nature. "My dear compadres," he began slowly, drawling out his words with an effort, "I have called you for one purpose, and one alone." The dying man paused for a moment to gain strength. This served to whet the curiosity of the two men still more. "For what purpose, compadre?" one of them asked. Having recovered part of his strength, the dying man answered: "I wish to have the bliss of Our Lord, Jesus Christ, that of dying between two thieves. Now

I die happy." So saying, he closed his eyes in the eternal sleep of death.

"Tio Jose Rafael," as he was generally known, was a pioneer farmer of the lower Desmontes District. He acquired all of the lands between the Arroyo Hondo grant-line, on the west, and the Watson place, on the east. He was known for his wit and humor, which always found its way into all his business dealings. Once, a man by the name of John Anderson (name fictitious) approached him with the intention of buying a piece of land from him. As has always been the general custom in carrying out such transactions, the land is first measured, or surveyed, then the deed drawn, before the money or other consideration is paid by the buyer to the vendor. In this case, Tio Jose Rafael called his two compadres aforementioned, who lived close to his farm, to help him and Anderson in measuring the land. The unit of measure mostly used at that time was the Spanish vara (about 33 inches) and the men took along with them a vara (33-inch rod) to use in measuring. Anderson assumed that, after measuring the land, the deed was to be drawn and the money agreed upon as the price of the land, paid by him to Tio Jose Rafael. Tio Jose Rafael took the rod in his hands and measured the first vara, then paused and looked expectantly at Anderson. Anderson failed to comprehend his intent and suggested that they continue measuring the land. "Vara medida, peso a la mano" (vara measured, one dollar down), meaning that, for each vara measured, Anderson was to pay, then and there, one dollar to the shrewd seller, till the full price of the land had been paid; then, and not till then, the deed was to be drawn. Disgusted by this requirement, Anderson refused to go on with the deal, and the land remained in "status quo."

Jose Rafael Vigil died about the year 1894. Fantastic stories of fabulous hoards of money, said to have been left by him, buried somewhere in the lands that he owned, have lured many a person to dig the ground in several places in an effort to locate the money, but without favorable results.

An old well that he dug in an arroyo, in quest for water, still exists, where, it is said, he buried some of his money, in the side wall, eight feet down. Nothing has ever been found. No doubt, some of the money that he accumulated during his lifetime is somewhere on the farm lands he formerly owned, buried beneath the soil that yielded the produce from which it was realized, as Tio Jose Rafael never had faith in banks and deposited no money with them.

Source of Information: Personal knowledge of the writer.

P I O N E E R -- The Day of Petitions.

Many things were accomplished by petitions in the early days of Raton, New Mexico. An interesting tale was made possible by an incident which occurred in 1887, as a result of so many petitions being circulated.

Mr. "Chip" Chapman made a bet of $5 that he could get Mr. George J. Pace, a prominent local merchant, to sign a petition to buy a rope with which to hang the same Mr. Pace. Interest ran high in the wager.

Mr. Chapman petitioned the authorities to bridge the Sugarite River, out east of Raton, to make the journey, into Raton, of the Johnson Park people and others living east of the river easier. It was pointed out in lenghty and flowery language that it would increase business in Raton and create a better feeling between the Raton people and the Johnson Park visitors. At the bottom of the petition in a separate paragraph, much like the first several, the petition agreed that each signer should contribute one cent toward a fund to buy a rope to hang George J. Pace.   Thirty signers were soon secured and Mr. Chapman took the petition to Mr. Pace, who read the first paragraph, glanced down through the list of signers, and flourishingly affixed his signature to the paper.

Some hours later Mr. Chapman failed to collect Mr. Pace's penny, and the other thirty had already refused to contribute theirs, but "Chip" declares that he collected the $5 bet.

Mr. Chapman was even a welcome visitor to Mr. Pace's store after that gentlemen got over his first anger and pretended fear that "Chip" might succeed in collecting the thirty cents.

As told by W. £. Chapman, Raton.

"Pioneer: The Day of Petitions," Kenneth Fordyce, March 26, 193-,
NMFWP, WPA #188, NMSRCA

Early Settlers of Llano Quemado by George Torres

by L. Raines

Llano Quemado is a small community lying south of Ranchos de Taos and established shortly after the settlement of Ranchos de Taos. It is more or less a cordillera or string of houses from east to west. The houses extend for a distance of two miles along a ridge which overlooks the fertile Ranchos Valley.

The Romero, the Mondragon and the Martinez families were said to be the first settlers of Llano Quemado.

All these first settlers were stockmen and they brought sheep, goats, and cattle. Since the very early establishment of the village some Indian tribes gave trouble, among them the Comanches and Apaches. They often stole horses, cattle, and sheep. In most cases the thieves were left unmolested for fear that if any member of the tribe were punished the whole force would come in a mass and wipe out the few inhabitants.

I recall a story my grandmother told me about one of her cousins who was captured by the Picuris Indians while he was tending a flock of goats on the hillside. This little boy was held in captivity for several months but finally was able to escape with the aid of an Indian woman who used to take him his daily meals. She had always been kind to him and when she heard that her people were going to sacrifice him to the Spirits, she immediately conceived a plan to get him free. The night previous to the sacrifice she took him some Indian garments, furnished him food, and told him which trail to take.

Source of Information: George Torres.

José's Escape from the Indians

by L. Raines

Cut off from the outer world by her blindness, Mrs. Tafoya, aged nearly 100, lives in her little adobe house back from the highway near Cleveland, New Mexico. When the boys and girls went to her for reminiscences, her old face lighted. She had been living in the past for so many years that she was glad to have an audience for the thoughts that ordinarily surge through her mind.

"Yes, my brother José, he was captured by Indians, shall I tell you that?"

"Yes, yes, please do."

"Well, one day José was at El Rio del Pueblo when he was surrounded by a band of Indians who took him captive. But José, he watched close so as to find his way home again. The Indians were good to my brother, treated him kindly, and kept him for a year and a half to take care of their horses.

"One day, however, he saw the savages put up two poles on which they tied a captive and built a fire under him. José was so frightened that he wanted to escape right away. He had been so long with the Indians that they did not watch him any more. He knew their habits so well that when he saw they were starting out to hunt he knew they would be gone several days; and as all the horses were away he would be left to help the squaws in the fields. Soon after the men left he took his wooden hoe and left the squaws around the camp. Once out of sight he threw down the hoe and started for home.

"Back at camp his escape was discovered and an Indian runner sped to the hunters, who came in prompt pursuit. A long stretch of plain lay before José. He could hear the whoops of the Indians in the forest behind. There was no shelter for the boy except a large rock about 100 yards away. 'Oh, Saint Anthony, help me!' cried José. He hurried forward and crept under the rock. The fleet horses of the Indians were soon heard approaching. Around and around they rode, then went away a little distance, returned and rode again, but they did not see José. At last they rode away. José waited until dusk; then calling on his Saint Anthony again he ran toward home.

"The next morning after my mother had gone to a neighbor's house, my sister and I were very much frightened to see an Indian standing at our door. He had long bone earrings and was very dirty. Then José spoke and asked us if we did not know him. We were so happy. I ran for my mother but did not tell her why I wanted her. She did not know my brother either. When he spoke, she knew his voice and cried for joy. When he had cleaned himself, she took the old bone earrings and gave him a pair of silver ones, which he wore the rest of his life."

Source of Information: Romero.

Spanish Pioneer: The Captive Shepherd Boy

by L. Raines

My great-grandfather belonged to a sturdy type of Spanish settlers, who met many difficulties with the Indians. He had few advantages and never went to school because his parents were too poor. When he was a small boy he was sent out as a shepherd to herd his father's sheep.

The Indians of those days did nothing but kill, steal, and fight the Spaniards. Sometimes they kidnapped the boys who were out on the hills herding the sheep.

My great-grandfather was one of those victims. He was about seven or eight years old when two other boys of the same age were stolen when they were watching their herds. The other boys cried and were promptly killed by the Indians. My great-grandfather, however, was brave and made no outcry. He was taken away and adopted by a tribe of Indians, whose language and customs he soon learned.

My great-grandfather spent many years of his life with the Indians. When he had been with them for about fifteen years, he decided that he would escape from them, but he could not remember what way he must follow to go back safely to his father and mother.

Then one day a break came. A traveling Indian dropped by to spend several days with the tribe. He told my great-grandfather that his parents had offered him all the money they had if he could only bring their son safely home to them.

But my great-grandfather thought the Indian was going to ruin both him and his parents by taking away all their property. He knew that if he had only a little hint as to which way to follow he could go by himself without the aid of the Indian. One night, while making arrangements for the journey, the Indian told him which stars they were to follow on their homeward trip, which was to be made by night only.

My great-grandfather realized that his parents would be ruined if they lost all their property to the Indian. All their life's work would be lost; all their future would be wrecked. He, therefore, concluded to find his way home alone. One day he told the Indians of the tribe that he was going to look for some horses that had been lost. He asked for enough food to last him three days, as he calculated that time would be sufficient to find the horses and bring them back to camp.

Everything being arranged, he set out with three good saddle horses. The first three days of his journey were uneventful but on the fourth day—the time when he should have returned to the tribe—the Indians became suspicious and followed him. He traveled only at night through forests, through creeks, and through rivers so that his trail would not be easily followed. During the day he rested in good hiding places. Sometimes the Indians passed within a hundred yards of his hiding place. All sorts of hardship faced him. He ran short on food and finally had to depend on wild roots and water. When one of his horses got tired, he turned him loose and got another.

One day he came to a village which he thought was his home. He unsaddled his horse, put him in a corral, fed him some hay, and then, tired and hungry, walked up to the house. He could remember only a few words of Spanish but he managed to make the old woman who opened the door understand his needs. He was given some food but he had been without eating so long that he fainted on taking the first bite.

His parents, who lived close by, soon heard about the stranger. When they saw him they could hardly believe that this was their son. He had long hair and could speak no Spanish; but by certain scars on his body they were able to recognize him. Once more my great-grandfather was with his parents and his people after fifteen years of life with the Indians.

Source of Information: Robert Lucero.

Mora

by L. Raines

It is generally taken for granted that the country town of Mora was named after a Spanish settler who was supposed to have established his headquarters above the village of Cleveland on the Rio de la Casa stream in the early forties of the nineteenth century. The man's name was Mora. Although this version is given credence the real origin of the name of "Mora" applied to the town is altogether different.

The first settlers of Gertrude's valley between 1830 and 1840, below the settlement of Cleveland, were French-Canadian trappers who were looking for beavers. They found quite a colony of these industrious little animals near the location of the present Cassidy Flour Mill. Having dug a short distance from the river bank the trappers discovered a heap of human bones. Consequently, they named, in their French language, the present Mora River *L'Eau des Morts*, "The Water of the Dead." The few Spanish people who were then starting to settle in the valley of Saint Gertrude did not understand the meaning of the French phrase and caught only the phonetic sound of it; therefore, they applied to the valley as well as to the river the name of *Lo de Mor*. The native had only to change *Mor* to Mora in order to make a Spanish name out of a French word.

This interpretation was given to Father C. Balland, Mora, by two old French missionaries, Fathers Redon and Fayet, who came to this country in 1865 and 1860, and by the most Reverend Archbishop Salpointe, who was the pastor of the Mora parish from 1860 to 1865.

The records of the Mora parish substantiate their statement. The records of the baptisms, marriages and funerals, which may be consulted, mention the present town of Mora as *Lo de Mora* until 1861; then the name of Mora appears alone.

Spanish Pioneer: Mañana

by L. Raines

The night was black. Romero and his companion were tired. A journey of four hundred miles on horseback in the late "forties" through the outlaw and Indian-infested regions of New Mexico was quite different from a modern Pullman trip.

As the travelers neared Sapello, they smelled smoke and rode cautiously, instinctively clutching their six-shooters. A gust of wind blew the embers, and in the distance they spied some objects lying about the fire. Going upstream some distance out of their way, they crossed the river as noiselessly as possible so as not to disturb the campers. They journeyed on about a half-mile.

"Pablo, wait here and take care of my mule. I will be back soon," whispered Vincente.

He crept cautiously along until he came to a cliff overlooking the river. Imagine his amazement when the fitful glow revealed a band of sleeping Indians. His first impulse was to shoot. A moment's reflection, however, told him that this would be reckless. He stole quietly away to where he had left his companion. He was gone! The mule was gone!

For the first time he remembered the canvas bag, containing fifteen hundred dollars in silver, strapped to the saddle. What was he to do? How face his employer? His home lay nearly thirty miles ahead; a band of hostile Indians lay behind him. No time for inaction!

Fortunately his outdoor life had developed in him a keen sense of direction. After groping about for some time he found his mule with saddlebags intact. Riding cautiously so as not to awaken the Indians, he overtook his companion. Was he angry? Poor old Pablo begged for mercy. The Spaniard's inherent respect for the aged was all that saved the life of the old man.

Toward morning they reached Mora. The "Viejo" was glad

to part company. Mr. Romero, before retiring, aroused the justice of the peace, related his experiences, and urged him to summon the settlers and rout the Indians.

"Mañana, mañana," replied the sleepy officer of the law.

But mañana brought word that the band of Apaches had driven off several herds of sheep and had taken the shepherds captive.

The above incident was told by Theodosio Gonzalez, a grandson of the Vincente Romero mentioned in the story.

SCHOOL DAYS IN OLD TAOS

The first teacher in the grade school of Taos, about 1885, was hired at Twenty-five dollars a month. This job he sublet to another man for Fifteen dollars, making a neat profit for doing nothing. Each pupil at that time was expected to bring two sticks of wood daily during the winter months. The ones who forgot to bring their quota of wood were obliged to "go way back and sit down" along the walls while those who brought the wood sat nearest to the stove and enjoyed the warmth. These young students were soundly scolded for saying "Good morning, teacher" in English, for at that time it was not considered good etiquette for a younger person to address an older one in English. This applied to both Anglo and Spanish-American pupils but especially Spanish-Americans.

Sources of Information:

Frank T. Cheetham, in address to Taos County Teachers. September, 1936.

Personal recollections of Harry E. Anderson, Raton, New Mexico.

"School Days in Old Taos," James Burns, October 24, 1936,
NMFWP, WPA #233a, NMSRCA

The Horse Trader As told by Juan M. Romero

by Lester Raines

About twenty-five miles south of Taos, closely surrounded by mountains, lay the Picuris Pueblo, which was supposedly the home of Santiago, an Indian horse trader. This story of him has been related to us by our father; his father told it to him.

Santiago, besides being a horse trader was, it seems, a fun-loving gambler. During the days of Geronimo, the Apache outlaw, the Picuris Indians traveled often to Taos, sometimes in peace, frequently in deviltry, preying on the settlers, stealing their cattle, horses, sheep, and occasionally, children. Santiago, however, indulged in none of these forays. Next to himself he liked horses. He liked them so much, in fact, that he would give anything for a good saddle horse. Later I shall tell how he finally acquired a horse that he liked particularly well.

In one of his many trips to Taos, Santiago met my grandfather, whose horse, Alazan, was one of the best horses in the settlement. It was a beautiful animal, a trained buffalo hunter. Santiago quickly offered to trade horses. My grandfather refused. Santiago then offered to buy the horse. My grandfather still continued not to consider either a trade or sale and was deaf to Santiago's coaxing.

Santiago looked around for a while and was very pensive. Finally he spoke, "Benecio, my mother is with me. I give the mother for the horse."

"No, Santiago," came the answer, "I do not want your mother and you are not going to have Alazan. Get out of here!"

A few days later Santiago and his mother came to my grandfather's house. He had, he said, wagered his horse during the races at the Pueblo and had lost. He wanted to borrow a horse to go to the Pueblo and bring back some horses to take his mother and him home. My grandfather agreed to loan Santiago a horse but told him to be back in two days.

When Santiago left for the Pueblo, his mother cried like a baby. She was very old and had to be taken care of like a child. Two days passed: no Santiago.

On the third day my grandfather went to Picuris to get Santiago so that he could take his mother. He was by that time willing to give Santiago the horse if he would only remove his mother. Santiago was not to be found at Picuris nor any other place.

Five years after she had been left at my grandfather's home, Santiago's mother died.

Extracts from "The Story of Early Clayton, New Mexico by Albert W. Thompson"

by D. D. Sharp

"From the Parajito to Clayton, 125 miles, the trail lay up Ute Creek, where generally water and grass were abundant. A month after leaving the Roswell country, the Perico was reached. Then there was a mad ride into town, where, at Charlie Meridith's bar the cowboys washed the alkali from their throats.

"For a month or more the wagons of the southern cattle owners camped about Clayton. A favorite spot was beside the rainwater filled lake, which in the '80's extended from Front to First Streets, and from the site of the present (1932) Star Lumber Company's office, two blocks north to Main Street. About the lake in summer were the round-up wagons and trail camps, and in its waters floundered the ponies of the trail outfit. Cattle from the south rarely watered in this rainwater pond. They were driven to the Perico, or some other prairie lake, several of which dotted the plains about Clayton. Cooks filled their water barrels from the railway tank in Clayton. After their cattle had been sold and shipped, the southern trail men departed at once for their homes in southern New Mexico.

"Some of the dusty wagon bosses from the Pecos River who came over the dusty path to Clayton in the nineties are (1932) still living. One of them, Jack M. Potter, resides in Clayton. Another trail boss, who as a young man rode from Roswell to Clayton behind a herd of long horns, is the Honorable James F. Hinkle, ex-governor of the State of New Mexico. Governor Hinkle writes of his recollections nearly fifty years ago, 'I think I was first in Clayton in 1890 and several years thereafter while the cattle trail ran to that point. We were once holding a herd on the creek (Perico) south of town when a rain raised it to swimming proportions. About half the men were on the side opposite camp to which we had to cross on our horses. Naturally we were wet and cold when getting over. I do not remember even being warm up there in the spring except when we were practicing before the bar.'"

Mr. Thompson ends his picture with this:

"The lake bed around which camped round-up wagons forty years ago (1932) has been filled in, reclaimed, and is now dotted with buildings and shops. It is within the very heart of the Clayton business district. Street lights, set high on ornamental steel poles cast their all night glow where once faintly burned the fires of the cowman's camp, which the night wind often fanned into intenser brightness, reflecting as its blue blazes shot upward, the tents of sleeping cowboys, a trail wagon, and several saddled horses which stood patiently picketed nearby."

About the early wool business of Mr. Clayton, Mr. Thompson had this to say:

"Soon after the completion of the railroad in 1888 the railway company constructed a long wool house on the east side of its right-of-way on the street now occupied by the city hall. Here in June and July of each year, came many four-horse teams drawing wagons and trailers loaded with long sacks filled with wool. Wool was stored free of charge by the railway company until such a time as sale and shipment were made thereof, in which Boston and eastern buyers vied with one another in securing the desired commodity. Wool was carted to Clayton from the Canadian River and from the country about Tucumcari, from Ute Creek and from the districts north of Clayton, the Corrumpa and the Cimarron. The early large sheep owners of northeastern New Mexico were Otto and Schleter, Gallegos Bros., Bueyeros, Tequesquite, Henry White, and Lujan Bros., of the Corrumpa, and A. McKinzie of the Cimarron. Ewes in the 1890's sold for $2.00 to $2.50 and wool brought from 11 to 14 cents per pound. Mexican herders, two of whom looked after each flock of sheep, were paid from $14.00 to $16.00 per month and board. Many small ranchmen owned from 500 to 1,000 head of range sheep, while larger owners ran from 5,000 to 10,000 ewes. With free range the sheep industry prospered and the flocks made substantial gains.

"The advent of the Denver and Gulf Railway created new conditions as to northeastern New Mexico. I recall the long road, which those of us who lived in that district before the construction of this system, were obliged to travel in reaching a town where we could purchase supplies.

"Leaving the Bushnell ranch early in the morning behind a pair of work horses in our freight wagon, we drove 25 miles past the head of the Tramperos and a mile or so south of the present Pasamonte post office. Skirting the west side of the Don Carlos Hills, we reached Ute Creek a little past noon; here we camped for dinner, unharnessed, watered and fed our teams, built a fire over which coffee and meat were cooked, and rested about an hour. Then we pushed on up Ute Creek crossed the Old Santa Fe Trail moved up the Palo Blanco past the Bottle Ranch (McCuisition) to Mr. Young's where we arrived late this evening. We generally carried our camp beds with us. These we spread out in one room of Mr. Young's stone house. Mrs. Young, a fine type of New England womanhood—she and her husband had come from some town near Boston—, prepared supper for us. We were then half way to Raton.

"Next morning we started early for our destination. The horses were allowed to walk much of the way. At noon an hour was taken for rest and dinner was prepared. About dark we arrived in Raton after two days of uncomfortable driving, perched on the high seat of an open Bain of Shuttler wagon. A day and a half, and sometimes two days, were spent in Raton; then the slower return trip to Tramperos with our load of ranch supplies was begun. Sometimes neighbors joined us in these trips to town, when we all camped out as night overtook us. On the whole these journeys were not without their poetic sides. What once took us five days to accomplish, visiting town and buying supplies, may now be done in one day through the auto, truck and good roads.

"The scent of smoke from our bull-chip fire on the prairie over which sizzling bacon and fired potatoes at the side of which we boiled our coffee, welcome aromas always attended with keen appetites are, like the times and traditions of half a century ago in northeastern New Mexico, shadowy though nonetheless fragrant recollections of the past."

Below I give Mr. Thompson's account of the great snowstorm of 1889:

"Clayton was a year and a half old when northeastern New Mexico was swept by the worst blizzard ever recorded in the history of that district, or perhaps in the history of the West. The storm was accompanied by a fall of snow which covered the ground from two to seven feet in depth. It left in its wake a considerable loss of human life and destroyed many cattle and sheep.

"Blizzards and snowstorms driven by winds of hurricane proportions are not uncommon during the winter months in the prairie districts of the West. The late Thomas O. Boggs, Uncle Tom, peerless plainsman, who lies buried in Clayton, once told me of an experience of his in the winter of 1846 and 1847, with a northerner.

"Boggs left Santa Fe, New Mexico in December, 1846 for Fort Leavenworth, Kansas. He was a trusted bearer of military dispatches from General Kearney's lieutenants in Santa Fe to Fort Leavenworth. He and the men who bore him company on this journey were all well mounted on government mules. Boggs had been impressed by the officers of Fort Marcy, Santa Fe, with the necessity of making all possible speed in the execution of his errand. Above all else he was to protect and guard the messages entrusted to his care, which were important and confidential. They gave information as to the conditions in the newly acquired province of New Mexico and the progress General Kearney was making on his overland march to California.

"All went well with Boggs and his companion until after the beginning of the new year, 1847; the couriers had crossed the line of the present State of Kansas and were making good time in their ride down the Arkansas River when one night, as they lay in the camp, dark clouds gathered in the north and the wind began to blow. Soon a storm accompanied by snow, sleet, and intense cold struck them. Next morning found the little company buried beneath two feet of snow.

"All that day the blizzard raged and when a second morning

shone, Bogg's men dug themselves out from under their stiff buffalo robes to view a sad and amazing spectacle. Most of their saddle mules lay dead in camp, frozen to death. A few mules had wandered off in the storm, probably to die.

"When the blizzard had abated Boggs and his men left most of their equipment where it lay, packed the mail, and a few provisions on their backs and pushed on foot making their laborious way eastward through the snow. Finally they came to a settlement of Crow Indians, who gave the half-famished company food, aided them in making moccasins to replace their worn out shoes, and loaned them horses on which to finish their journey to Fort Leavenworth, which they later reached, and delivered their dispatches. Boggs never forgot this experience in which he and his followers narrowly escaped death.

"A happy sequel is attached to this story. Upon returning to Santa Fe in the spring of 1847, Uncle Tom learned that his pet riding mule on which he left New Mexico the winter before, and which he supposed had died in the blizzard on the Arkansas, had returned to Fort Marcy. She had drifted from camp during the storm and making her slow way across country, reached the Santa Fe trail, later to be picked up and brought to the Territorial Capital."

District Two: Buster Degraftenreid as Buffalo Hunter

"I never knew him by anything but Boots. In those days you didn't ask a man his name and if he told you you wouldn't believe him."

From "Buster Degraftenreid as Buffalo Hunter"
by Mrs. Belle Kilgore

Camp Maddox

by H. P. Collier

𝔄 sinister message went swiftly across the country, one which caused the scattered population of southwestern New Mexico to rethink and retell all the bloody Indian stories handed down to them from generation to generation. How the husband and father had died and had been scalped while trying to protect his family; how a mother had been struck down and her long, beautiful hair taken while her arms still held her six months-old baby; how another family had been murdered and the house burned while their lovely sixteen year old daughter had been carried away into captivity and a living hell!

These stories and many more were retold because Geronimo and his dreaded band of Apache Indians had quit the reservation and had gone on the war path. Where would he strike first? Men cleaned and oiled their guns and say that the supply of ammunition was sufficient. Women and children rarely left the yard; men ceased to ride the range; the air was oppressive with expectancy. Rumors of where the Indians were and what they had done and were doing, grew larger as the distance traveled grew greater. A bunch of W. S. cowboys returning hurriedly from a roundup on the Blue, brought word that the Indians had murdered the Luther brothers and had also killed their own tired, worn out ponies after supplying themselves with fresh range animals. The cook at the W. S. ranch told these returning cowboys that the Indians had, that day, rounded up a bunch of W. S. saddle horses west of the ranch house and had driven them away toward the northeast, which meant that they were headed for their old hunting ground in the Black range from which they would come forth to murder and steal.

Soon after this, Troop C of the 8th U.S. Cavalry commanded by Major Sam Sumner, accompanied by Dr. Maddox and Lieutenants Williams, Fountain and Cabell rode up to the W. S. ranch house and asked concerning a camp site. They were shown a place five miles northeast of the ranch where there was a two room adobe house, plenty of big shade trees and a cool spring of clear water. Major Sumner was delighted with the location and soon a small city of orderly arranged tents appeared.

The following day another menace to the welfare of the troops, besides the Apache Indians, appeared. A rickety old wagon drawn by a decrepit horse and a shaggy burro, driven by an old, gray bearded man accompanied by a large mannish-looking woman, arrived and set up camp about one fourth of a mile from the soldiers' camp. They unloaded from the wagon two barrels of vile whiskey into a torn, dirty tent from the top of which floated a banner bearing the inscription, "Fort Nasty." The following day Major Sumner asked Captain French, manager of the W. S. ranch, to have these people move off the W. S. property. Captain French went to "Fort Nasty" and told the man he was trespassing on W. S. property and that he would have to move. Then out of the tent came the mannish woman with green eyes, a cavernous mouth partly filled by a vile tongue and two, long, yellow teeth that did not strike and plainly told Captain French where he could find a hotter climate than the Mohave Desert. Captain French retreated dejectedly. Later, "Fort Nasty" was removed by Major Sumner, assisted by his troops.

Major Sumner's Camp was officially named Camp Maddox after the "Soldier Hill" massacre in which Dr. Maddox lost his life. He was a true soldier and rode with Troop C.

"Uncle" Bill Jones and George Pickett

(of Last Chance Canyon and Sitting Bull Falls, Southwest of Carlsbad)

by Allen B. Cooke

It was said by Kit Carson that the Indian's cunning in leading his enemy into a natural trap—a region without water, a river whose banks were lined with quicksand bogs, or a canyon whose steep sides afforded a perfect site for ambush—accounted for more tragedies than his marksmanship. And, to such cunning, the Last Chance Canyon, cut east and west, deep and sheer in the Guadalupe Mountains, approximately forty-eight miles southwest of Carlsbad, owes its name.

Grandpa Jones and Ma, so affectionately known in Western lore, in 1867 drew up their oxcart, with all their worldly store, to a gurgling spring on the bank of the Seven Rivers. With them were their stalwart sons and a group of settlers, who had trekked their way across the continent from Virginia. They unloaded and decided to make the spring their headquarters, only to be shot at by a band of Indians who claimed prior rights to the precious water. A pitched battle took place and the Jones boys and the others succeeded in chasing the Indians to what is now Rocky Arroyo, about ten miles to the west.

As the needs of the settlement of Seven Rivers (no longer existent) grew, several of the homesteaders, in 1881, squatted in the Rocky Arroyo and, as before, the Indians disputed their right. Another battle ensued and this time the wily Apaches drew the frontiersmen into a long and deep canyon while they repaired to the lofty mesas of the Guadalupes to watch. The Virginian settlers, not knowing the country, searched for days in vain and became lost in the maze of intertwining canyons.

Prodding their jaded ponies from the rim of one vast canyon

to another, peering down into their colorful depths for a vestige of water, they saw only heat waves rising in mockery from the furnace-like depths of the gorges.

No water! Death was inevitable. The Indian's trickery!

Looming in the distance was their last chance—a high, yellow, jagged canyon whose valley might contain water. To get there would be their last effort. So they pushed on, struggled to the rim and peered below.

Eureka! Water! They reeled down an old Indian trail and found life on that August day in 1881—in sparkling delights of the cool river.

So the canyon was named by these thankful men—the Last Chance Canyon—and to this day it is so known.

Uncle Bill Jones, the lone survivor of the group, son of Grandpa Jones, still rides the far mesa reaches and has been helpful to the many expeditions that have dug and scraped the sides of Last Chance and its many tributaries, since its discovery in this region of exceedingly interesting archaeological remains.

The naming of the canyon and the falls is spiked with humor. Bill Jones was quite a wanderer in his day—the "Daniel Boone" of the colony and upon returning from his many excursions, he would sit around the table in his father's house at Seven Rivers and regale the folks with what they termed "fantastic stories and plain lies"—or just "bull."

One of these stories concerned the falls mentioned in the foregoing and his brothers, in disgust of his exaggeration, shouted, "Well, Sitting Bull, I'll tell you if there is a falls there we will name it after you." In due time the spinner of yarns proved its presence and, from that time on, this canyon has been named Sitting Bull Canyon and the falls, Sitting Bull Falls.

In one of the caves, about six miles from the eastern entrance of the Last Chance, George Pickett holds forth. From all outward appearances, he is a hermit and this cognomen is a source of pride to him. Nothing is known of him and no one has been able to break down his exterior beyond the point of "don't you think I look like Bill McGuinness," a bad member of the Black Jack gang, who roamed the valleys and climes of New Mexico, four decades ago.

A member of an archaeological expedition, of whom the hermit was especially fond, engaged Pickett in a conversation and he told of his wanderings since ensconced in the Last Chance cave. He told of a visit to the environs of Amarillo, on the heaths of the Llano Estacado and of his being "stashed" for the night on a lonely ranch. Asking the ranch owner for lodging, he was brought to the kitchen of the homestead and introduced to the cowhands and members of the family.

"The young girl who was doing the cookin' began crying," George recounted, "and kept it up for some time and it seemed that every time she looked at me she began to cry 'worser.' I didn't know what to make of it but I asked the 'bossman' and he told me she was the sister of Bill McGuinness and she figured I was him come back." And Pickett avers he had quite a time proving he was not Bill McGuinness, who was paroled in 1906 from the State Penitentiary. The resemblance, those in the 'know' about Carlsbad say, is striking. Bill McGuinness does live. . . . . and so. . . . . . "talk is cheap." George Pickett is a law-abiding citizen of Last Chance Canyon.

Source of Information: Personal interview with Carl Livingston, Assistant Land Commissioner, Santa Fe, New Mexico.

Pioneer Story: Daniel Carabajal

by Edith L. Crawford

I was born at Lincoln, New Mexico, December 12, 1872, and have lived in Lincoln County continuously since that time.

My father, Jesus Sanchez Carabajal, was born at Tomé, New Mexico, which was just across the Rio Grande river from Belen, New Mexico, in the year 1807. My father and mother were married in Belen, New Mexico. (I do not know the date.)

My father joined the army about 1862 and served part of his time at Fort Stanton, New Mexico. While a soldier at Fort Stanton father moved his family from Belen, New Mexico to Lincoln County in 1870. They lived at the Torres Ranch, which is about three miles southeast of Fort Stanton, New Mexico.

I have heard my mother tell about the ox teams they drove from Belen County and how slow they traveled and were always on the lookout for Indians, as the Indians were pretty bad at the time. Soon after moving his family to Lincoln County my father was discharged from the army. He farmed on the Torres place and plowed his fields with ox teams and used a forked stick for a plow.

My father died about a month before I was born. I was the youngest of seven children, all of whom are dead except myself. My mother moved to Lincoln, New Mexico, soon after my father's death and I grew up there. I remember seeing Billy the Kid leave town the day he killed Bob Ollinger and J. W. Bell, his guards at the old courthouse in Lincoln. We lived just below the old Torreon in Lincoln at the time. I was up town playing with some boys just across the street when he killed the guards. We hid behind a picket fence and watched Billy ride out of town. We were too scared to go and see the two men he had killed; we were afraid that he would come back and shoot us. All the people in Lincoln were afraid to come out for a long time after Billy the Kid rode away towards Fort Stanton. I wanted to go and see the men he had killed but I was too afraid to go.

I was married to Lugardita Chavez, November 3, 1898, in Lincoln, New Mexico, by Father Jose. There were eleven children born to this union: Juan, Juanita, Ysa, Aurora, Rufina, (Aurora and Rufina were twins,) Leborio, Baldimar, Regina, Adelia, Bonny, and Manuel. All of our children were born in Lincoln, New Mexico, except Bonny, who is in the C.C. camp at Carrizozo, New Mexico.

I have farmed, cut wood and herded sheep to make a living for my family.

Narrator: Daniel Carabajal, Lincoln, New Mexico.

June 23, 1938   ALBUQUERQUE JOURNAL

Old Timers Who Saw Coffin and Knew Pall Bearers Say Billy the Kid Is Dead

Pawnee Bill and Frontiersmen, Probing Story Outlaw Still Lives, Reported Coming Here

"I know two men who were Billy the Kid's pallbearers and consider that is pretty good evidence that he is dead," Elfego Baca, famed peace officer and veteran of several gun battles, said Wednesday afternoon.

That was his comment when told that Major Gordon W. Lillie, better known as Pawnee Bill, is coming here with a party of old timers to run down a rumor that the famed outlaw who figured in the Lincoln County war was not killed in 1881, but still lives.

Old Timers Coming

Coming here with Pawnee Bill are the Rev. J. W. E. Airey of Houston, Tex., president of the National Frontiersmen's Association, and B. F. Barbert of Taos. All are cronies of Baca, and they had a hot time together last November in Houston, when the frontiersmen held a picturesque convention.

"I'll tell 'em that Martin Sanchez, who died in Santa Fe, and other man who is still alive but whose name has slipped me, were pall bearers for the Kid at Ft. Sumner, where he was shot by Sheriff Pat Garrett," said Baca.

The old timer had just left a hospital, where a cataract was removed from one of his eyes. The one eye that peered through a hole in a black bandage that encircled his head, sparkled as Baca recalled other days.

Man Claims He's Billy

He said he'd heard a report that an old man had approached Bob R. Lewis, town marshal at Magdalena, and claimed to be Billy the Kid. The man told Lewis he was living in the country not far from Magdalena, Baca said he was told.

The Kid, whose name was William Bonney, went by the name of Baca for several years, Elfego said, and spoke Spanish fluently. If alive now, he'd be posing as a Mexican or a Spanish American, in Baca's belief.

Oldtimers in Clovis said Wednesday that there are at least two men in Ft. Sumner who saw the Kid in death. One of these is Jesus Silva, who is said to have made the Kid's coffin. Deluvina Maxwell, Navajo servant woman, who was in the Pete Maxwell home when the Kid was slain there, died two years ago. She often related the story of the killing.

"Old Timers Who Saw Coffin and Knew Pall Bearers Say Billy the Kid is Dead," Albuquerque Journal, June 23, 1938, NMFWP, WPA #211, NMSRCA

Pioneer Story: Mary Lee Queen

by Edith L. Crawford

My father, Captain John Lee, was born November 27, 1835 in Edinburgh, Scotland. His parents came to the United States when he was eighteen months old and lived in Moodus, Connecticut. When he was fourteen years old he ran away to sea. He followed the sea for many years and came to own his own sailing vessel. He traded extensively in the South Seas and dealt mostly in copra. He went around the world three times in a sailing vessel, and discovered a small island that was called Lee's Island. When I was a small girl in school at White Oaks, New Mexico this island was shown on the maps of my geography.

My father married Mary Purcell, who was a daughter of an English missionary of the Church of England, and a graduate of Oxford. My mother was the granddaughter of King Mata Afa, who was king of the island of Samoa. My father and mother were married at Apia Samoa. They owned a plantation near Apia and lived there for several years. They had nine children born on this island. Father decided that he wanted his children educated in the United States, so they left Apia on a sailing vessel for the states. They were six months on the sea. They ran into the "calms" and were delayed for days and weeks. Their water and food supplies got short and they were put on short rations. Just before the food was entirely gone they made the port of Honolulu and the vessel was restocked. They landed at San Francisco about the year 1879. After visiting my father's family in Connecticut and traveling around a good bit they decided to settle in Richmond, Virginia.

Father bought a farm near Richmond and lived there for about a year and a half. Mother and the children had chills and fever and were sick so much that they decided to move. Father had always wanted a cattle ranch, so they moved down to southwest Texas and bought a cattle ranch about twenty miles from Brackettsville, Texas. The family came by train from Virginia to Texas and had been there only a short time when I was born on June 1ˢᵗ, 1882. About two years later my mother had another baby girl and she and I were the only children born in the United States. While we were living there Father met a man named McBee who had a ranch at White Oaks, New Mexico. He was always telling Father what a great country New Mexico was so in 1886 my father sold out his place in Brackettsville and started for New Mexico.

Our family consisted of Father, Mother, and the eleven children. My two oldest brothers and my oldest sister were married, so they and their families came with us to New Mexico. We were in five covered wagons drawn by horses. Father had about 200 head of cattle and about sixty horses. The boys drove the stock and the ladies did the cooking. I was about four years old at the time but one or two incidents stand out very clearly in my memory. We were very much afraid of the Indians, as we had heard of the terrible things that they had done to wagon trains. We were not molested by them at all tho' we saw them on several occasions. I remember waking up one morning and hearing my mother crying. I looked out and it seemed to me that I saw piles and piles of dead stock all around us. The cattle and horses had died from drinking the alkali water. This happened where Seven Rivers emptied into the Pecos river. My father was very much discouraged and took what was left of the cattle and horses and went up on the Penasco in New Mexico. He bought a farm and we lived there for about a year. We raised lots of potatoes that year and the boys sold them. Father decided to go on to White Oaks, New Mexico, to where the McBee's lived so he sold out the farm and what cattle he had left and moved to White Oaks. My married brothers and my married sister and their families moved back to Texas. We went to the McBee ranch which was about two miles from White Oaks. We lived on this ranch a year and Father ran a dairy and sold the milk in White Oaks. At the end of the year Father got us a house nearer town, just above the Old Abe Mine pump station. He opened up a meat shop in town. We children went to school and I remember one teacher especially, named Wharton. The geography that we studied showed Lee's island on the map and the teacher often told the class that it was our father who had discovered this island. My brother Bob married and worked in the South Homestake Mine. He drilled into a "dud" (a precision cap that had not been exploded) and it blew up and killed him. This was about 1892.

There was such a big family of us and all the married ones settled around my father and they called the place Leesville. There were about five families of us. Father used to drive the stage to Socorro. I remember once that he did not get home when the stage was due and my mother got very uneasy. The stage was often held up and we were afraid it had been held up and my father killed. He was a night and day late and just about the time my brothers and some friends got their horses saddled to go look for him we saw the stage coming over the hill into White Oaks. They had run into a terrible snowstorm and the horses could not pull the stage through the storm. It was very cold and my father and the passengers were almost frozen. He stopped the stage at our house and the passengers came in and got warmed up and drank some coffee before Father took the stage on into the town. Father wore a beard and I remember that it was all covered with ice and snow and you could only see his eyes.

I grew up with Edward L. Queen in White Oaks and we were married in the Methodist Church there on January 1st, 1902, by the Reverend Sam Allison, who now lives in El Paso, Texas.

We have three children, two boys and one girl, all married, and one grandson and one grand-daughter, who all now live in California. Of my father's family there are only three left: myself, one brother, Jim Lee, who lives in Douglas, Arizona and one sister, Mrs. Ray Lemon, who lives in Carrizozo. My father died in Douglas, Arizona in 1920, at the age of eighty-five years. My mother died in Carrizozo at eighty-one years, in 1925.

Mr. Queen and I leave White Oaks sometimes for years at a time but always come back. We have our home here. Judge Andrew H. Hudson, who owned the property in White Oaks known as Leesville, made me a gift of a deed to this property in 1936. I am very glad to own our old home.

Narrator: Mary Lee Queen, White Oaks, New Mexico, aged 56 years.

Pioneer Story: Nellie Reily

by Edith L. Crawford

I was born in Grapevine Texas, in 1877. I was six years old when we left Grapevine in April 1883. My father, Seaborn T. Gray, mother, four children, two boys and two girls, my father's two sisters and their husbands, Mr. and Mrs. John Lowery and Mr. and Mrs. Henry Manning and three cowboys, Henry Pruitt, Jim Carlisle and Johnny Ricker were in our party.

Pat Garrett was a cousin of my father. He came to Grapevine Texas to visit us in the early spring of 1883. He had a cattle ranch on Little Creek, which is now part of the "V" ranch, near Ruidoso, in Lincoln County, New Mexico. He persuaded my father to move to New Mexico and move his cattle where there was lots of good feed and water and open range. Cousin Pat mapped out the trail we were to travel as he had hunted Buffalo out on the plains and had made the trip several times and knew all the watering places. We traveled in four covered wagons, drawn by two horses to each wagon. One wagon was a chuck wagon and carried the provisions and the cowboys' bedding. There was a chuck box in the back of this wagon. The three women did all the cooking. The chuck wagon could stop at each town and load up with provisions to last until we got to the next town. The rest of the wagons did not go through the towns as we had two hundred head of cattle and twenty-five head of horses with us. We could only travel about fifteen miles a day on account of the horses and cattle having to feed on the way. We camped out in the open each night. The men would take turns standing guard over the camp and the stock each night as the Indians were bad in those days and Father was afraid they would come by some night and steal all of our horses and cattle. The families slept in the wagons and the cowboys made their beds on the ground. We used lanterns for lighting and cooked over a campfire in Dutch ovens. The only fresh meat we had were antelope and buffalo. They were very plentiful. I remember when we would see a herd of Buffalo we would drive until they could see us, then the wagons would stop and father would hang a red blanket on the side of one of the wagons. The Buffalos would become curious and keep edging up and when they got in shooting range father would get his Winchester and pick out a nice fat yearling and kill it. They would skin him and all we would take was the hindquarters and the hide.

After we reached the plains the only fuel we had was buffalo and cow chips. Every day when we stopped for dinner and at night my oldest brother and I had to take tow sacks and gather the chips. Mother made sour dough biscuits twice a day and corn bread for our noon meal. She baked it in Dutch ovens and my brother and I would watch to see if she dropped any of the chip ashes in the bread while baking it, for we thought it was awful to have to use the buffalo and cow chips to cook with. We never saw any Indians or traces of any on the whole trip out here and we were on the road five months. It was awful dry and hot crossing the plains. We ran out of water one day and we and the stock too suffered terribly from thirst. The cattle would not let us stop to eat dinner or supper. They put their heads down and traveled in a trot most all day. It was after dark when the cattle smelled water and they all struck out in a run for this watering place. It was just about dry when we reached it and we had to drink water from cow tracks that night. When we got up the next morning and saw the kind of water we had been drinking we children all tried to get sick. There was not enough water left in the holes for us to make coffee the next morning so we started on our way looking for fresh water. We drove about two miles when we got to the Canadian river with the nicest clearest water, so we camped on the bank of this river for three days and rested ourselves and the stock. Mother and my two aunts did the family washing and the men folks caught lots of nice fish.

One day while mother was driving along my two brothers and I were playing in the back of the wagon and I fell out. My oldest brother called to mother and said "Mamma, Nellie is out." Mother stopped the wagon and looked back and there I lay in the middle of the road screaming to the top of my lungs. She thought that I was half killed but I was not hurt at all, just scared half to death.

When we reached Fort Sumner, New Mexico the Pecos river was running bank full of the muddiest water. We had to dip it up in barrels and tubs and let it settle before we could use it. We had to lay over there ten days waiting for the river to go down. We camped in an old adobe hut for it was raining when we got there. We got so tired of waiting to cross the river that one morning father decided that we could make it so the cowboys rounded up the cattle and horses and jumped them off in the Pecos river. They swam across with only horns and faces showing but we lost only one cow in crossing. When it came time for the wagons to cross the women folks and we children were awfully scared. The wagons crossed one at a time. One of the cowboys tied a rope to the horn of his saddle and to the tongue of the wagon and guided us across. The water came up to the bed of the wagon and some ran into our wagon.

While we were in Fort Sumner waiting to cross the river we visited Billy the Kid's grave. I remember it had a board at the head with his name, age and date he was killed. He had only been dead two years then.

After leaving Fort Sumner we found wonderful grass and water for the stock. It was about the middle of August and was the rainy season in New Mexico. We were on the road a month from Fort Sumner to Little Creek, New Mexico. We traveled by way of the Jicarilla and Capitan Mountains and crossed the Salado flat which is about eleven miles west of Capitan, New Mexico. We arrived at Pat Garrett's ranch at Little Creek, New Mexico in September 1883. We had been on the road for five months. Mother was so homesick when we first came for we had to sleep in a tent in Pat Garrett's back yard and we ate with the Garrett family until we found a place to live in. When we did find a place to live in it was a log shack and it leaked. Mother had an awful time trying to keep our bedding dry when it rained or snowed. It was awful cold the first winter we spent at Little Creek as it is situated at the foot of the White Mountains. We lived there about a year and in 1884 father filed on a homestead on the Salado flat where he raised cattle and fine horses until 1900. That year he sold all his cattle and horses and laid out the town of Capitan, New Mexico.

Father was born in Coosa County Alabama, October 31, 1851 and died in Capitan New Mexico, July 23, 1915. Mother was born in Arkansas April 26, 1855 and died in Carrizozo, New Mexico, October 16, 1935. Father's two sisters did not stay very long in New Mexico; they did not like it here so they moved back to Texas and I do not know what ever became of them. The three cowboys stayed with us for a while and then drifted away and I do not know where they went. I was married to William M. Reily October 31, 1894; seven children were born to this union, five girls and two boys. Mr. Reily died in Carrizozo, New Mexico, March 9, 1931.

Narrator: Nelly B. Reily, aged 61 years, Carrizozo, New Mexico.

Pioneer Story: Jose Apodaca

by Edith L. Crawford

My father was Severanio Apodaca and my mother was Juanita Sanchez, both were born in Old Mexico and were married there. They came to the United States soon after they were married. (I do not know when they were born or when they married or the year they came to the United States.) They came to Lincoln County, New Mexico, for a while ands moved from there to Agua Azul, New Mexico, (which is now called Blue Water, New Mexico.) Agua Azul is located on the south side of the Capitan Mountains. Father moved there about the year 1872, and took up a piece of land and built a two-roomed hut on the place.

He had a few head of horses and cattle and farmed the place. There was lots of wild game in the Capitan Mountains in those days and they always had all the fresh meat that they wanted. About the first day of January, 1873, while my parents were living at this place, a friend of theirs by the name of Marcial Rodriguez came to go on a hunting trip with my father. They got up at daybreak one morning and went out to look for their horses. The men had to cross a flat which was between the mountain and the big arroyo. The Juniper trees, which had covered this place, had limbs that grew very close to the ground. While my father and Marcial were crossing this flat a band of Indians were hidden in the Juniper trees, and as the men came out in the open the Indians began shooting at them. They hit Marcial in the back and my father in the leg. The two men fought with the Indians all day and as it began to get dark Marcial told my father to make a run for the arroyo and try to get away and save himself, as Marcial felt that he was going to die and there was nothing that Father could do to help him. It was best for Father to go for help. Father made a run for the arroyo with the Indians after him, but as it was dark he was able to get away from them. Father walked most of the night and came out at the Casey ranch, which was about four miles north of Picacho. He told the Casey men about the Indians and that he had left Marcial Rodriguez seriously wounded on the flat at Agua Azul. Father was anxious to get back to his home and to my mother.

The Caseys formed a posse and sent word up and down the Rio Bonito for every man that could go, to meet them at Agua Azul and fight the Indians. The posse left Casey Ranch just at daybreak and went as fast as possible to Father's house to see about my mother, who was expecting a baby. When they got there they found that the Indians had been there and taken my mother away with them. The posse, headed by my father, took up the trail of the Indians. When they got to the flat at Agua Azul they found the body of Marcial Rodriguez. The Indians had scalped him and cut off his right arm. The posse dug a grave and buried him where he lay. By this time several others had joined them and they started out after the Indians again. They overtook them at the west end of the Capitan Mountains and the Indians and posse had a fight. Several of the Indians were killed but some of them got away. Someone in the posse noticed two squaws had my mother and when they saw the white men coming and knew that they could not get away with my mother, they split her head open with an axe and the squaws made their get away. When the men got to my mother she was dead and they found that she had given birth to her baby, which was alive and a boy. The posse dug a grave and buried my mother right there on the mountainside.

My father took the baby to Lincoln, New Mexico, and gave it to a woman named Tulia Gurule Stanley to care for. She raised this baby and called him Jose Apodaca.

The Indians that killed my mother were Mescalero Apaches. My father was killed by the Harrell Brothers, on the Ruidoso River, about where the town of San Patricio, New Mexico, now is. My father was on the way to the Dowlin Mill, which was on the upper Ruidoso. He was taking a wagon load of grain to the mill to be ground. This was about a year after my mother was killed.

The Harrell Brothers were from Texas and had settled on the Ruidoso River. They had trouble with the Mexican people over water rights, which terminated into what is known as the Harrell War.

I grew up in Lincoln New Mexico and was married there to Evangelesta Gamboa, in 1900. There were no children born to us and my wife died in Lincoln in 1916 and was buried at Raventon, New Mexico. I have lived all my life in Lincoln County. I am now living at Carrizozo, New Mexico.

Source of Information: Jose Apodaca, Carrizozo, N.M.

Pioneer Story: Mrs. Annie E. Lesnett

by Edith L. Crawford

I have lived in the State of New Mexico for sixty-one years. I lived in Roswell, Chaves County, for twenty-five years and in Lincoln County for thirty-six years.

I met my husband, Frank Lesnett, in Chicago, Illinois, when I was sixteen years old. He was born in the state of Ohio. He joined the regular army at Fort Selden Ohio, in 1870, for a period of five years and was sent to Fort Stanton, New Mexico, to serve his enlistment, fighting the Indians. He was discharged in 1875 from Fort Stanton.

He came back to Chicago, Illinois, and we were married July 19, 1876. We lived in Chicago for a while but Frank was never satisfied, for he loved the west and wanted to come back to Lincoln County, New Mexico, so he left me in Chicago with my people and he came back to Ruidoso, New Mexico, and bought a half interest in the Dowlin's Mill. This mill was owned by Paul and Will Dowlin at the time. Frank stayed here and sent for me and our baby son. I came by train from Chicago to La Junta, Colorado, and from La Junta to Fort Stanton, New Mexico on Numa Raymond's stage coach, drawn by four horses.

Numa Raymond and his bride, who was from St. Louis, Missouri, were passengers on the stage with me. I do not remember any of the places that we stopped except Jerry Hocradle's place, where we stayed all night and changed teams. We had a very pleasant trip, no scares from Indians or desperadoes, although I was very much afraid of the Indians. My husband told me so much about them and how they would go on the war path, but at the time they were supposed to stay on the Mescalero Reservation.

My husband met me at Fort Stanton. He was driving two big bay horses to a Studebaker hack. The horses were named "Bill Johnson" and "Bill Dowlin." How happy I was when my husband met me and we drove up the beautiful canyon toward the White Mountains. It was in May 1887. We went by way of the Pat Garrett Ranch, which was located on Little Creek, and on by Alto and down Gavalon Canyon to the Ruidoso. When we arrived at Dowlin's Mill I saw some blood in the front yard. Frank told me that a man named Jerry Dalton had shot and killed Paul Dowlin the day before. Dalton left the country and was never heard from again.

My new home was a four-room log house, with a big fireplace in the front room, which we called the parlor. We used kerosene lamps and candles for lights. A man by the name of Johnnie Patton cooked for us. We boarded several of the men who worked in the mills and helped on the farms. We raised hogs and sold them to Fort Stanton. We raised our own feed to fatten the hogs and in the fall of the year the farm hands would butcher about a hundred hogs at a time. I would get some of the neighbor women to come and help render out the lard. We used a big iron pot and rendered up the lard out in the yard. I raised lots of turkeys and chickens and sold them at Fort Stanton.

I was always so afraid of the wild beasts that roamed around the hills. I remember one time, my husband and the cook had to go to Lincoln to court, and left a Mrs. Johnson with me and my three children, to stay alone at night. One night after we had all gone to bed, Mrs. Johnson heard something prowling around the house. We lay real still and listened, for we did not know whether it was Indians or wild beasts. We did not have to wait long to know, for it was a mountain lion and when he got up real near the house he let out a roar. We all most died of fright for we were afraid that he would break the windows and come in after us. We moved all the furniture and barricaded the doors and windows. The lion kept walking around the house and roaring. After a while he left and went down to the cow pen and killed one of our milk pen calves. I told my husband when he came home the next day, that I would never stay home with just women folks again, and I never did while we lived on the ranch.

The Mescalero Indians from the Mescalero Reservation used to come to our place and trade. My husband had a small store and was postmaster at Ruidoso. I saw four buck Indians have a fight in front of our store one time. They pulled each other's hair out and fought with quirts. They fought for about an hour, although the Indians never did bother us. I was awfully afraid of them, especially when I first came to Ruidoso. I was always good to the Indians. I gave them doughnuts and cookies when they came to the Mill and it was not long until all the Indians were my friends. Geronimo used to come to our place quite often. Once he brought me a big wild turkey and another time he gave me a nice Indian basket. I gave the basket to Mrs. Hiram Dow and she still has it.

There was usually a crowd of young people at the Mill and we used to ride horseback fifteen and twenty miles to a dance, and never thinking anything of it. In 1882 my husband bought out the interest of the Dowlin brothers and he was sole owner of the Mill, with the old water wheel, about two miles from the town of Ruidoso. At that time we had a grist mill and a saw mill.

I went back to Chicago, Illinois on a visit to my people in 1879, but I did not stay very long as I was anxious to get back to my western home that I loved so well.

I remember the Chicago fire well. I was sixteen years old, and when our mother woke us up that night and told us to get up quick and get dressed because our house was about to catch fire. We all got dressed and were gathering up the things that we wanted to save and when I got outside all I had in my hands was the bird cage, with the bird in it. Our home burned that night. That was in 1871.

In 1887 we sold our ranch and the cattle on the Ruidoso to the Crees, who owned the "V V" outfit. We moved to Lincoln, New Mexico, where we could have better schools for our children. We lived on the Ruidoso all during the Lincoln County War but my husband never took sides with either faction. I did give Billy the Kid several meals when he would come to our place, but my husband never knew anything about it, for he had warned me not to feed any of the men from either side, but I did it anyway as I felt sorry for them when they said they were hungry. Lincoln County was a wild country when I first came here and at first I used to get home for my people in Chicago, but after I had been here a few years I liked it and never cared to go back to Chicago to live.

Five of my children were born on the Ruidoso, one in Chicago, and one in Lincoln. We lived in Lincoln until 1890 and then moved to Roswell, New Mexico, and lived there for three years and moved back to Lincoln in 1893. I have lived in Carrizozo for the past ten years. Two of my children live with me. I am content and happy to spend the rest of my days here in Lincoln County.

Narrator: Mrs. Annie E. Lesnett, Carrizozo, N.M., aged 83 years.

Pioneer Story: Clerdo Chavez

by Edith L. Crawford

$\mathfrak{I}$ was born in 1880 at Las Chozos, New Mexico, which is located seven miles southeast of the town of Lincoln and have lived all my life in Lincoln County. My father Cleto Chavez was born April 26, 1845, in Socorro, Texas which was just below Franklin, Texas (which is now known as El Paso, Texas.) His father died when he was six months old and his mother when he was twelve years old. He was left to make his own way early in life. He went to Franklin, Texas and earned his living the best he could doing odd jobs. One day he met a man by the name of George Neblett who owned and operated a sawmill on the Mescalero Reservation. He had freighted some lumber to Franklin by ox teams. He offered Father a job to work around the mill at ten dollars per month and his keep. He also taught him to speak English. This was 1870. Father went back to Mescalero with Mr. Neblett, traveling by ox team. They were always on the lookout for Indians in those days as they were always going on the warpath. At night when they stopped to camp they formed a circle with the wagons and put the oxen inside the circle and one or more of the men kept watch during the night. Father said that they did not see an Indian on the whole trip back to Mescalero.

One day after arriving at the mill Mr. Neblett put Father on a horse and told him to ride just as fast as he could to Tularosa, New Mexico and warn the settlers that the Indians had gone on the warpath and were headed for Tularosa. Father said that he rode as fast as the horse could go all the way. Just before he got to Tularosa he met Marino Ruiz riding horseback. He was going up the mountainside to cut some wood. Father told him that the Indians were coming and to turn back. He paid no attention to him but went on up the road. About the time Father reached Tularosa he heard the Indians giving their war whoop and he knew that they had killed Marino Ruiz and sure enough they found his body the next day. On this same trip Father saw Benito Montoya coming on horseback but he was too far away to be warned. Benito heard the Indians coming tho' and he rode into some tule grass which grew awfully rank and was tall enough to hide him and his horse and the Indians passed him by. Benito told me this same story years after it happened and he remembered seeing my father on his way to Tularosa. (This same Benito Montoya was one of the jurors when Billy the Kid was tried at Mesilla New Mexico for the killing of Sheriff Brady.)

The people of Tularosa had built barricades to protect themselves from the Indians. They dug deep trenches and would fight from these trenches. They fought the Indians off on this occasion without much loss. When the Indians went on the warpath they always left the reservation. Mr. Neblett was a fine upright man and never had any trouble with the Indians. He sold his sawmill to A. N. Blazer in 1873 and it was later called Blazer's Mill.

Mr. Neblett, his wife and son were killed on the east side of the Organ Mountains. They were on their way to Old Mesilla to locate. They all three had been shot and their bodies left where they fell. The only thing missing was the team and until this day no one has ever known who murdered the Neblett family. Father had left the employ of Mr. Neblett in March 1872 and moved to Picacho, New Mexico where he worked on the farm of William Casey and tended the horses and cattle. In October 1872 he left Casey and went to work for Jack Price who owned a farm at Picacho. In October 1874 Father married Prudencia Miranda and they moved to Los Chozos, were Father took up a homestead of one hundred and sixty acres. He farmed and raised cattle and horses. He was living at Los Chozos during the Lincoln County War but he took no part in it. He and Jose Miranda his father-in-law used to laugh and say that when they were with Murphy and Dolan they were for them and when they were with McSween they were for McSween but they never were involved in any way in the war.

My Mother was born on May 10, 1855 in a small town called Acacio in Socorro County and came to Lincoln County with her parents in 1862. They came in a wagon drawn by oxen by way of the Gallinas Mountains and while crossing the mountains they met a band of Indians. It was just about night and at this time there were about fifteen wagons in the train, as each day other wagons met and traveled on with the Mirandas. When they sighted the Indians the wagon train stopped and made camp for the night. They formed a circle with the wagons and put the families and all the stock inside the circle, and prepared to give the Indians a battle. The Indians had stopped on the mountainside and were watching the people in the wagons. They did not attack at once and there was a fellow in the crowd by the name of Juan Lucero who could understand and speak some Indian, so he went out to within hollering distance of the Indians and asked them if they were ready to fight and the Indian chief replied that they did not want to fight then but would be back the next day at noon to fight. The wagon train laid over in this camp for four days waiting for the Indians to come back but they never did show up, so the wagon train went on their way to Lincoln, New Mexico.

They traveled very slowly and some of the men folks rode ahead of the wagon and some behind, to protect the train from the Indians in case they were in the mountains waiting for them. They never saw any more Indians and arrived safe and sound in Lincoln. It took about two weeks to make this trip by ox team from Socorro to Lincoln, New Mexico. Jose and his family went on to Las Chozos, seven miles east of Lincoln and took up a homestead. He went to farming and raised horses and cattle, but during 1865 the Indians got so bad they would come into the fields where Jose was plowing with oxen and unyoke the oxen and drive them away, and they stole all of his horses and cattle. After the Indians were quieted down the government paid Jose Miranda (my grandfather) for all of the horses and cattle that the Indians had stole from him. These incidents were told to me by my father and mother. I was a very small boy at the time.

Jack Gillman and David Warner were drinking and they went to a house of ill fame and were raising a roughhouse. Someone went to Juan Martinez who was the constable at the time, and told him to go to this house and stop the rough stuff. He walked up to the door and called Jack Gillman who came to the door. Juan told him he was under arrest for disturbing the peace. Gillman said, "All right Juan, anything you say is all right with me." About this time David Warner came up and said to Gillman, "Don't you surrender to him, you don't have to obey any orders from him." Juan Martinez reached for his gun and so did David Warner. Both fired at the same time and both fell to the floor mortally wounded and died in a few minutes.

Gillman was so scared at the outcome that he made a dash for the river and hid in some brush. The people of the town were so mad about the killing of the two men that they formed a posse and went to hunt for Gillman and when they found him some one in the posse shot him on sight. Later they found that Martinez had shot Warner and Warner had shot Martinez and that they had killed an innocent man when they shot Gillman but it was too late then.

My father died in Carrizozo, New Mexico, November 1, 1932 at the age of eighty-seven years. My mother is eighty-three years old and is living with one of her granddaughters in San Francisco, California. I have served as Probate Judge in Lincoln County for eight years and have been Justice of the Peace in Carrizozo for four years.

Narrator: Elerdo Chavez, Carrizozo, New Mexico, aged 58 years.

Frances E. Totty
Related by Otho Allen
Age 54

February 25, 1938
c1-- 171

EARLY DAYS IN THE SOUTHWEST, By Otho Allen

Billy the Kid

John Cummings told me the first time he saw Billie the Kid was in Cochise. The Kid came into town and went to a saloon and said he was hunting work. The boy saw some men gambling and was soon in the game he was a stranger in the country, and as he seemed to have all of the luck and was taking all of the money; one of the men made a nasty remark. The Kid drew his gun and killed two of the men around the table and injured another. He walked out of the saloon as he had just been the place for a drink, and walked over to his horse as unconcerned; looked back, and then jumped on and rode away. The men at the saloon had thought of him as a mere lad and were taken back when they found him quick on the draw. The boy left Cochise and was never seen there again.

"Early Days in the Southwest, By Otho Allen, Billy the Kid," Frances E. Totty, February 25, 1938, NMFWP, WPA #212, NMSRCA

Buster Degraftenreid as Buffalo Hunter

by Mrs. Belle Kilgore

"One of the most interesting periods in my life," said Mr. Degraftenreid, "was the winter of 1882, when George and John Causey made their last trip as commercial buffalo hunters, stopped their wagon train at our place on the Alamogordo.

"The heavy wagons were pulled by oxen, and the man who took care of the 'loose steers' had quit. So George Causey asked me to take the job, and I did.

"The Causeys had come from Kansas to Las Vegas, New Mexico because of the absence of trails to the part of the Texas Panhandle to which they were going.

"At that time, however, there weren't many buffalo left of the countless thousands that once roamed the Great Plains. From 1875 to 1880 were the great years of buffalo hunting. By 1882 the great herds of buffalo were reduced to scattered bunches of five or six and seldom more than ten or twelve.

"The hunters had to scour the countryside on horseback to find them. When they sighted a bunch they would maneuver to get on the down wind side, then they would sneak up on them, taking advantage of every bit of cover the country afforded. They would pick out a bull and shoot him, and while the others were milling around uncertainly or attacking the wounded animal they would shoot as rapidly as possible. Sometimes, however, the buffaloes would run. In that case the hunter would shoot as long as they were in sight, then chase them on horseback, jumping off to shoot every time they got within range.

"And the range was surprisingly long," said Degraftenreid. "I've seen old man George Causey turn a buffalo end over end nearly a mile away. Those old .50 caliber buffalo guns shot an awfully big cartridge. The guns were so heavy barreled that a man couldn't hold one up and shoot it like he would an ordinary gun. He had to carry a couple of sticks tied together to make a forked stand, and when he got off his horse to shoot it would put those sticks in the ground for a rest. They shot them so fast that the barrel would get blistering hot and wouldn't shoot straight anymore. Then they would pour water in them from a canteen and I've seen them hot enough to boil the water.

"The Causeys killed only a couple of hundred buffalo that winter (1882). However, in previous years the hunters saved only the hides and the tongues, which sold for 25 to 50 cents apiece in the big cities, but that year they saved all the meat and even the tallow. The meat was salted down in pits which were lined with buffalo hides hairy side to the dirt. Hides were also used to build the houses in which the hunters lived. They built a framework of poles and stretched the hides over them, the hairy side in.

"I got to kill quite a few of the buffalo, but most of the time I went along to hold George Causey's horse while he was shooting.

"I've heard men tell of roping lots of buffalo, but I can say from experience that if a man roped one buffalo he wouldn't want to rope another. I took out one day after a 'spike' bull, about a three-year-old. I didn't have any gun but an old cap and ball pistol so I decided to rope him. I had to chase him about two miles and a half before I could throw my loop, but I made a lucky catch around his neck and one horn.

"I threw him just like you would a steer, but he got right up and charged my horse. With those sharp horns he could have killed a horse in a minute. A lot of people imagine a longhorn steer would be dangerous, but he couldn't hurt you unless he happened to hit you with one of those horns as he turned his head. A buffalo was a lot more dangerous.

"Well, I kept throwing that buffalo every time he got up, but he would jump up and come right back at me before I could wind him up in the rope. Finally my horse got so tired that he could hardly get out of the way, and I was about to let that buffalo have my rope when I happened to throw him in such a way that one of his front feet was caught. I started dragging him with my horse keeping the rope as tight as I could. He gradually choked down, but even when he quit moving I kept dragging him.

"Finally I was sure he was dead, but I still didn't want to get off and take that rope from around his neck. I just leaned over and cut my rope. When I went back to camp the boys didn't believe I had roped a buffalo, but I took them over there with me the next morning and there he was dead.

"After the buffalo hunters that spring, I went to work for J. W. Lynch, who was running some cattle at Spring Lake. Lynch had a tough outfit, and the cowboys were giving him trouble. It finally got so bad that Lynch wanted to pay them off and get rid of them, but they wouldn't take his checks. Neither would they let him go get the money so things were at a standstill. Lynch even had reason to fear for his life.

"At last, he took what appeared to be the only 'out!' He sent me all the way to Las Vegas, New Mexico for some money. It was a long and hard ride even for a grown man. And I was still a boy and an undersized one at that. I didn't weigh over 100 pounds. I took letters from Lynch to some prominent men in Las Vegas and they fitted me out with new clothes and fresh horses and sewed a fat money belt into my clothing. I didn't know how much money I was carrying and when I got back to Spring Lake I found that it was $1,700.

"After paying his troublesome cowhands off, Lynch left for several months and put me in charge of the ranch. One afternoon that winter, a squat heavy-set Indian, riding a badly jaded paring horse stopped at the ranch while I was out. He wanted to trade horses, but he was told he would have to wait and talk to the boss.

"When I came in that Indian's eyes sure did get big; he couldn't believe that such a little kid was the boss. We both spoke Spanish so we got along fine and had quite a visit. He said he was going from Fort Sill to the Mescalero reservation, but his horse was almost dead. He wanted to trade, but he didn't have anything to give as 'boot' except his .44 Winchester rifle and his six-shooter, and of course he didn't want to give them up. I could not let him have one of our winter horses (a winter horse is one that has been fed up all summer for winter use), but I finally decided to let him have a sorrel that was a good circle horse but was too crazy for anything else (a circle horse is one that is used only for long rides)."

Traded With Geronimo

"So we traded, and he asked me for a bill of sale so nobody would accuse him of stealing the horse. I had him give me a bill of sale, too, but he couldn't sign his name. He made his mark, though, and told me to write "Geronimo" by it. I didn't think much about it until I heard later that Geronimo the Apache chief had escaped from the soldiers at Fort Sill, Oklahoma, and had gathered a band of warriors in the mountains of New Mexico.

"I saved that bill of sale with his name on it for many years but it got away from me. Apparently Geronimo remembered me, for years later, about 1905 or 1906 he sent me a good luck ring through the mail from Florida. It was a plain bone ring with a swastika (Indian good luck sign) carved on it. I broke it several years ago and when I looked for it one day to have it fixed, it was gone. I have never seen it again."

Not long after trading horses with Geronimo, Degraftenreid moved back to near Vernon, Texas, and married and settled down for a time. He came back to New Mexico several times, and in 1888 or 1889 he built a house on what is now known as the Hart ranch seven miles south of Melrose. It was then known as the Horn ranch, after Lonnie Horn or "the Toole" after the 'toolies' or high grass that grew there. Later it was known as the Pigpen Ranch.

That old ranch house contains the same floors, timbers and windows that were in the Pete Maxwell house in which Billy the Kid was killed at Old Fort Sumner. At the time Degraftenreid built his house, Fort Sumner was abandoned and the buildings of the old military post were allowed to fall into ruins or were wrecked for their materials. So it happened that Degraftenreid bought the Pete Maxwell house.

He built one room of his house exactly like the one in which Billy the Kid was killed in order to use the same materials without alteration and waste. One of the window casings has a bullet mark on it and Degraftenreid said he was told that it was made by a bullet the Kid, mortally wounded, fired at Pat Garrett as the sheriff dived out a window close on the heels of Pete Maxwell. Those who were there, however, said the Kid only half drew his guns from their holsters before he died.

Degraftenreid built the ranch house in 1888 or 1889 but did not move his family out here until 1892.

Trouble with Sheep Men

About that time cattle men were having lots of trouble with sheepherders.

"After we had a big rain in this country, sheepherders would drift over from the Pecos River and ruin our grass," he said. "They didn't own any watering place so when the surface lakes dried up they moved back to the river.

"The cattlemen didn't kill any sheepherders if they didn't have to, but they would beat them until they couldn't come out. If a man happened to kill one of them, he skipped over into Texas. The Mexican deputies couldn't follow them there, and the white men wouldn't pay any attention.

"One day we heard that there was a bunch of sheep a few miles away, and one of my hands we called 'Boots' said, 'I've been hearing about how you handle these sheep men. Let me take care of it for you.' So he left, and I didn't see him for three years.

"That night, though, the Mexican deputies came to the ranch looking for him. I went over to the sheep camp with them, and he certainly had done a good job. He had beaten up four sheepherders, burned their tents, scattered groceries all over the place, and shot three or four burros and fifteen or so sheep. He hadn't killed anybody, but he had done such a thorough job of wrecking the place that he had to lay low.

"I didn't hear from him for several months; then I got a letter saying he was sick in Sweetwater, Texas. I owed him $43 wages when he left and he asked for the money. He said he would return my horse the first time he came that way, and sure enough, he came riding in on it three years later.

"I never knew him by anything but Boots. In those days you

didn't ask a man his name and if he told you, you wouldn't believe him. I sent that check to him made out just to 'Boots' and the bank paid it. We called him Boots because he wore high top boots that came nearly up to his knees.

"Beating up sheepherders was a rather dangerous pastime, for those sheepherders had good rifles, were instructed to shoot anybody who came around and molested them. Sometimes when a cowboy rode up they would drop behind a clump of bear grass and start shooting without ceremony."

One of Degraftenreid's best stories is about the time he was accused of shooting out the light in a Fort Sumner dance hall.

"I was the only white man there, and everybody was having a big time. Five or six Mexicans got in a fight and some dirty skunk shot out the light. Everybody piled out the door, but when we checked up nobody was dead. So we lit candles and went on with the dance.

"The next morning the Mexican deputy sheriffs came and arrested me for shooting out that light. They took me before the justice of the peace—*alcalde*, they called them—and had a trial. They didn't ask me whether I was guilty or anything. One of those Mexicans, including old Salidon Trujillo, were brought in and they looked at me and said they didn't see me shoot out the light but I was the only white man there and I had a six-shooter.

"When they got through, the old *alcalde* said that there wasn't enough evidence to convict me but that the court believed I was guilty and the fine would be just $10, enough to pay for the light.

"That old *alcalde* could just look me in the eye and tell that I shot out that light."

As told to Clovis News-Journal Reporter. Mr. Degraftenreid told me that he would be glad to have it reported for he was not able to give his experiences again this summer. I have sent it with the permission of the Clovis Evening News-Journal.

A Last Steal—Pioneer Story

by Mrs. Benton Mosley

In recalling Indian raids, two stories are frequently heard here as being that of the last steal made in this country or of the last horses from a raid brought here by the Indians.

One of these has to do with Mescalero Apaches stealing into the camp of the first Anglo settler enjoying squatter's rights at Four Lakes (a man named either Carter or McCarthy), cutting the stake ropes and hobbles of his dozen or so horses and fleeing with them. In this instance, one Joe Champion is credited with having trailed the horses and Indians to Monument Spring, and on some distance toward Pecos, recovering the horses and restoring them to their owner. Whether Champion did this alone or with assistance from others is a matter of some disagreement.

The other story is that of a raid reported as having occurred in 1884, which is in all likelihood the last, with the incident recounted above happening very little earlier. The distance of full fifty miles between Four Lakes and Monument Spring—with scarcely an inhabitant between at that time—explains somewhat the paucity of determining knowledge.

This latter story is of horses stolen from ranchers west of the Pecos River, near the point of the Guadalupe Mountains. The raid was made in the fall of the year when most of the ranchers had only "winter," or the grain-fed horses about their camps. Most of these were stolen from two or three ranches and camps; with so few mounts left to get around on, much time was lost both in learning the extent of the raid, and in getting enough horses to trail the Indians and stolen stock.

Four mounted men (Jim Ramer, Joe Nash, Boston Witt, and Tom Fennessy), with a pack horse carrying beds and food, took up their trail at John Aiken's Camp, found they had crossed the Pecos near the mouth of the Delaware River, and followed them north and northeast across bleak desert, sedge grass ridges, grassy prairies, and deep sand, for more than seventy miles; then climbed the cap-rock and coming out on the high plains soon sighted three Indians with the twenty or more stolen horses at a point near the present site of Pearl; apparently they were headed for Monument Spring.

The Indians sighted the ranchers just as quickly and moved out, pushing the horses before them, but when the ranchers crowded them and fired a few shots—though they were far out of range—the Indians abandoned the horses and fled. The Anglos, elated at regaining the horses, rounded them up and turned them back west in a stampede, then gave chase to the Indians. The Indians had by now gained a lead of perhaps a mile, and were apparently on fresh horses, while the Anglo ranchers' horses were of course badly jaded.

Soon the Indians went out of sight over a slight rise, the ranchers pursuing hotly in the direction they had disappeared in. After some two miles of such travel without coming in sight of the Indians, the ranchers pulled up to reconnoiter—in time to look back and see the wily Indians, who had taken advantage of a sharp turn and a shallow though protecting draw, rounding up the recovered horses at high speed and turning them north.

With the first dawning of what had happened each rancher dug his spurs in and headed either in the direction of the activity or where he thought he might be able to head off, or cut in on, the horses and Indians. All their attempts were futile; the ranchers had been led too far out of the way, and their mounts were too nearly spent. In a very few minutes, both horses and Indians were gone like a puff of dust—right up to the cap-rock, heading for Mescalero Spring. And bobbing along among them went the ranchers' only hope for sustenance or comfortable rest—their pack horse, with food and camp beds. His rope had been dropped when they first came upon the Indians, and in the excitement of shots and general melee he ran into the bunch of stolen horses when the ranchers had turned them west.

Soon the straggling ranchers, left there on the prairie, with given-out horses, came together. With dispirited faces and dark looks, their first phrases for each other were, "Why didn't you...?" "What did you...?" "Why in the world...?" "If..." and "Now, we're in the helluvafix!" Until like so many other situations of early plains life the grimness was so intense as to become ridiculous, and someone grinned at the way Old Big Foot, one of the Indians, had out-generaled them, and soon all were smiling wryly at his coup.

As a survivor recounts, there was nothing to do but limp on into Monument Spring for water—which came near being buffalo soup but wasn't. There was a dead buffalo lying in the edge of the pool at the spring, and they drank from this pool through a far from clean handkerchief, to keep back the insects. "Best water I ever tasted, too," this narrator declares.

The ranchers rested as best they could while at the spring, in the old rock "chosey" (a *chosa*, meaning a one-room camp house) built there by buffalo hunters, but didn't see any food till they had completed the slow and tiresome two-day trip back to the Pecos Valley.

The Indians in this raid were renegade Mescalero Apaches; and some of the horses were later recovered at the Indian Agency by a writ of replevin, and a long stay in Lincoln. The story is told oftener now perhaps than at the time of its occurrence, for the recounting survivor chucklingly declares, "We didn't talk about it; we were ashamed of it!"

Sources: Mr. G. W. Witt, Lovington, New Mexico, who is the "Boston" Witt of the story. (This story is often placed in another location—just north of Monument Spring some miles, but this survivor places it west—near Pearl—, so be it.)

Plains Man Whips His Wife Seventeen Miles

by Mrs. Benton Mosley

Had there been a Humane Society in southeastern New Mexico in the very early nineties, investigators would doubtlessly have been out Ranger Lake way, investigating certain injuries received by Mrs. Hester Backus. That is, if Mrs. Backus had chosen to expose the evidence, which consisted of many black and blue welts across her lower limbs—plainly marks of a doubled rope, and allegedly inflicted by her husband, Jeff Backus.

A conviction in this case would have been difficult to secure, however—circumstantial evidence being what it is.

The Backuses, who made their home at Ranger Lake (then a part of the LFD Ranch) had just finished their noon meal when Mr. Backus, looking out the front door, saw several Comanche Indians approaching. His wife almost simultaneously espied others approaching from the rear. As she turned into the room to apprise her husband of her discovery, she also glimpsed the Indians out front.

Backus gave her one terrified glance, and the choked command: "Come on! . . . we may be able to make it to Buckskin."

With all possible haste he hoisted his wife up behind his saddle, on the little dun horse that was standing tied at the front gate—with the saddle on—at the time. And the two fled to the east— the direction of the nearest neighbors, some seventeen miles away. As they rounded the lake and topped a rise, Backus exclaimed, "My lord! Hester, there's another one," as another Indian bobbed up, in another direction. The Backuses had grown up farther east, along the Texas frontier, and Indian raids had been the dread of their youth.

So busy were they with flight that there was little time for looking back. At first they had heard the yip-yip-ing and ky-yi-ing of the Indians, and saw that several fell in behind them, in hot pursuit, and with much waving. More than this they did not know. Mrs. Backus, with arms tight about her stalwart husband bounced and jounced and bobbled, as the breeze whistled past their cheeks and ears. Be it said to her credit that in this emergency she is said to have actually straddled their steed—a thing unseen and unknown, for a woman, in those days.

On and on toward OHO (another ranch and their destination), they sped. The Jerry Dunnaways lived at OHO. Buckskin did the first few miles with comparative ease, then under the double load he began to lag. Backus, glimpsing the mounted Indians in the distance, loosened more of his rope—which he was using in lieu of a quirt—and doubled it. With this he lashed Buckskin across the hind legs—up one side and down the other. For miles and miles, Buckskin, tough little Spanish pony that he was, did his terrified, panting best under the stinging lashing, and the urgent digging-in of Backus's spurs.

The increasingly nervous urgings of the frightened wife was a repetition of "Oh, Jeff, hurry! Can't you do something to keep him going . . . faster . . . faster." Backus was encouraged by the fact that the Indians had not yet overtaken them. Buckskin must really be good; Indians always had good horses. Their escape, if they made it, would likely cost the life of Buckskin, but . . . what more heroic death for a horse . . . than saving the lives of his riders, and possibly those of the neighbors ahead.

When they drew up at OHO, the horse was spent and useless. Backus was so agitated he could hardly make clear what had happened; and his wife was black and blue and raw red from having received the brunt of those unmerciful lashes intended for Buckskin.

Their breathless tension melted into a relaxed collapse, when casually the neighbor said, "Indians? Why they won't hurt you . . . they come by every year . . . once or twice . . . They're reservation Indians that cross the Plains, to hunt and visit, on a permit or pass issued by the government agent. That's what they was trying to show you. And tryin' to catch you for . . . I don't know what makes them surround a house the way they do, unless it's for old times' sake."

Backus, observing the spent condition of the horse, is said to have remarked that it was a shame to so treat such a horse, but that he had "had to whip him every jump to out run them Indians." And it is also told that just here his wife, rubbing her legs—too sore and swollen for walking—and raising the voluminous calico skirts of her day, to better the determine the extent of her injuries, turned upon him with, "You mean you whipped me 'every jump of the way.'" Neither of them seemed cognizant of the licks in their fright.

It took Mrs. Backus several days to recover from the beating sufficiently to walk; and her husband insisted it took him even longer to get over his scare. Contrary to expectations, the buckskin horse did not die from the effects of this wild ride. Hester Backus always added, "... because I caught most of the blows."

Source of Information: Mrs. Nancy Dunnaway, Lovington, New Mexico. (Have heard the story from several others also—but she knew more of the particulars.)

Blizzard Happenings

by Mrs. Benton Mosely

If there is one word sure to evoke the recounting of early day experiences from south plains pioneers, that word is blizzard. And whether they tell you of the blizzard of '84, '88, '96, 1903, 1906, 1918, or of the big freeze in 1933, memories are suddenly stirred to keenness, while eyes take on the far away look of one remembering, and words often reflect a sense of awe.

**

The story may have to do with a lone rider, lost in a blizzard and snowstorm, riding continually for three days and two nights, over uncounted and unfenced miles—without food or fire or sleep—and without coming upon human habitation, person, or landmark, during that time.

**

Or it may be about cattle—piles of them—drifting for miles in a storm, along the old drift fence, and at its end stumbling blindly off the edge of the cliff to death two hundred feet below.

**

Or the heading of sheep flocks toward the cap rock, seeking to get them "under the hill" for shelter; and how the snow whipped into banks many feet over their heads; and that for fourteen days owners and herders, guided by small air holes melting through, were taking out live sheep.

**

A few can tell you of the thousands of cattle, of open range time, drifting with a blizzard for days—some for three hundred miles—in an unbroken stream across the plains to the Pecos.

***

Others will tell of the two cowboys, strangers, lost and partially frozen, who were saved by one woman's humane custom of keeping lamps burning in her windows on such nights.

**

And the story of the young rancher who brought cattle here from a milder climate, in winter, and when spring came he had not a tenth part of them.

**

Or of drifted, frozen cattle piled so high in the southwest corners of pastures that other cattle walked on over dead cattle, fences and all—as bridges from one pasture to another—not from a few pastures, but from many.

**

One hears of the travelling camper and his young son, who, seeking their team—during a breathtaking blizzard, with visibility no more than an arm's length—lost their way and perished only a few yards from their camp.

**

And of frozen herders (most of them Mexicans) running into the 'teens from one blizzard—for a herder must stay with the flock, regardless of death risks.

**

The "fortunate" ones in 1918, whose fat cattle and those in sand pastures, were at first apparently unharmed, but many of which later lost their feet and had to be shot.

**

Some one is sure to recall the homesteading woman who lost her way between home and the barn.

**

And that evening before the big freeze (1933) was the warmest for weeks: a fire and the usual bed covering being uncomfortable: yet before dawn the lowest recorded temperature of this section (around 30 below) had been experienced. The freeze destroyed many of the prettiest landmarks in the country—huge weeping willows, many of them a quarter century old, and this the first proof that they could not survive here.

**

Besides all these things, one is told of devious and ingenious ways in which the cold was outwitted, one's bearings regained, and life sustained—by cowboy, freighter, or sheepherder.

It is the trickiness of south plains weather that wreaks such havoc—the whimsicality of it and its suddenly variable temperatures. In the north where steady cold prevails, one is more prepared and somewhat acclimated.

Residents, formerly of the north, declare the same low temperatures in a more broken country and where cold is more common are not nearly so keenly felt, nor do they cause such suffering and livestock losses as these stinging, lashing furies that sweep across the high plains bring. A fierce blast of the north's real winter, in a place where it can do more harm than in the real north itself—a place more accustomed to the south's sunshine.

Such death-dealing blizzards come only once in several years—hence little adequate preparation for, or protection against them, is made. The usual milder temperature makes all flesh feel the cold more severely, and the unbroken expanse of the plains greatly increases the velocity of storms.

It is out of all this that so-and-so's experience in such-and-such blizzard comes.

The vengeance of such storms is usually soon spent, however. Ground-freezing is unusual, and never of more than a few days' duration. Almost as suddenly as it came the blizzard is over. The sun breaks through; and with warmth again prevailing, it would be easy to feel that Lea County citizens, lacking fishing and big fish as a topic for tall tales, have merely resorted to the weather as a substitute—with blizzards the high spot of interest.

Sources of Information: The experiences enumerated above all came under the personal knowledge of the writer; occurring to friends, acquaintances, or well known people in the vicinity.

The Round Mountain Fight

by W. L. Patterson

The Round Mountain fight, "the battle that saved Tularosa," between the settlers and a handful of U. S. troops on one side and the Mescalero Apache Indians on the other, occurred on April 17, 1868. Round Mountain, a small conical-shaped hill or butte about six miles northeast of Tularosa, gave its name to the battle, although it was a running fight extending over several miles.

The original settlers of the Tularosa colony, Spanish-speaking emigrants coming from the settlements on the Rio Grande in 1862, located in the foothills a mile or so above the plain on the Rio Tularosa, but later for the purpose of better defense against the Indians, moved further down to the plain near the present site of Tularosa. At the time the Indians roamed over the region robbing, burning, killing and destroying property at will, and considered the new settlers interlopers to be robbed and exterminated.

The original colony, consisting of twenty families, was exclusively Spanish-American, and was the only settlement between El Paso (then the village of Franklin) and this country adjacent to Fort Stanton, including what was then the flourishing town of Lincoln.

What precipitated the Indian attack at that time was the sending of a four-horse wagonload of supplies from nearby Fort Stanton to Fort Selden on the Rio Grande. A detail of six troopers of Company H, 3rd U. S. Cavalry, was sent along as protection against the Indians, who habitually attacked every freight or supply team unprotected by troops. The soldiers accompanied the supply wagon until it was thought beyond the danger of attack, almost down to the Tularosa settlement. Turning about to return to the fort, they had only gone a mile or two when they encountered a large band of warring Apaches. Sergeant Glass, in charge of the soldiers, seeing his small force greatly outnumbered, hurried one of his men back to the Tularosa settlement for reinforcements, in the meantime putting up the best defense possible. When the settlers got word of the oncoming Indians, like the Minutemen of the American Revolution, they rallied to the call and were instantly on the move to meet their traditional enemy. According to accounts, never did men show greater nerve and valor than these citizen soldiers fighting in defense of their home, lives and families. With the six regular soldiers they fought the Indians back inch by inch, killing and wounding many. The battle raged around Round Mountain, some of the pursuing army gaining the point of vantage of a crumbling old fort erected for the protection of the first settlers, the walls of which were still standing. Strange to say only one citizen, Jose Luran, was killed, several being wounded mostly by arrows.

During the fight an old Indian warrior, probably to inspire his men by his bravado, jumped into the doorway of the old fort, and was killed by the guns of his enemies. Many dead Indians were found upon the field after the battle.

A big celebration was held at Tularosa the evening after the battle, and the settlers danced all night to celebrate the victory, which saved the colony from destruction, and virtually put an end to Indian warfare against the settlement.

The Indian version of the affair, as related by one of them some years afterward to a pioneer citizen, Mr. John Meadows, long a resident of Tularosa, now deceased, was that they had accumulated enough guns and ammunition to have won that fight, but they didn't know how to operate the guns. They put the powder on top of the bullets, instead of vise versa. The Indians, Mr. Meadows was told, had 500 warriors in reserve several miles away. These were to wait till the attacking party had overturned the wagonload of supplies, then all were to join in the attack on the Tularosa settlement, and massacre every man, woman and child.

Round Mountain is directly on U. S. Highway 70, about six miles northeast of Tularosa.

Sources of Information: *History of New Mexico*, Vol. 2, p. 823, Pacific States Publishing Company, Los Angeles, Chicago, New York. As to first permanent settlers of Tularosa. Also other reliable sources. John P. Meadows of Alamogordo, New Mexico, recently deceased. Recollections published in Alamogordo News of January 30, 1936.

Pioneer Story: Dick's Hat

by Katherine Ragsdale

During the wild and wooly days of Seven Rivers, the cowboys from various ranches would come to town and swap yarns, drink, and gamble. They would generally find someone to tease, too.

It so happened there was a cow camp across the Pecos River and the cook at the camp needed some groceries—so he called a youngster named Dick Eaton and told him to ride over to Seven Rivers and get them for him.

Dick was only 10 years old and loved to wear the old hats that belonged to some of the cowboys, and one of the boys had given one of his old hats to him—several sizes too large for Dick, but he was proud of it even if he did have to tie it on. And also, it was his only hat.

Dick tied his hat on, got on his horse, swam the river and rode into Seven Rivers for the groceries. Just as he was getting off his horse, eight or ten cowboys came out of the saloon and spying him came over and asked him where he was from. He told them some county in Texas and they argued that there wasn't such a county, and almost made him believe he wasn't in Seven Rivers.

Then one of them remarked about his good looking hat, and asked to see it, so he took it off and handed it to the cowboy. After looking at it for some time the cowboy threw it in the air and shot a hole through it, another fellow spoke up and said he only hit it once, so again and again it was thrown in the air and shot through. Poor Dick was almost in tears when one of the fellows said, "Son, was that the best hat you had?" and Dick answered "It's the only one I have." They took him in one of the stores and bought him the best hat they could find.

Filled with happiness mingled with fear, Dick rode back to camp with the groceries and his new hat.

Source of Information: Mr. Mark Corbin.

A. J. Ballard: Buffalo Hunter 1875-1876

by Georgia B. Redfield

Slaughtering of the buffalo on the Llano Estacado (Staked Plains) by hunting parties in "big kills" of hundreds and thousands at a killing, had practically ceased by the year 1877.

Long before the extermination of the buffalo the Comanche Indians had been crowded from their buffalo hunting ground east of the Pecos Rivers, by hunters from the east and by Spanish settlers from the Rio Grande Country.

The Rio Grande settlers came in gay hunting parties, clad in picturesque leather regalia, carrying betasseled lances, and riding fleet footed lance ponies. They made these food hunting expeditions in the fall, times for reverie, in which hunting prowess and athletic stunts were features of all the buffalo camp hunting days.

The Indians' hunting expeditions conformed to religions, ceremonials and buffalo dances. In both the dances and prayers "The Great Spirit" was asked to send many herds of buffalo for their winter's food.

While 1878 is generally conceded to be the year that marked the extermination of the buffalo, there were still many herds that roamed the western plains east of the Pecos River, until after the early eighties.

"I saw small herds of them myself after I came to New Mexico in 1881," said Mr. J. A. Manning.

"It was in 1882 that Dan Lucas roped two buffalo calves out of a herd of several hundred and had them driven over to Arizona with a herd of cattle.

"Old Hot-Tamale Charlie—who still lives here, in the Chihuahua district—worked in nearly all the buffalo camps. I have known Charlie for nearly sixty years. He was one of the best skinners in the camp of John W. Poe, and was one of the fifteen skinners who worked for L. B. Anderson on the Staked

Plains in 1875 when they worked over three and four hundred buffalo on many days.

"My wife's father A. J. Ballard hunted buffalo in 1875.

"The buffalo ranged south-west as far as the Pecos River in the fall, and north-east in summer.

"Mr. Ballard spoke often of using very little of the buffalo meat. Hundreds were killed, skinned, and the meat left to waste. It was impossible in those days to dry or use such great quantities. He sold the skins for robes only as the leather was too porous to be used for shoes or other purposes.

"The hunters made tepees of the buffalo skins, for use in the hunting camps. They were very good for this purpose until there was a rain, when they would shrink and pull out of place, leaving gaps through which wind and rain often damaged bedding and provisions.

"Mr. Ballard liked all he saw of New Mexico during the buffalo hunting expeditions. He returned in 1878 with his family to make a home in this part of the state.

"My wife, Bert Ballard Manning, was a small child when they moved here, but she remembers some of the buffalo hunting experiences her father enjoyed.

"Some places on the plains in the seventies were often black waves of moving buffalos for several miles.

"I was never much of a hunter myself. I liked to see the buffalo free, roaming the plains, but they were doomed for extermination in order to rid the country of hostile Indian hunters, and to save the buffalo grazing lands for stock of cattle men who were settling in 'The Lower Pecos Valley.'"

Source: Given in interview by J. A. Manning—410 South Richardson Avenue, Roswell, New Mexico.

Buffalo Hunting in the Seventies

by Georgia B. Redfield

Buffalo hunting on the Llano Estacado (staked plains) brought a few brave early-day settlers to the Lower Pecos Valley. Settlements and homesteads were established long after other districts in New Mexico because the buffalo hunting territory of hostile Comanche Indians lay from the Pecos River which marked the western line of feeding range of the buffalo to the Texas line on the east.

Because of hostilities of these Indians, who resented the coming of the 'pale face' to their hunting grounds, the buffalo were doomed for extermination.

It was claimed that if this district was ever to be a white man's country the buffalo must go, for then the Indians would have no interests on the plains east of the Pecos River.

It was said the cattle men were responsible for this thought, because of the buffalo grazing on lands desired for their stock.

J. F. Ballard and John W. Poe were two buffalo hunters coming from Fort Griffin, Texas, who saw the fine grazing land of this district, and returned to make homes in this promising stock-raising country of the lower Pecos Valley.

From the coming of John W. Poe in 1873 until the extermination of the buffalo in 1878, there were times when they would say there were so few buffalo one would swear there were none and at other times there had been more buffalo on the prairies than there had ever been cattle in the half century of ranching that followed the extermination of the buffalo.

Horace M. Albright—a manager of the potash industry of Carlsbad district—describes a colorful buffalo stampede of the early days.

"We were camped for the night," said Albright, "when the stampede started. We didn't have time to leave, so just had to stay and shoot it out. We got under the wagons and killed 'em as they came. The slowest shooters loaded the guns while the rest of us let 'em have it. When our guns got hot we changed to cool ones. The next morning the buffalo were stacked so high all around us, it took hours to move the bodies so we could get through. When we were on our way again we heard a rumbling like thunder, and there came thousands, really the main part of the herd."

John W. Poe told of seeing countless thousands of buffalo milling around a water hole. The hunters were not molested. Four miles were covered and they had not passed through the herd.

John W. Poe and his friend, John Jacobs, killed four hundred buffalo on their first two months hunt. The hides brought from one to three thousand dollars, for robes.

The Indians then, in 1873, were not hostile to those who were supplied with guns and ammunition, but the men who took chances without plenty of firing arms were the targets for attacks.

A band of Indians escaped from the Fort Sill reservation and attacked their first buffalo hunting camp, but shots from the buffalo guns sent the Indians to cover.

At night nothing was left lying around, for under cover of darkness Indians came quietly and helped themselves to anything in reach.

A team was stolen by them and another team of mules was brought and tied to a wagon wheel two feet from the sleeping hunters. One morning they found the second valuable team of mules was gone and moccasin tracks were left to mock them for all the precautions they had taken to protect their teams.

Success of the buffalo hunters was largely due to their marksmanship.

One particular morning John Poe, hiding on the windward side of a herd where the buffalo could not scent him, killed eighty head on a space of ground not more than an acre in extent.

The best skinners, equipped with a supply of good skinning knives, skinned from fifty to sixty buffalo a day.

When John W. Poe and John Jacobs broke camp on their second expedition, they had eleven hundred hides. These they sold for one dollar each.

Source of Information: *Sophie Poe—and Buckboard Days*—By Sophie Poe, 1936.

Interview: William Cooley Urton

by Georgia B. Redfield

I was born in Cass County, Missouri, and am the son of W. C. Urton and Maria Worrell Urton, who were married in Missouri in 1875.

When six years of age, in 1884, my brother, Benjamin Worrell Urton, and I left Missouri and came to New Mexico with our parents, and established a ranch home, in the Cedar Canyon country sixty miles northeast of Roswell. The outfit, a part of the Cass Land and Cattle Company holdings (my father, W. C. Urton, a stockholder) became widely known as the Seven H. L. Ranch.

The branded cattle ranged from the Texas line south, almost to Las Vegas on the north. There was no railroad closer than 150 miles, until ten years later our coming to that part of New Mexico.

In 1894 a part of the Santa Fe Railroad system was completed from Eddy, now Carlsbad, to Roswell.

I have often wished to express in writing all the different excitements we experienced in this new country of southeastern New Mexico, with its Indian hostilities, cattle thieving, and land and water feuds. All these proved only thrills and joys for us, little lads, but must have been hardships and anxieties for our parents.

When the men brought in a herd of cattle from Fort Griffin, Texas, and turned loose on the grazing lands 3,000 head of two year old heifers, we little fellows joined in the celebration and fun of the cowboys who immediately, on arriving safely with the cattle, started a contest to see who could brand the first calf of those born on the trail from Ft. Griffin.

All of us on the ranch, known as the Missourians, had pretty hard sledding the first few years, though we were blessed with plenty of water and good grazing for the stock, except during long drought periods.

I remember once very soon after arriving at the ranch we

were without supplies. Someone told us there was a wagon load of jerked (dried) buffalo meat, on a trail nearby. We bought and ate some, by candlelight. The next morning we found the entire lot of meat alive with hide bugs.

We got our groceries by ox wagon from Las Vegas, 150 miles. Once supplies ordered by mother for Thanksgiving arrived the following April.

The post office was at Fort Sumner. When we could go for mail it was usually old when we received news from back home. Father's mother, sick in Missouri, had been dead three weeks before we received the letter saying she was sick.

One time mother was bitten by a mad dog and was taken by buckboard, 60 miles to Roswell, and was sent from there to Abeline, Texas, for mad stone treatment.

Once on Friday a messenger was sent to Roswell for Dr. E. H. Skipwith to attend Brother Ben who had measles. Dr. Skipwith, arriving the following Sunday noon, said he knew the boy would be well or dead so he had taken his time.

Mother must have often been very lonely. Sometimes six months would pass in which she would not see a white woman. She would lose count of time. One time she worked hard all day Sunday preparing for the Sabbath which she thought would be the next day and observed the Sabbath on Monday.

Some members of our family were once stricken with ptomaine poisoning. A cowboy happened in and gave his special emergency treatment without which, some of us might have died.

For schooling, a district school and teacher were established on the ranch. The teachers and expenses were paid for only three months of school. For the rest of the term it became a private school paid for by my parents and many parents of children on our ranch and neighboring ranches.

My brother and I one day saw the first Indian we had ever seen. He was standing stately and silent on a big rock, in the place now known as Romeroville. We got away from there as quickly as we possibly could, and when we had reached a safe distance, brother Ben said, "Let's go back and shoot that ol' Indian!"

A thrilling sight, one day after Indian uprisings, was 500 Indians with sixteen soldier guards passing the ranch; the Indians were being changed from one reservation to another.

In 1889, J. J. Cox on the adjoining ranch died. His ranch and the ranch holdings of some others who grew discouraged were bought and the Cass Land and Cattle Company became the largest and most important cattle owners on the Pecos River in New Mexico. The stockholders were J. D. Cooley, Lee Easley and my father, W. G. Urton.

The name of the ranch changed from Seven H L to Bar-V.

There were always a number of cowboys working at the ranch who were called by new names, selected by them when they came to the new clean country, where they wished to start with a slate wiped clean. According to the well known tradition of the west, no questions were ever asked at the Bar-V Ranch.

Some criminals who came never reformed. For two years "Black Jack" Tom Ketchem and his brother Sam (who were two notorious desperadoes) worked on our ranch.

They stole and were raiding Bar-V horses when they robbed a train at Folsom in 1900 or 1901. That was the last train robbed in New Mexico. Sam was shot in an arm and died later of bloodpoison from the wound. "Black Jack"—Tom—had one arm shot off, but was captured, tried, and hanged—his head jerked entirely from his body by a clumsy hangman.

About forty cowboys were employed at times, and five hundred saddle horses were used by the outfit.

My father would not keep a dangerous horse. He protected the men in every way he could. In all the time—twenty-seven years—he was in the cattle business, there never was an accident, nor a death among his men.

We moved to our present home three miles northeast of Roswell in 1900. Mother died here in 1909 and father in 1928.

I, W. C. Urton, was married in 1915 to Miss Mamie Spencer. We have one daughter, Frances, born in Roswell in 1920.

My brother, Benjamin Worrell, was married in 1909 to Miss Bess James. One son was born to them, whom they named Jason

James. Bess James Urton died in 1929. Ben's second marriage, to Mrs. Underwood, took place in Altus, Oklahoma in 1932.

Source: William Cooley Urton, 3 miles northeast of Roswell. Some dates checked from *First Ranches*, New Mexico Magazine, June, 1936, page 47. (They misspelled name Urton).

"Chihuahua" District Roswell: The Hot Tamale Man

by Georgia B. Redfield

Many picturesque characters, of the Spanish American people, live in the district called Chihuahua, located in the southeast portion of Roswell.

Charlie Fowler—known as "Old Hot-Tamale"—lives in one of the many little adobe houses of the Chihuahua district, which make this section of the city different with their clean swept dirt floors, white washed walls, and tiny fireplaces tucked in a cozy corner—homes typical of the New Spain, which were built in New Mexico after the coming of Coronado in 1540.

Old Hot-Tamale insists that if there were a drop of Spanish or Mexican blood in his veins, he would let it out. He was married in his early years to a Mexican woman, who made her departure from his home leaving behind mysteries, lies and many unpleasant situations for the man to battle with, alone, until a woman with a heart came into his life, married him—mothered him—and was a real companion for many years.

"Now I am eighty years old and need her," said old Charlie, "and she has gone from me forever. Since she died I am helpless like a little child without her. After she was took from me I just went to sleep and didn't know anything for a long, long time. Now I can't pull my wagon of hot tamales, like I used to do, and the Roswell people miss the ol' tamale man they say. They like me. Friends come to my door often to pass the time of day. Some men took my pictures just yesterday, and the finest painters come from away off and paint me and my tamale wagon, and they want to write stories about me. I haven't told any of them what I am going to tell you, and you must get it all down good, for it's history, and they want to keep it here in Roswell, anyways.

"They are stories of things that happened, and things I saw and heard in these parts long before you was born, when there wasn't nothing, anywhere 'round here closer than Fort Stanton.

"I guess now you must bear with me some, for my recollection gets to dodgin' 'roun' and 'roun' when I try hard to remember important places and times.

"I been burnt out here two times by a low Mexican, for revenge when he got mad at me. You're right mam, I don't talk like Mexicans talk, for I ain't Mexican—thank God! I'm Indian mostly. My mother was full blood Choctaw Indian. Don't make no difference what other blood I had. I am just a man of honor and of my word.

"The first man I ever worked for in my life, besides my folks, was John Chisum when he lived in Denton County, Texas.

"I was leader of pack out-fits on horses for him in 1867 and we would be gone five or six days at a time, working cattle. I had seven pack leading horses and five other pack men had six.

"We would lead some and drive some, when we came to New Mexico by way of Castle Gap east of pontoon bridge on the Pecos River, where the old T X Ranch used to be at Horse Head Crossing. We came up from there on the west side of the river, to Bosque Grande, about thirty five miles north east of where Roswell is now, but it was all wide dry prairie then, and lots of coyotes and prairie dogs and nothing else living until you got to six mile hill west and found antelope. The Pecos River was the deadline for buffalo. I never saw one west of the river in my life.

"I was with General McKenzie's outfit in 1872. He was a great Indian fighter, even before the time Geronimo commenced his murdering and stealing. Geronimo was a terrible hard Indian and all New Mexico dreaded and feared him. But they say there's honor even among thieves, and I never heard of him harming a woman or a child.

"He was a bitter old man after he was in captivity at Fort Sill. He would stand for hours facing his old hunting ground, with his arms hanging helpless never saying a word. It ain't because I have Indian blood in me I say it, but the whites crushed the Indian people who were here in this country first. Do you know what become of the Lost Tribe which came up missing when Moses was leading them through the wilderness? Well they swung around that mountain (it was Mt. Ebo I believe)—and they wandered 'round and 'round and finally crossed the narrow channel in the Canada course. They was the beginning of the Indian people Columbus found when he came. Once a lawyer asked an Indian where he got some of his masonry. The Indian said, 'We always had it,' and I believe they did have it before the whites.

"In 1874 I was with General Davison in U.S. 10th Calvary trying to capture Lone Wolf a bad Indian who raided with the Comanches. We had eleven companies of soldiers, 2v pieces of artillery (cannon), 78 head of cattle, and nine cow-boys. We pulled in and fixed up for a camp at White Fish, where we were going to cross McClelland Creek, and here come a stampede of buffalo. We fought buffalo from nine to eleven at night. We had to block the charging buffalo with the dead ones as we shot them to keep them from running through our camp out-fit. We had been short on supplies, eating only one hard tack for a meal. After that we had plenty of meat.

"What with Indians and buffalo you had to travel with your eyes open those days.

"I was manager of the bull ox train, for L. B. Anderson, buffalo hunter on the Staked Plains in 1875. I was one of the fifteen skinners in camp. We worked over three and four hundred buffalo some days. In September the general course of buffalo traveling was south-west and in summer it was north-east.

"I have skinned buffalo, herded sheep, cooked, drove bull ox wagons, and barbequed here in Roswell. The last three years have doubled up on me for I've had it so hard since my wife died. I am all tired now. Someday I will tell you more. We will write a book of all the things I saw and did, before I was the old hot-tamale man."

C. D. Bonney: Old-Timer Interviewed

by Georgia B. Redfield

When this investigator on Writers' Project District 2 asked C. D. Bonney, old- timer of Roswell, for a story of some early-day experience, he at first looked amused and then a little reluctant.

I had always heard Mr. Bonney never liked to talk of his achievements or adventures and it was very apparent he did not like to appear a hero, as many stories told by others prove him to be.

Mr. Bonney was one of the first settlers in the Pecos Valley, coming to Roswell from Mississippi in 1881.

At the time of his coming to Roswell he was a young man, courteous, chivalrous, brave. He made many friends in the valley because of his bravery. He was not afraid to enter into any adventure or business enterprise planned, during the progress and growth of the town.

In 1881, the year of his coming to Roswell, he purchased an interest in the store owned by Captain J. C. Lea, organizing the firm of Lea, Bonney and Company. This store was across the street from where the courthouse now stands. The goods for the store came over from Las Vegas by ox wagons. In 1884 Mr. Bonney sold his holdings in the store to Lea, Poe and Cosgrove, and bought a ranch thirty miles west of Roswell on the Hondo River. At one time he owned fifteen head of horses on this ranch. This bunch of horses and all his ranching interests he sold to R. F. Barnett and engaged in the real estate business. He laid out a tract of 250 town lots, into "Riverside Heights." Establishing a power plant on Spring River, he furnished this tract with electric light and water. He then purchased 120 acres west of Roswell which he sold off in five and ten acre tracts.

During the time of the Indian uprisings and raids (in connection with all of his business enterprises) he served as Indian scout, under Captain Scott. He can tell of many thrilling experiences with the Indians, and interesting stories of the first stockmen—their feuds and fights over grazing lands and the waters of the springs and rivers.

"Well I guess I am an old-timer all right," said Mr. Bonney, when told that we wanted a story—preferably of Indians.

"I located a mining claim the other day," he continued, "a gold mine in Cox Canyon, about four miles east and a little south of Cloudcroft in the Sacramento Mountains. I named this mine 'The Fifty-five,' for that day (June 4th) was the anniversary of my arrival in Roswell fifty-five years ago."

Mr. Bonney rose and closed the door against the hot wind of the first real warm day of this summer of 1936. When he turned to resume his seat there was a little twinkle in his eye.

"So you want a story about Indians do you? Well I could tell quite a few. One of them is of the time we chased a band of Indians on just such a hot day as this—some hotter—it was in July, in 1882." Mr. Bonney resumed his seat. Quiet a moment, he gazed on an oil painting—a splendid picture of an Indian. The painting was done by Mrs. Bonney, his wife, who is an artist whose pictures would grace, and be outstanding for its life-like naturalness in any art collection in New Mexico, or in the United States. Mr. Bonney was remembering, thinking of what would be interesting to tell of trails of adventures he had traveled in the beginning of his life, on the plains, when a young man, over half a century ago.

"One night, about nine o'clock," he firmly resumed, "we were sitting out in front of the hotel, it was the first hotel built in Roswell, and it was in front of where the court house is today. It was just a four room adobe house, owned by Captain J. C. Lea. Paying guests slept in the attic upstairs. We were enjoying the cool evening breeze, when an orderly came with a message from Captain Scott, to come down to their camp. Captain Scott had just arrived with a troop Calvary. I had known Captain Scott before that time, in Fort Stanton," said Mr. Bonney. "I went down to his encampment and the first thing he said to me was—'Bonney, have you seen any Indians around here lately?' I told him I had seen some, early that very morning, at Bitter Creek, which is ten miles northeast of Roswell and Captain Scott said—'Bonney, you must go with me, we just have to get those Indians! If I don't catch them I will be court-martialed.' He then told me that a runner had overtaken him at Picacho that day with orders for him to go back to Colfax County and turn his command over to Lieutenant Penn. Lieutenant Penn had just arrived from West Point. There had been an Indian uprising over in the northern part of the state. 'If I catch those Indians, Bonney, it will be O.K. even if I did disobey orders, by coming on here, but if I don't catch them—well, I will be court-martialed.' That's the way of the world: one is rarely ever given credit for trying, for doing their level best, but achievements bring glory and one is overwhelmed with honors and praise.

"Well," continued Mr. Bonney, "I told Captain Scott I would go with him, but he would have to leave his buglers behind, for you could never catch Indians with noise like they made. I told him to select five of his best tried men and to leave the rest in Roswell, and at 2 o'clock the next morning to send me one of his best horses, I had my own saddle, bridle, and gun. He was to send the horse where the corner of Main and Third Streets now is. Captain Scott's encampment was in an old corral a block north, about what is now Main and Second Street. Captain Scott did send a good horse. We left Roswell at 2 A.M. and crossed Comanche Draw at sunup, where we struck the Indians' trail. We pressed on and caught up with them, just outside of the sands, between Comanche Draw and Mescalero Springs. The Indians made a stand in the sand hills. It looked for a while like we would have to shoot it out with them. They were part Comanches and part Apaches—forty-seven in all. One old Indian, the leader, threw up his gun to fire on Captain Scott. I saw him just in time to throw my gun on the Indian who then was afraid to shoot. I got down, walked around, and made a quick grab and got his fine gun and the old fellow came at me with a knife. We finally got the knife away. Then there we were standing in that hot July sun, which about cooked us, when Scott walked up and said—'Bonney, you saved my life.' But you better not put that in," said Mr. Bonney. Why not, I thought, for he deserved all credit for the capture of those marauding Indians. If Captain Scott had been killed the Indians would have made short work in taking the other six of the little detachment of soldiers, and would have gone free to raid and plunder at will.

"Well," continued Mr. Bonney, "we then disarmed all the Indians, who soon gave up, after we had caught their leader, and they had pretty good guns too. We went on over to Mescalero Springs and camped all night. We divided the Comanches from the Mescaleros and sent the Comanches to Fort Sill and took the Apaches back to Mescalero Reservation.

"Yes, we got them, and everything was O. K. for Scott, I guess. He wasn't court-martialed even though he didn't turn his command over to Lieutenant Penn as ordered." Lieutenant Penn was afterwards made General and was here as inspector of the New Mexico Military Institute. Captain Scott was afterwards made Major General.

"We didn't have such good luck every time we went out after Indians," said Mr. Bonney. "One time a band of Comanches stole fifty horses from a corral in the Capitan mountains and came out to Mescalero Springs. We got so hot on their trail, the Indians stabbed twenty-seven of the horses when they tired out."

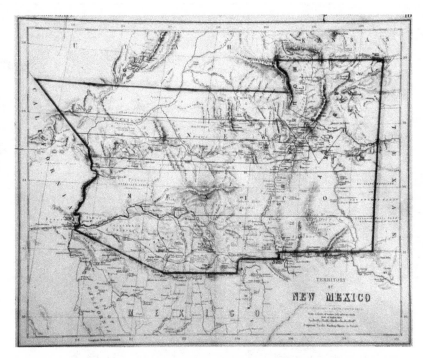

Territory of New Mexico, ca. 1857 by A.D. Rogers (artist), A. Keith Johnston (artist), Fray Angélico Chávez History Library #78.9

Johnson's Ranch, Canyoncito, NMHM/DCA #008840

Jay Hawk Store, Taos, July 1897, Philip E. Harroun, NMHM/DCA #011496

'Wool Bags,' Taos, July 1897, Philip E. Harroun, NMHM/DCA #005458

Pigeon's Ranch, Glorieta, New Mexico, June 1880, Ben Wittick, NMHM/DCA #015781

September 1895, Mora County, NMHM/DCA #022460

Adobe home, New Mexico, NMHM/DCA #070827

"Navajo Camp Group," 1880–1890?, Ben Wittick, NMHM/DCA #015930

"Navajos at Home," 1880–1890?, Ben Wittick, NMHM/DCA #016016

"Return of the Bear Hunters, Navajo," 1880–1890?, Ben Wittick, NMHM/DCA #015931

Southeast corner of Santa Fe Plaza with the Exchange Hotel (center) and Seligman & Clever Store (right), 1855?, NMHM/DCA #010685

The Elsberg-Amberg wagon train on the Santa Fe Plaza, October 1861, NMHM/DCA #011254

A Santa Fe Trail wagon train on San Francisco Street at the Plaza, c. 1868, NMHM/DCA #011329

Plaza of Albuquerque, New Mexico, Engraving from *El Gringo* by W. W. H. Davis (1857), NMHM/DCA #713895

Camp Alice near Fort Wingate, New Mexico, 1880–1900?, Ben Wittick, NMHM/
DCA #015761

Geronimo, Chiricahua Apache
taken before his surrender to
General Crook, C. S. Fly,
NMHM/DCA #002115

"Chatto, Sub-chief of Chiricahua Apaches. Murderer of McComas family near Silver City, New Mexico," 1880–1900?, Ben Wittick, NMHM/DCA # 015915

'Mexican Gamblers playing Monte,' December, 1895, Philip E. Harroun, NMHM/DCA #012240

District Three: The Snow Bride

"Beneranda was well wrapped in a large black tapalo (shawl) and it was no easy task to get her and the hoop skirt on the back of the burro."

From "The Snow Bride as told by Rumaldita Gurule" by Mrs. Lou Sage Batchen

The Burial of Old Jose As Told by Christiana Baros

by Mrs. Lou Sage Batchen

Old Jose Gutierrez lay dead in his house. Outside the storm raged and the snow piled up all over the mountainside. La Madera was all but lost under the white drifts, and no one knew what to do. Jose must be buried. The little cemetery was hip-deep in snow and the icy wind, which swept over them, had crusted the top. No grave could be dug there. Then Nicholas, old Jose's son, made up his mind. He and his father had brought in all the timbers and the windows and the doors, which went into the building of the little church. They had helped to build it. Their wives had helped to lay the cement-like adobe floor and helped build the altar. He would bury his father there. So the men dug a grave in the adobe floor. They broke a path to the church door and carried the home made box which contained the body of the old patriarch into the church and there the mourners held the last rites and buried him.

Within a short time the priest came to them on his monthly visit. He learned in consternation of what the people had done. He ordered the body removed at once and left the village. Another month rolled round, the priest returned to find, to his greater consternation, that nothing had been done. His order had been ignored. He lectured them soundly and demanded that without delay the body be taken from the church. Again he came on his monthly visit. The body of old Jose was still in its grave in the church floor. He commanded Nicholas to remove it. The man remained obdurate. The priest appealed to others but they refused to do anything contrary to the wishes of their friend Nicholas. The matter went to the Archbishop at Santa Fe. Then the church at La Madera was closed and the monthly visits of the priest suspended until such time as the orders were obeyed. Time passed, one year and then many, when voices were no longer lifted in prayer or in the singing of mass in the La Madera church. And then—the

Archbishop was found dead. Another succeeded him. The case of La Madera came to his attention. The years of silence in that little church was considered punishment enough. The regular monthly visits of the priest were reestablished and again there is heard the lifting of voices in prayer and the singing of the mass in the little church.

Source of Information: Christiana Baros, age 33, of Placitas, New Mexico, a descendant of one of the twenty-one families to receive the San Antonio de las Huertas Grant from the King of Spain in 1767.

The Peace Plot As told by Patricio Gallegos

by Mrs. Lou Sage Batchen

The settlers of Ojo de La Casa had been in their new homes but a short time when the quick wit of Valentino Zamora, El Jefe (the leader), averted a panic and saved the settlement. His son-in-law possessed a span of burros. In those days—the Civil War Period—burros cost not less than fifty dollars a span, and fifty dollars in Ojo de La Casa in those days was no small fortune. Burros could scale mountains like goats, they could carry heavy loads of wood on their backs, in short, they could be driven to do any sort of work and they were the only burros in the settlement, therefore they were a community charge.

One stormy night Nicholas herded them into a sheltered canoncito (little canon) to graze. They would be safe enough there, and he would get up very early in the morning and bring them in. When he left the settlement about dawn, no one but old Valentino saw him. He hurried along, for the high wind of the night before still swooped down on them from the mesa, and the air was frosty. He had not gone far when he sighted one of his burros. Where was the other one? He ran as hard as he could to the canoncito but he found no sign of the beast there. He ran along the trail they had made for their goats. On and on, searching the ground for tracks. He stopped short. What was that red stain there on the ground? Blood! And here were tracks of tewas (moccasins). The Indians! They had butchered his burro for meat and carried it away. In his grief and rage he shook his fists and swore vengeance. He would rouse the men and they would track down the Indians and kill them. He started back to the village, then stopped. There was Valentino coming to meet him. Nicholas called out, "Come quick, see where the Indians have killed my burro." Together they looked at the blood stained earth. "We will hunt them down and kill them. We will make them pay for my burro. Now I go to get the men." He gave a bound, the strong hand of the elder man stayed him, "Sh-ee, sh-ee, my son," and he laid a finger across his lips, "Sh-ee, not one word of this or Juanita (the old man's wife) will stir up the women. You know if they hear that an Indian has been here in the night, not one of them will stay. They were afraid to come to this hidden place, one word of this and they're gone. We'll cover this spot, and I'll lead them to believe the burro wandered off. Wandered down to that shaft we discovered and fell in and broke his neck. The earth is loose around there. It is dangerous to go there. They will not investigate." With hope of revenge dying in his heart, poor Nicholas walked silently back to his house.

Source of Information: Patricio Gallegos, age 60, of Ojo de La Casa, son of Juan Maria Gallegos.

Juan y el oso ladron (Juan and the Robber Bear)

by Mrs. Lou Sage Batchen

The beauty, the grandeur, the strength of the eternal hills (The Sandia Mountains) around Las Placitas afforded very little if any pleasure but created many problems for the villagers in the old days.

Wild turkey and deer were plentiful throughout the region and that was especially true around the watering places. But also in those same mountain retreats, lurked the bear. A four hundred pound bear was not a rare inhabitant of the Sandias. The bear was an enemy of the hunter and the herder. They could not cope with the bear, they could merely keep out of the bear's way, or outwit him in any manner they could devise. When the bear came upon their flocks of sheep or goats, there was nothing they could safely do, but to allow him to depart with a loudly protesting member of the flock. The bear was out to get himself a dinner. If he were allowed to take it peacefully, he carried it off and there was an end to his thieving, at least for the time being. Meanwhile the herders removed their flocks to another region and protected them the best they could.

Always the shepherds carried bows and arrows, and a gun if they had it—and plenty of lead slugs. But the muzzle loading gun was no weapon to turn upon the bears. But then, few indeed were foolhardy enough to tempt Providence or the saints by such an act.

When herders were compelled to remain in the mountains with their flocks, they constructed strong refuges of heavy logs, laid upon the ground and built up in the manner of a corncrib. These places were made so low (for the purpose of strength) that they were comfortable only when the occupant was lying down. But there were other places to give safety and built for more comfort; cabins built atop tall, heavy stilts. The occupants of these cabins perched so high from the ground, always had a gun. But then there was a chance to take careful aim at any bear found climbing one of the poles and also there was time to reload the old gun, should the first shot (slug) miscarry. The bears that attempted to climb those poles leading to the cabins must have been few, as but one instance can be recalled. Juan Maria Gallegos of Ojo de La Casa killed a small bear, about a two-hundred pounder, when it attempted to climb the pole which led to a point of the cabin where a sack of cheese of goat's milk was suspended.

However, these cabins did not become refuges from bears until after there were several guns in the community.

It does seem strange that in Las Placitas and immediate vicinity, located at the very foot hills of the Sandia Mountains where bear abounded, that there should have been but one famed bear hunter. To this day, the older citizens like to tell of his exploits. His name was Juan Archibeque. He did not seek to avoid the bears: he openly hunted them. His only weapon was one of the old muzzle loading guns. He was a good marksman and quick as a flash at reloading his gun. But even at that, hunting bears with such a weapon was dangerous business. Who could tell when something would go wrong, right in the face of a bear that had been injured by the shot and not killed? So his family and friends worried about him, whenever he picked up the old weapon and announced that he was going bear hunting.

In the Sandia Mountains in the region of Alameda was a cañon infested with bear, Cañon del Oso (Bear Canyon). Juan was determined to go there. He told the women of Las Placitas that he would bring them some bear grease from Cañon del Oso; he did not mean it as an idle boast.

Nicolas Gurulé and José Mora, his two close friends, tried to dissuade him from making the dangerous attempt. He laughed at their fears, so they decided to go along with him. When they reached the bear infested cañon, Juan had little difficulty in dissuading them from entering the cañon with him. They knew only too well that few hunters even with good guns risked their lives in hunting bear in Cañon del Oso.

So it was that they watched their friend enter the place as he called back to tell them not to worry about him, that he would get his bear and so make good his word to the women of Las Placitas.

Nicolas and José passed the first few hours of the wait, very pleasantly. But as time passed and the afternoon shadows grew long, they became anxious. Could it be that Juan had met his last bear? But they stayed on outside the cañon because there was nothing else for them to do.

Then suddenly he appeared. What did he bring? Something heavy all wrapped up in a beautiful bear hide. They hastened to meet him. What a bear hide it was! Juan was as good as his word. He had killed a bear. It was a huge animal. He had taken off its beautiful coat, carved many choice cuts and plenty of fat from the carcass, and there it all was. He would show the women of Las Placitas that he meant what he said. The three men divided the burden among themselves. Each portion proved to be as much as any man could carry the long way back to Las Placitas.

Now Juan was a hero for true. He had got his bear in Cañon del Oso. What more than that could any hunter do to prove his prowess?

After that Juan went away to hunt bigger and meaner bear, and herd sheep in the interim. He was gone several years, years which wrought a change in the life of the people of Las Placitas: abolition of peonage and the centralization of the Navajos on a reservation, brought about by new laws. With the menacing Indian raiders safe in the hands of the government, the villagers need fear them no more.

And now that the people no longer could turn to the patron's store and receive credit, unless they were employed by the patron, the very fact that they were well rid of the thieving Navajos gave them heart to clear and cultivate land wherever they could find it: that was, within reasonable distance of the village.

Just to the South and to the West of Las Placitas lay a flat area abundantly watered by the stream from Ojito Blanco (White Springs). The land was studded with oaks and brush and stones. They called the place Los Montes (The Wilds). A low range of hills concealed it from most of Las Placitas. But that mattered little now under the new conditions. So the men set to work to clear the land, and to divide it into fields. It was rich soil for corn, and with water to spare, the place was a real promise land. In the very early Seventies it became a land of waving green corn. A welcome sight to the corn hungry people of Las Placitas.

But it happened, as it usually does, that the serpent came to Eden. Men irrigating the fields found precious ears of corn broken from the stock. Many ears yet green were lying about the fields. Woe to them, a thief was invading their fields. A thief in many ways, more difficult to deal with, from their point of view, than the treacherous Navajo. They must now fight and kill a bear. A big bear, if the tracks about the fields told the truth.

They improvised a trap. The bear cunningly side-stepped it. They ingenuously prepared falls, but never a bear track did they find in those vicinities. Yet the corn was stolen or wasted. The situation grew desperate. Not one of them would risk his life in attempted killing of the animal with a gun. Something must be done.

Then they decided to send a runner into the Jemez Country to find and fetch Juan, their own great bear killer. Who but Juan could help them in this kind of trouble?

It is not remembered how many days passed before Juan came in haste to Las Placitas in answer to the summons for him. It was recalled that he lost no time in surveying the lay of the land and in making his plans to kill the raider. So before dawn of the morning which followed his return to the village, he went to Los Montes and hid himself on top of a low hill, at the lower Southwest part of the land. From that vantage point, he had an unobstructed view of the fields as well as the trail from the mountains. In that cool of the very early morning he saw the bear's approach. He was indeed a huge bear, and he seemed hungry for his breakfast, as he was coming at a lively pace.

Juan waited motionless, measuring distances with his eyes and waiting for the bear to attain a good position from the hunter's view point. But the bear had scarcely penetrated the outlying corn field until he paused to take observations. Juan felt that the moment was right for him to take aim. He moved. Before he had time to fire, the bear was headed full speed up the trail to the mountain.

With but one thought in his mind, Juan leaped down the hill and went in full pursuit. He would not be outwitted by that bear. Up the mountain trail he dashed, the bear ahead of him, bent on keeping his distance. The trail grew steeper, more narrow; but on went the bear trailed by his pursuer, the hunter who had no notion of giving up the chase. He had killed bears before, and he would kill this one. He kept his weapon ready in case the animal should turn on him.

Now they had reached the giant pines. It became harder to keep track of the bear; as the great trunks of the trees became hiding places.

Between trees, Juan thought he had found his chance. He took aim and fired. The slug missed its mark. For the first time in his hunting career, Juan missed his bear. For a second he was stunned. But he had no time to think of his bad aim; he must give all his attention and energy to the matter of saving his life. The injured bear was at him. Juan dodged behind the trunk of a tree. The bear was the pursuer now. Juan stepped lively, then fairly leaped around that tree, that race track of some twelve and a half feet. The bear made fearful sounds and Juan could almost feel his breath as he came on, round and round the track, as determined to get Juan as Juan was to get him.

As Juan ran around the tree he refilled his gun. He gave a bound, put a wee more distance between himself and his enemy. He whirled about and fired. There was a flash. That was all. In a twinkle of an eye, Juan had jerked himself about and was on his way again. What had he done? Nothing. That was the trouble. In his excitement and worry—he was worried now—he had forgotten the slug—the powder was all he had put into his gun.

Juan felt like a condemned man for just an instant. Then he did reload his gun again, kept his mind upon what he was doing as he skipped around the track, a jump ahead of the suffering bear. A bear infuriated and eager to kill him.

As the bear kept his pace, there was nothing for Juan to do

195

but speed up, put enough distance between him and his enemy to take another shot at him. He had to get the bear this time. He had to do it, and he would—and he did.

But with that victory came a general slump in Juan's overtaxed mind and body. And it was thus that his friends Nicolas and José who had tracked him to the spot found their more famous than ever Nimrod, his faithful weapon and the big brown bear, the thief of Los Montes corn fields.

Sources of Information: José Gurule, age 90, Las Placitas, New Mexico, son of the Nicolas in this story. Benino Archibeque, age 73, Las Placitas, New Mexico. youngest brother of the hero, Juan Archibeque, of this story. Benino was born after Juan was grown up. Patricio Gallegos, age 62, Ojo de la Casa, New Mexico, son of the Juan Maria of this story, who was a friend of Juan Archibeque. Venturo Escarcido, age 64, Las Placitas, New Mexico. He knew Juan Archibeque and grew up with his younger brothers.

The Snow Bride As told by Rumaldita Gurule

by Mrs. Lou Sage Batchen

All the old timers of La Madera delight to tell the story of Beneranda Gutierrez and Terencio Lucero. Beneranda was seventeen. Terencio was twenty. It started one day in late autumn in the year 1881. That autumn day was summery, a perfect day for the trip such as Terencio planned. He and two of his friends started early that morning from their home in Placitas to walk to La Madera. Terencio was dressed in his fiesta best, not that it was a fiesta day but that he was going a-hunting a bride. The maidens of Placitas had failed to quicken love in his heart and he wanted a wife and a home of his own. He owned a flock of goats and some land and he worked often for his patron, Pedro Perea, of Bernalillo. He was a tall broad shouldered youth and he looked well in his suit, which was bought at a store, and his brand new leather boots which had been ordered specially for him. He took care as they walked along rocky Perdizo Cañon (Partridge Canyon), which was the road through the Sandias from Placitas to La Madera, that he did not scuff them. He wished to charm some maiden; then he must look the caballero (gentleman).

They reached La Madera in mid-morning, for the distance was only a little over five miles. Terencio had never been there before and he looked about him, wondering where he might find someone he knew. And then he rubbed his eyes and stared. Never had he seen such a lovely maiden. Down the trail she came like a little frightened deer. Her feet were bare and the dust rose like little clouds about her slender ankles. She steadied a tinaja (pottery vessel) on her head with her two graceful arms. She was on her way to the spring a half mile from the village, to fetch water for her family to drink. Her heels kicked out her many petticoats as she hastened along and the flush deepened in her cheek as she thought of the audacity of the young man staring at her, and of her own ill looks on such a momentous occasion. Not often did a maiden see such a handsome youth. The young man sighed as she disappeared among the trees. "Who is she?" he demanded of his companions. "Beneranda Gutierrez," said one of them. Without another word Terencio turned on his heel and started for his home. He had found his bride. The rest was up to his father.

The next morning father Lucero, accompanied by a small delegation of good citizens of Placitas who would vouch for the reputation and financial standing of his son, appeared in La Madera before the house of Jose Gutierrez. Jose saw them and came out to offer greetings. For a long time the men spoke together in low confidential tones; then they went into the large kitchen where Beneranda was making tortillas, for it was nearing dinner time. "This is my daughter, my friend," Jose said to father Lucero. Before Beneranda knew what it was all about, father Lucero asked, "Do you wish to marry? My son says he will have no other wife but you." Visions of the handsome youth she saw the day before filled her mind. "Yes," she said. Her father accompanied the men back to Placitas. The next day the two fathers went to consult the priest in Bernalillo and the date was set for the wedding and the plans made. Now, the rest was up to the young man and his family. They had but two weeks, as the wedding had been set for an early date.

Meantime Terencio was busy. Senor Pedro Perea of Bernalillo had need of him there, so he could not call upon his promised wife. But, according to the old Spanish custom, he bought her wedding finery and it came to her at La Madera via burro. It was a bewildered bride-to-be that looked at her wedding dress. The curious about her shook their heads. The dress had hoops in the skirt. The fashion had finally made its way into the heart of the Rockies. Beneranda was the one to introduce it in her section. The dress was of cashmere and the veil of sheerest lawn gathered into a small wreath of wax flowers. For her feet, were zapatos de Castellan (shoes of Spanish fashion) as the people called shoes from the store in those days. The other dress, and there must be one in every trousseau, was of blue sateen.

The day before the wedding was cold and snowy. Late in

the afternoon Terencio and his two friends, who were to attend him, arrived from Placitas on burros. Very early the next morning the wedding party left for Bernalillo that they might reach the church for the sacrament before the marriage ceremony at eight o'clock. Beneranda was well wrapped in a large black tapalo (shawl) and it was no easy task to get her and the hoop skirt on the back of the burro. The burros, six of them, for there were four padrinos (attendants or godparents), padded through the snow down Perdizo Cañon. They passed through Ojo de La Casa before the village had stirred from its sleep and on through Placitas like ghosts in the cold gray dawn.

When they reached Bernalillo it was snowing. When they came out of the church the storm was raging. By noon the sky cleared and they started for home. It was a long, cold, and difficult ride but at last they emerged from Perdizo Cañon in sight of home. According to custom, the groom's family had prepared the wedding feast and brought it to the home of the bride to serve it. All was ready and the guests waiting to welcome the bride and groom. When they saw them coming they rushed out to meet them. Old Pedro, the simple one, had loaded an old gun and as the burros approached he fired to the right and the left clearing their path of evil spirits. The burros took fright as the bullets cut the air about them, and became unmanageable. Beneranda lost her tapalo when her burro jumped and kicked up the snow and made a sudden rush forward. The hoop skirt bounced up and down. It was a funny sight. The gentle ripples of amused laughter fell upon the ears of old Pedro. He thought it was the crowd's approval of his good work. Up went his old gun and he blazed away again and again. The people shouted at him. Beneranda screamed hysterically as her burro kicked high in the rear and gave a sudden nose dive. Off she went in the snow, her veil somehow caught in the animal's flying hoofs. He hook skirt was wrecked, her bodice torn. Her groom carried her into the house and the women repaired the damage to her wedding clothes the best they could. But the bride had another chance to look fresh and lovely. At midnight there was a pause in the dance and her two padrinas (lady attendants) took her away and arrayed her in that other dress and put her hair on her head in a knot. Until now it had been down. This putting the hair up in a knot on the head indicated that she was no longer a maiden, and the change of dress had a similar significance. Then she returned to the dance.

This old custom is no longer observed, and the other dress has completely lost its meaning. But the old Spanish custom of the man buying the trousseau for his bride-to-be still prevails, as well as the custom of the groom's family furnishing and preparing the wedding feast and serving it at the home of his bride.

Source of Information: Rumaldita Gurule, age 67, of Placitas, New Mexico, a descendant of one of the twenty one families to receive the San Antonio de Las Huertas Grant from the King of Spain in 1767.

History of Juan Tafoya (Marquez)

by A. A. Carter

The Town of Marquez, or Juan Tafoya as it was originally called, was settled in or about the year 1860. It is on a secondary road out of Old Laguna on U.S. Highway No. 66, and the trip into Marquez should not be attempted during wet weather, for it is about eighteen miles over a stretch of mesa country from Old Laguna, and some of the arroyos may be too high for motor transportation. During fair weather the trip may be made very comfortably.

The Caves of Juan Tafoya

People from Moquino and Seboyeta found Juan Tafoya a good place in which to carry on agriculture, so they would go there during the planting season and stay until the harvest was over. At that time the Indians were still harassing the native people with raids, and thus made the lives of these agriculturalists quite dangerous. So to protect themselves they had to make their homes in the most secluded places they could find, and here in this canyon they found a very appropriate place to live at "Las Cuevas"—the caves. These are cave-ins formed in the solid rocks of the mesas through some geological phenomenon. The natives divided these caves into several rooms by building stone partitions, and they thus became the first Spanish-American cave-dwellers in this section of the country.

These people lived in this manner for a known period of three years. Three sentinels were always kept at different points to guard against any surprise Indian attacks. Several Indians were reported killed at different times while trying to creep up on these caves.

According to the best information now available, there were fifteen families living at the caves of Juan Tafoya. Among them was a man named Manuel Cassias, who became their leader in every way.

Story of Manuel Cassias

No one seems to have ever heard where Mr. Cassias was born, but it is known that he lived at Los Lentes before getting to Juan Tafoya (Marquez). He had married an Indian maiden at Isleta, went to the Indian village of Paquate near Seboyeta, and from there went to Juan Tafoya or Marquez.

There are many things for which Mr. Cassias is remembered. He was the founder of Juan Tafoya; he was the schoolmaster; he was instructor in the Catholic religion; he was the only settler who could read or write; he was the local judge and justice of the peace. No one seems to know where he was born, but he died in 1917 and claimed at that time that he was about ninety years old.

The Town Prospers

These farmers were very successful during the three years they were at Juan Tafoya and lived in the caves. They were so successful and happy that they decided to stay and make their permanent homes in Marquez, so they cleared the forest round about, built adobe houses, and started a town.

After it was seen that the town was prospering, Mr. Cassias invited the attention of the people to the need for a church and so they had a meeting, where it was agreed to start working on that project. To be sure that the building of the church was carried out to the finish, Mr. Cassias made every man sign a warrant whereby each one would be obliged to work toward that end until completion of the structure.

Punishment for Slackers

As the construction of the church got on its way, some men, as is always the case, would slack on the job. These slackers, however, were not let off any too easily. If Mr. Cassias knew that there was no good reason for their failure to report for duty, he would punish them severely.

For punishing purposes, he had installed in front of the church site a large strong pole with a branch joint just where the head of the average man would be when standing erect, and a device on the pole for holding the man's head in this Y-like joint or branch. When persons broke their agreement or some rule regarding the construction work which was grave enough to warrant this kind of punishment, that person was tied up to the pole with his head securely fastened there for a period of hours consistent with the offence—in the opinion of "Judge" Cassias. If it was an aggravated offence, or had been committed several times by the offender, such violator was also beaten and flogged, and in this manner the church was ultimately finished and completed by the local population. Incidentally, it must be kept in mind that each of the families consisted of an average of ten persons, all of whom, except the very small children, were compelled to do some share of the work . . . .

Pioneer Story: Henry Lutz

by Edith L. Crawford

I left Ratisbon, Germany either the 15th or 16th of January, 1881, on the steamer Wertha, and landed in New York City the 3rd day of February, 1881. I stayed in New York City about ten days. I went from there by train to Trinidad, Colorado, where I got a job as clerk in a general store owned by Rosenwall Brothers. I worked for them a couple of years. I quit this job to go to work for a Polish Jew by the name of Cohen. I did not stay with him very long as he wanted me to go out on the streets and pull the customers into the store and make them buy. There were a lot of coal miners from Starkville and Angleville, Colorado who came into Trinidad to do their buying. I left this job and went to work for the Circle Diamond Cattle Company of Thatcher, Colorado, as a cowboy. I only stayed through one roundup, as I knew nothing about cattle and riding. I sold my saddle, bridle, spurs and bed to the roundup cook and borrowed a horse and rode him bareback forty miles to Thatcher. I met a friend of mine, John Pfluegen, who now lives at Santa Fe, New Mexico. John and I were going to seek our fortunes in Old Mexico. We got as far as Albuquerque and both found jobs. John went to work for Ilfeld Brothers, and I for Spitz and Schuster. I stayed with them for awhile and then went to work for E. J. Post & Company of Albuquerque, the largest hardware firm in the southwest. The next year I went to Santa Fe to work for better wages for Speigle-Berg Company. They were in the retail and wholesale mercantile business. I stayed with them until they sold out and went to New York. In March 1886 I met R. Michales in Santa Fe, who had a store in Carthage, New Mexico. He offered me the job of helping him move his store from Carthage to Roswell, New Mexico. We had two wagonloads of goods drawn by a span of black mules and a span of gray horses. We camped out at night and took turns guarding the wagons and horses, as there was lots of stealing going on in those days. When we got as far as Lincoln the prospects looked good so Michales rented a building next to the old Courthouse and opened up a general merchandise store. I stayed with him until I saved up some money and I bought out Charlie Beljean's interest in the Jaffa Prager Company who handled merchandise and livestock. I took care of the live stock end of the business. I sold my interest to Jaffa Prager Company and went into the sheep business for myself. I made good money while in the sheep business. I went back to Ratisbon, Germany in 1890 to see my mother. I had been in the army in Germany and had a two year leave of absence when I came to New Mexico in 1881 and as I had stayed nine years instead of the two, I was a deserter. When I got back there I went to see my mother but did not stay at home for fear someone would recognize me and report me to the military authorities. I saw one girl when I got off the train that I had gone to school with and I always thought that she had reported me for the authorities found out that I was back there on a visit. After staying with my mother for a few days I went to Munich, Bavaria to see Miss Mathilda Speath. We became engaged and gave a big party to announce our engagement and set the date for our wedding. About twelve o'clock the night of the party, my brother in law, John Brunero, told me to leave the country at once as the authorities at Ratisbon had found out that I was in the country and were looking for me for deserting the army. I went at once to the home of my girl's father and told him just what had happened. It was very embarrassing for me to have to do this but it was the only way out for me. I asked him for his consent for us to be married in Switzerland. He gave it and I went to Rahrchach, Switzerland to make arrangements for our wedding but on my arrival in Rahrchach I looked up the Mayor and told him that I wanted to get a marriage license, that I was an American citizen and my girl was Bavarian. He informed me that we could not marry in Switzerland as we were not subjects of Switzerland. When I returned to the hotel I met an Englishman who told me I might be able to get married at the American Consulate at Zurich, Switzerland. When I got there I was told that there had been a law many years ago where an American citizen could be married at the

Consulate but that the law had been abolished, and that it would be impossible for us to be married in Switzerland. I sat down and wrote my girl how things were and told her that I was going to leave at once for Paris, France. I found out when I got to Paris that I would have to go through so much red tape that it would be at least six weeks before I could get a marriage license, so I gave up that idea. I wrote my girl that I wanted her father to bring her to South Hampton, England and that we could get married there. Her father was afraid to cross the English Channel so that ended our trying to get married in the old country. I wrote her that I was leaving Paris on the Normandy, for the United States. When I got back to Albuquerque, New Mexico, I wrote my girl that if she still wanted to marry me she would have to come to the United States. I bought a store at Cerrillos, New Mexico. I wrote my girl that if she would come to New York that I would meet her there and we could be married at once on her arrival. She wired me when she left Germany for New York, but when the time came for me to leave to go meet her my clerk quit and I had no one to leave with my store. I wired a friend of mine by the name of Fletcher to meet my girl and show her the city and when she was ready, to put her on a through train for Las Vegas, New Mexico. I met her on her arrival at Las Vegas and we were married in the parlors of the Plaza Hotel, by Chief Justice O'Brien, in August, 1890.

Charles Ilfeld, Max Nordhouse and some of the salesladies of the Ilfeld Company store were at the wedding. After the ceremony we went to the home of Charles Ilfeld to a big banquet. We left the next day for our new home in Cerrillos, New Mexico. We lived there for one year and then went back to Lincoln, New Mexico. I bought out the Jaffa Prager Company store and ran sheep as a side line. I bought the James J. Dolan home which was one of the nicest residences in Lincoln. My wife and I had five children, three girls and two boys, of which only two girls are left. Mrs. Lutz died in Carrizozo in September, 1930.

Source: Henry Lutz, Carrizozo, New Mexico, age 74 years.

Tales of Old Timers: Harry Coddington

by Mrs. Eleanor DeLong

Mr. Harry Coddington, who had a ranch in the Sandia Mountains in 1883 and one in the Zuni Mountains in 1885 and afterwards lived in Gallup for nearly twenty-five years, gives the following reminiscences of the early days in the vicinities.

"Coolidge was a red hot town during the construction of the Atlantic and Pacific Railroad. There were killings and robberies and hold-ups at that time. After the railroad division point was moved to Gallup, Coolidge died overnight. General Carr, famed as an Indian fighter, was at one time Commander-in-Chief at Ft. Wingate. Ft. Wingate received its name from Capt. Wingate who lost a leg at the battle of Val Verde on the Rio Grande where Federal troops were defeated by Confederates. The surgeon with the troops wanted to remove Capt. Wingate's leg after the battle. His reply was "Never, if I go to hell I'll take both legs with me" and he died soon after.

One of the pioneer characters at Coolidge and owner of the ranch called Bacon Springs—two miles east of the present site of Coolidge—was "Uncle Billy Crane," one of Kit Carson's scouts and teamsters. Later he married and settled on the ranch from where he obtained contracts for cutting hay and delivering it at Ft. Wingate for the cavalry troops' horses. Owing to this fact Indians called him "Hosteen Cloe," the hay man. Upon receiving his check he would promptly proceed to lose it in a poker game with officers at the fort. A tale is told of Billy Crane in a poker game with Roman A. Baca, a wealthy sheepman and father of Roman L. Baca, for many years speaker of the Lower House in the Legislature in Santa Fe, and a strong politician. The game was played at Bacon Springs and the cowboys there favored Uncle Billy to win so they hung a looking glass back of Baca's chair. Cowboys say it is the only time Uncle Billy won in poker.

Before the days of the railroad it is told that Uncle Billy stopped his buckboard and examined tracks in the road ahead of them. Upon returning to his seat in the buckboard the stage line official inquired as to his apparent interest in the tracks. Uncle Billy looked very mysterious and dignified and replied, "There is a grey mule and a brown horse pulling a buckboard, I can see from the tracks." The stage officer expressed some doubt as to his ability to discriminate from the tracks, and the argument was concluded by a bet of five gallons of whiskey to be paid at Santa Fe upon arrival there. Upon reaching Santa Fe they learned that such an outfit as Uncle Billy had described had arrived in Santa Fe the previous day. Uncle Billy won his bet of five gallons of booze and while under the influence of liquor told how he had seen them pass his ranch two days previously.

Personal interview with Mr. Harry Coddington.

Albuquerque Pioneers: Merchants and Citizens of the Past Era

by B. W. Kenney

Many who came to Old Albuquerque in the town's younger years were men who afterward became well-known throughout the state and in some instances became national characters. Among these was Major Melchior Werner. He escaped from Germany (1848) after having been condemned to death for his part in the German revolution of that year. A military man, he enlisted in the United States army, and eventually he was transferred to the post at Albuquerque. He later left the army to open a mercantile business in Old Town, and in time became one of the largest merchants in the Territory. He was postmaster of the town for many years, and died in 1883.

Other men who had business houses included Spruce M. Baird, Sydney A. Hubbel, John A. Hill, and Henry Connelly. Mr. Connelly became territorial governor (1861-66), and the names of other men continued to crop up whenever city and state affairs commanded the attention of such leaders.

The "first" Anglo merchant in old Albuquerque was supposedly a man named Winslow. Information concerning him is very meager, but it is known that he arrived via the Santa Fe Trail, and conducted a store in Old Town many years before returning to his former home somewhere in the East. John Hill, already mentioned, clerked in Winslow's store. Hill then became Territorial Deputy U. S. Marshall.

The largest known stock of goods in the territory prior to the Civil War was owned by Rafael and Manuel Armijo. Their rambling adobe building housed approximately a half a million dollars worth of merchandise.

Advent of the Civil War brought its share of excitement to Albuquerque. New Mexico as a "border state" was divided in opinion, and Albuquerque shared the same civic feeling in regard to sympathy for the two causes. Slavery existed to a degree within the state. There were those who therefore opposed the abolishment of slavery while others were bitter in denouncing slavery, or peonage, as it was generally termed in New Mexico. As the feeling heightened, bitterness grew; old friends became sudden enemies, families were divides; hatred, suspicion and distrust predominated.

The city as a whole was inclined to favor the Northern cause, influenced by the presence of a Union military post. But there were those who espoused the cause of the South, secretly planning to render whatever aid they might be able to offer.

Captain Enos was in charge of Albuquerque post, and kept himself informed by means of couriers as the Texans advanced northward in the territory toward this city. Then came a courier to announce that the Confederate General Sibley and his Texans were approaching Belen, thirty miles away. Enos well knew the strength of the invading army. He knew his own little troop at the post would be no match in case of conflict. Rather than lose his men and the post supplies, Enos chose to evacuate the city. Hastily he loaded all the available wagons with stores and supplies, sending them ahead toward Santa Fe. He and his men remained, but before daylight the following morning he ordered all the buildings and remaining stores burned. Making certain nothing of value could fall into enemy hands at the fort, Enos departed with his men for Santa Fe. And a few days later General Sibley occupied the city without opposition. The Confederates remained in Albuquerque two months (March-April, 1862). Then word was received that Colorado troops were advancing toward Albuquerque from the north. Sibley made immediate preparations for a hurried departure. With too much impedimenta for flight, Sibley had his troops burn and bury certain equipment. Eight cannon (Napoleon guns) were buried in a hole dug for the purpose near the post. The cannon were guns which had been captured by the Confederates earlier in the war. Although the cache was well concealed at the time, in after years citizens searched until the spot was found. The guns were dug up, none the worse for their burial in the dry earth. The local G.A.R. post was placed in charge of the relics. Two of the guns are at present in Robinson Park, 8th and West Central Avenue.

Sources: from old newspaper files.

Albuquerque in 1853
From the Personal Writings of Franz Huning

by B. W. Kenney

When I came to Albuquerque the town had 2 Companies of Dragoons, 2 Companies of Infantry, and a Regimental band. There were also the Chief Quarter-Master and Commissary Departments, as well as the Military Hospital and the Purveying departments. The inhabitants of the town, exclusive of the military post, number about six hundred, made up mostly of clerks, ex-soldiers, teamsters, laborers, besides the usual number of gamblers and camp followers.

There were of course plenty of stores and saloons, and all of them did a thriving business, for money was plentiful. Major Carleton was in command of the Post until he was later transferred to California. It was he who put up the flagstaff that stands in the plaza of Old Town at present. He also built an attractive sun-dial, but it was ruined soon after he left.

I started to work for a man named Rosenstein, who had a store on the south side of the plaza in the house of Manuel Romero. We soon thereafter moved into another building owned by Santos Garcia. It was the same corner where Mr. Borradail now lives. At that time the Old-town plaza was much larger than it is now, it extended farther south and east. It was large enough to permit the soldiers to use the ground for their drills. The plaza was also much lower than it now is, and after every heavy rain a pond would form. Many times when I opened the store early of a morning I saw wild ducks on the plaza pond.

An old-timer, William Pool, had a saloon and boarding house just east of the church. Peter Saxel was sutler and lived in the rear of the quarters of the commanding officer, in the building next to the church on the east. The quarters of the Dragoons were in buildings that stood near the present Santiago Baca residence, while Infantry quarters were located where the Pohmer house now stands. The largest commercial house then (and until 1860) was the firm of Rafael Armijo. They carried a stock of about two-hundred thousand dollars, and they had their own mule-train to bring their goods in from Kansas City. Armijo's store was located where the two Catholic school-houses are now standing.

Albuquerque was a lively place in those days. The soldiers spent their wages freely, there was hardly an evening without a fandango—often two or three—and as a result there were often quarrels, fights, and even killings at some of the dances.

One discomfort the town experienced was due to the fact that water for domestic use had to be brought from the river or the acequia. It was always more or less muddy, and in winter water hauling was a disagreeable task. No one then thought that some day Albuquerque would be a large city, with fresh soft water that is pumped from deep wells instead of the muddy river water we used in those days.

I was with Mr. Rosenstein about a year when we moved into another building on the west side of the plaza. John Hill was the carpenter who acted as chief engineer in charge of the raising ceremonies.

Many of the army men's names have escaped me; but I recall Major Rucker, the Quartermaster; Paymaster Major Frye, who was later relieved by Major Longstreet. Longstreet was the same man who distinguished himself as a Confederate general in the Civil War. There was a Lieutenant Sturgiss of the Dragoons, who later joined the Union army; a Major Sheppard of the Infantry, and General Garland. Colonel Summer had his offices at the Pablo Montoya ranch, east of town. The Quarter-master corrals and buildings were located where the old Fairgrounds and the Horsecar barns are now (1897) situated. Another of the officers was Colonel Bonneville, who had been a well-known explorer in the Northwest Territories. (Note: the great Bonneville Dam, government project, was named in his honor.) The Colonel loved music, and as long as he was here we always had a regimental band.

The famous Judge Benedict Kirby was presiding over the entire district from Albuquerque to Mesilla (Las Cruces). The Judge did not belong to any temperance society and in addition to that fact he greatly enjoyed playing cards for something besides mere pastime. The judge was somewhat rotund and he always carried a walking stick. He was too portly to stoop over, even when sober; and after his card game he would always walk home with his stick in hand as an aid to his faltering steps. Occasionally he would drop the stick. Thereafter he stood helplessly still, waiting for somebody to come along to pick up his stick. He was unable to walk without it, and he knew that if he stooped over to attempt picking it up, he would fall on his face. The only thing he could do was to stand still, cuss like a trooper, and wait until some friend—man, woman or child—came by and helped him out of his difficulty.

Sometime about a year or so later I left the store and went with Judge Kirby Benedict in the capacity of Interpreter and Deputy Clerk of the Circuit. The Court clerk was Vincent St. Vrain, a son of the famous Colonel St. Vrain. We held our first session of court at Tome (Valencia County), next to Socorro. We traveled on horseback with pack mules to carry the grub and bedding. We had many adventures, especially whenever we camped out at night. At times the mosquitoes became unbearable. With the first attack of these pests, somebody in the party suggested that we rub whiskey on our hands and face to repel insects. Some of us tried it, but the Judge explained solemnly that there was only one place to put the whiskey—inside. This he proceeded to do.

When we returned to Albuquerque I rented a room which I made into a sort of office. There I did all of the Judge's writing—correspondence and his records. The spare time I had was spent in studies, mostly languages.

In the summer or early fall of 1857 I bought a small stock of goods from Elberg and Amberg, at Santa Fe. The merchandise was hauled to Albuquerque, where I started a little store. A year later Manuel Garcia built me a store room on the plaza. My business was a small affair. I was my own "chief cook and bottle washer." While I did not make much actual money, there was little or no expense, as I did my own work even to cooking my own meals. I was still in this plaza building when in 1859 my brother Charles came from

California to join me. We formed a partnership, and thereafter the firm name was F and C Huning. Our expenses were still small and we improved our condition rapidly, so that in about a year's time we had to move into larger quarters next door.

Before we moved into the new store I became acquainted with Don Antonio Sandoval, a rich old native who lived in Barelas, just below the present town of Albuquerque. Sandoval gave me a letter of credit, endorsed by Henry Connelly (who became Territorial Governor in 1861), but who at that time was a merchant at Peralta. The draft was on a St. Louis bank and was good for five or six thousand dollars. With this credit I went to St. Louis and bought a stock of goods. I was able to buy at great advantage in this way, prices were reasonable and the selections were extensive. While buying goods in St. Louis I got acquainted with a young man, E. D. Franz, who was later to become well-known in New Mexico affairs. Franz bought a buggy and a pair of mules so that he could accompany me back to New Mexico. The merchandise went by boat from St. Louis to Kansas City.

My brother and I put all the new stuff into our new store and thereafter we did a hustling business. Our profits were greater, due to cheaper cost prices; and the large stock enabled us to supply a greater number of customers.

The following year I bought my own ox teams and made trips back and forth between Albuquerque and Kansas City. This was kept up each summer for several years, but meanwhile we people of Albuquerque began to wonder about certain movements among the military. One by one different commanders left the post—some went north, some south. The cloud of Civil War was forming, and thereafter I could see plainly that trouble was coming rapidly to a head.

On one trip east I went to Emporia, Kansas. It was a small town, but a merchant there provided excellent camping quarters for my outfit. So I camped there but went on to Leavenworth, near Kansas City. Leavenworth was full of soldiers. Fugitive slaves were coming in every day. There was a noticeable tenseness in the air.

On my return trip to Albuquerque we passed through the

town of Lawrence, Kansas. A few days later the little town was sacked and burned by the notorious bushwhacker, Quantrell. All the time I had been hearing rumors of trouble in New Mexico. On one trip to St. Louis I heard the newsboys yelling of a "Battle in New Mexico." I bought a paper and read of the encounter at Fort Craig. This caused me great uneasiness. I decided the Confederates would probably go down to Albuquerque before long and I feared they might commit depredations in such an event. As fast as possible I hurried home, and along the road we met the first mail coach that was able to come through after the battles. In the coach was E. D. Franz, our partner at Los Lunas. He had letters for me from my brother.

The news I received was a great relief. Franz reported that the Texans had come and gone without doing much damage in Albuquerque. When I finally arrived at home I found it was an opportune time, as all stocks in town were practically exhausted. We soon disposed of the goods at good prices.

Source of Information: Extracts (pertinent to Albuquerque) from an old mss, the personal writings of Mr. Franz Huning, deceased, who came to Albuquerque in 1852-53.

Franciscan Fathers
Post Office Box 107
Cuba, New Mexico

Sept. 30, 1940

Mr. Charles Ethrige Minton
Santa Fe, New Mexico.

Cuba

My dear Mr. Minton

Your letter, regarding the founding of Cuba, to the Post master was referred to me. Am giving you what information I have from the local people.

The first settlers, families by name of McCoy and Atencio, Came here in 1879. They called the place "Nacimiento" in honor of the birth of the Blessed Virgen Mary. They settled about 2 miles east of the present town and Came from Jemez. Those who settled on the present site of the town Came in 1880 also from Jemez. There were two attractions here at that time — ranching and Cattle-raising.

The name Nacimiento was Changed when the Post office came to Cuba. The people tell me it was Changed because there already was another Nacimiento with a Post office.

Franciscan Fathers
Post Office Box 107
Cuba, New Mexico

Why was it given the name of Cuba?
A small locality across the river
(Rio Puerco) was called Cuba even
today people refer to it as Old Cuba.
and I think that was the reason
for taking that name. I do not know
exactly when the name was changed
but I do know that as late as 1915
all mail was directed to Nacimiento
Cuba P.O. Probably the Post Office
Department at Albuquerque or
Washington D.C would have more
information.
I hope that this will give you
some information. If I can give
be of further help do not fail to call
Sincerely yours
Rev. L. Holtkamp

Letter from Franciscan Fathers, Rev. L. Holtkamp, September 30, 1940,
NMFWP, WPA #223, NMSRCA

A Navajo Superstition Leads to the Killing of a Negro Slave

Santa Fe, New Mexico July 1865

Dr. Louis Kennon Sworn:

Am a resident of New Mexico; have been for twelve years past; am a native of Georgia; am a physician by profession.

I think the Navajos have been the most abused people on the continent, and that in all the hostilities the Mexicans have always taken initiative with but one exception that I know of. When I first came here the Navajos were at peace, and had been for a long time. There was a pressure brought to bear upon the commander of the department by the Mexicans, and all Americans who pandered to that influence to make war upon the Navajos. General Garland was commander of the Department at that time, and if you asked the Mexicans any reason for making war, they would give no other reason, but that the Navajos had a great many sheep and horses and a great many children. General Garland resisted their pressure until the unfortunate killing of a negro belonging to an officer at the post. The circumstances as to them are these:

Among the Navajos there is a great equality between the men and women; women own their own property independent of their husbands, and having property, are entitled to vote in councils. They are also at liberty, if dissatisfied with their husbands, to leave them at will; but when they do so the husband asks to wipe out the disgrace by killing someone. A case of this kind occurred.

An Indian of a wealthy and influential family had been deserted by his wife in this way, and he having had some real or imagined ill-treatment from this negro slave belonging to Major Brooks, of the 3rd infantry, killed him. A demand was made for the surrender of the murderer, or war would follow. He was secreted by his family. The Indians killed some other Indian and brought in his body, insisting that it was the body of the murderer, killed while escaping from arrest. But the soldiers knew the murderer well, and they knew the folly of this pretense, so the demand was still insisted upon.

Meanwhile some Navajos near Albuquerque were murdered and robbed by some Mexicans, and the Navajos made demand for the surrender of the murderers by General Garland. This was refused, and the surrender still insisted upon the Indian who murdered the negro. The Indians offered to pay for the negro, but failed to surrender the murderer. War ensued, and there has been no permanent peace since. There have been intervals of quiet, but no substantial peace. Previous to the killing of the negro, the post had been in command of two very able and philanthropic gentlemen, Majors Kendricks and Backus, who kept the Navajos at peace by keeping the Mexicans away from them.

I was in the service of the United States as acting assistant surgeon, and was stationed at Fort Defiance in 1858, and was on a campaign against the Indians under Colonel Canby, and was in active service two months, scouting over the country, and therefore I knew something about the country. In the old Navajo country the grazing facilities are inexhaustible. I saw no evidence of minerals; it is a red sandstone country, in which minerals do not exist.

I think the number of captive Navajo Indians held as slaves to be underestimated; I think there are from five to six thousand. I know of no family which can raise one hundred and fifty dollars but what purchases a Navajo slave, and many families own four or five—the trade in them being as regular as the trade in pigs and sheep. Previous to the war their price was from seventy-five to one hundred dollars. But the other day some Mexican Indians from Chihuahua were for sale in Santa Fe. I have been conversant with the institution of slavery in Georgia, but the system is worse here, there being no obligation to care for the slave when he becomes old and worthless.

Battles of the Civil War in Apache Canyon

by Bright Lynn

On March 22nd Colonel Slough's army of 1,342 men, including 300 regular troops, marched from Fort Union toward Santa Fe, encamping at Bernal Spring on the 24th. On the 25th the advances of 400 men, half of them mounted, encamped near the old Pecos ruins; and a scouting party under Lieutenant Nelson captured four men of the enemy's picket, five miles farther west at Pigeon's ranch. Next morning Major Chivington advanced with all his force, and about a mile beyond the rancho, at the mouth of the Apache Canyon proper, found a Texan battery posted, which opened fire. This was about 2 p.m. The federal infantry, deployed to the canyon slopes as skirmishers, advanced to the attack, the cavalry remaining behind a spur in the ravine, with orders to charge when the cavalry showed signs of retreating. The battery presently fell back about a mile or more, but Captain Howland failed to charge as ordered. The new position of the Texan guns was at a bend in the canyon, across a dry arroyo-bed, supported by the infantry, strongly posted among the rocks and on the summits. Chivington repeated his former maneuver, but dismounted Howland's and Lord's men to strengthen the infantry on the flanks, he left the cavalry charge to 100 Colorado horsemen under Captain Cook. After a sharp fight on the flanks the battery yielded, and Cook dashed forward, his horsemen leaping the arroyo with a yell, and charging through and through the enemy's ranks. Cook fell, severely wounded, but Lieutenant Nelson took his place. The infantry, under Captains Downing and Wyncoop, cooperated most effectively; the Texans were driven from the field, and the fight of Apache Canyon was won.

Statements of casualties are conflicting; but the federals seem to have lost from five to fifteen killed, and the confederates from 20 to 40, with nearly 100 prisoners. Chivington before night fell went back to Pigeon's rancho to bury his dead, care for the wounded, and send back the prisoners, with a message to Colonel Slough and the main army. That night or the next morning he retreated four or five miles farther, to Kolosky's rancho, where the water supply was better; and here he was joined by Slough and his troops in the night of the 27th.

On March 28th Slough pushed forward with his full force; but Chivington, with 400 or 500 men under the guidance of Lieutenant-Colonel Manuel Chavez, was detached to cross the mountains and attack the enemy's rear. His success will be noted presently. The rest of the army, 700 or 800 strong, met the Texans, sooner than Slough expected, half a mile beyond Pigeon's rancho, about 9 a.m. From the first the federals were outnumbered, acted on the defensive, and though fighting bravely for about five hours, were forced back to the rancho, to a new position about half a mile farther east, and finally to Kolosky's. Had the enemy known the number of troops opposed to them, or had they not been somewhat over-cautious as a result of the former battle, the federal repulse might have been a disastrous defeat . . . . Scurry, the Texan commander, instead of following up his success, sent a flag of truce, asking an armistice for the purpose of burying his dead, and caring for his wounded. This was granted by Slough, and the Texans took advantage of the opportunity to fall back to Santa Fe, which position they presently abandoned and retreated down the Rio Grande.

The cause of Sibley's retreat, notwithstanding his apparent victory, must be sought in the operations of Chivington. This officer, on the 26th, with 370 Colorado volunteers and 120 regulars, had been guided by Chavez over the mountains to the rear of the enemy, where they arrived about noon. Descending the precipitous cliffs in single file, they drove off the Texan guard, capturing several of their number, spiked the canyon, killed the mules, burned 64 wagons, and destroyed all the enemy's supplies, thus rendering it impossible for the confederates to continue their offensive operations.

Source: *West American History*, Vol. XVII, pages 694-697, by Hubert Howe Bancroft.

Wetherell's Death

by Bright Lynn

"This story was published once. I don't know what the name of the magazine was that carried it but I know that it was not a true account. I was there when it happened and I also attended court afterward. The story as I tell it is true to the last detail and you can write it as I tell it."

This is the introduction that Tom Fallon gave me to this story. He was reared on the mountain and has taken an active part in the development of the cattle and lumbering industries of this section. He is the typical old cowboy of the west whose type is rapidly being replaced by the rancher who uses the automobile more than the horse.

"Me and this boy went to look for a stolen horse. It was the 22nd of June, 1910. I was herding down near Chaco Pueblo Bonita. The horse belonged to Dick Wetherell. An Indian stole the horse. It was a frame up. Me and Bill Finn found the horse in the flat and caught him. We rode up to the Hogan and called. A squaw came out and said that the old man was not there. I was sitting on my horse and could look into the hogan. It was dark in there but I could see the old man lying on a blanket. I told Finn.

"Bill Finn could talk Navajo and he called him out. Dick Nanasazi, the Indian, came out. They talked. The Indian grabbed him by the throat and Bill hit him over the head with his six-shooter. We sat there a few minutes and I got off my horse and turned the Indian over to see if he was dead. He was not dead but was stunned by the blow.

"I was not armed. Bill had only one round of cartridges for his gun. We rode away driving the stolen horse with us. Soon an Indian, riding very rapidly, passed us. Another Indian rode up behind us and told me that three or four Indians were coming and they were going to kill some one to avenge the blow that had been struck.

"I was riding for T. P. Tallard who was camped on the Escavada and I had to ride back over the trail we had just used. As I went back through the Indians stopped me. They were going to tie me up, but when they found that I had no gun I was able to talk them out of it.

"I rode on and saw Richard 'Dick' Wetherell and Tallard riding down a hill. I turned so as to meet them. Tallard told me to go on and cut certain horses out of the herd that was being held until we got the horses we wanted out. Talland and me rode over to the herd and cut out the horses he wanted.

"Wetherell left us and went on. As we started back with the horses we met an Indian coming up the 'dug way.' He told us that there had been a fight and Wetherell had been killed. He would not tell us where the body was. We began to look for him as we went down the road.

"We found him lying on the right hand side of the road. Both thumbs had been shot off. He was shot over the left eye and through the chest. It appeared that he had fallen from his horse when he was shot through the chest and that an Indian had then walked up and shot him in the head, leaving the powder burns on his face.

"Tallard rode over to Fort Wingate after the soldiers and I went to the settlement, if it could be called that, to protect three Mexican women, a widow, and a school teacher until the soldiers could arrive. I took the horses on to the ranch and later went down to Los Lunas for the trial. Finn was fined and the Indian who shot Wetherell was given ten years. I think he received a suspended sentence."

Source of Information: Told to Elisabeth Lee Morgan by Tom Fallon.

The Navajos As told by Sarah Garcia

by L. Raines

My great-grandfather's house was a low adobe structure with a wide veranda on three sides of the inner court and a still broader one across the entire front, which faced the south. These verandas, especially those on the inner court, were supplementary rooms to the house and in them a greater part of the family life went on. There the women said their prayers, took their siestas, and wove their laces. There the herdsmen and shepherds smoked and trained their dogs. All the family life centered around the verandas, with no fear of the Navajos, as the house was well protected by a high adobe wall.

One starry night everyone was seated on the veranda. My great-grandmother was telling her children about her childhood days in Spain. Suddenly there came the whoops of a band of Indians, their fiendish yells coming nearer and nearer. My great-grandfather was a brave old man. He ordered his children not to move, confident that the high adobe wall would keep out invaders. My grandfather, who was the youngest of the family, gave a loud cry and pointed to the wall. His mother looked up and saw about fifty Indian warriors clambering over the wall. She sprung from her chair and called for help. She seized the younger children and ran to a neighbor's house to ask for help. Her husband and the older boys stayed to fight.

When help came, it was too late, for the Indians had already left, taking with them everything they could. The house, before comfortable and beautiful, was now a ruin, and, worst of all, two of the Garcia boys had been killed in the struggle.

Mr. Garcia thought he would take revenge by going into the Indian village and attempting to lay it waste. A month afterwards, he and some friends departed for the Indian camp. There Mr. Garcia lost another of his sons, whom the Indians took prisoner.

Unable to rescue the boy, Mr. Garcia returned home. Before the party left, however, they seized a little Navajo girl, whom they brought home with them.

The girl grew to be a great help to the family. Later she married a Spanish youth. She died only a few years ago, living to survive her a daughter, whom we love as if she were of our own blood.

Spanish Pioneer: Kidnapped

J. C. Roybal's Story

by L. Raines

My grandfather was a pioneer and an early settler on the Rio Grande between the pueblos of San Ildefonso and Santa Clara.

His main occupation was the herding of cattle. During the cold months the cattle were brought into the valley and kept there; then when the warmer seasons came, they would be driven up to the sierras, where he and the family went to live during these months.

One summer all the family went to tend the herd. Early one Monday morning all the family left except Martha, who stayed at home to do the chores. All day she moved happily about the house, intending to show her mother that she was a good, capable housekeeper.

At dusk, however, she remembered that the calves must be penned and the chickens locked in their coop. Lazily she moved to the barn, stopping to pet the barnyard animals as she did so. As she neared the chicken coop she began to sing but she was not half through the song when she heard a yell, so shrill and loud, close beside her that she fainted.

When she recovered from her faint she found herself lying on a goatskin in an Indian tent. She was so frightened that she began to scream, which brought all the Indian boys and girls in the village to her, all of them eager to see their captive.

Late that night the family came home and were surprised to find the house open and Martha gone. All hands joined in the search but to no avail. For weeks the house was as if haunted. Three weeks after the mysterious disappearance of Martha, Pete, one of the cowboys, wandered to the Indian camp to buy a horse from the chief, Little Head. He was well known to the Indians as a fighter.

They respected him for his prowess in battle and liked him for his friendliness.

As Pete came in the village all the children scampered to shelter. A little girl only remained playing, not minding who was approaching. As the visitor came near she greeted him with a glad, "Good morning." Pete was amazed, for he knew no Indian could speak English so well. He looked at her more closely and recognized his boss's daughter.

He went to the Indian chief, Little Head, but instead of buying the horse as he intended he bought Martha and took her home.

Source: J. C. Roybal.

Santa Fe Weekly Gazette—Aug. 12, 1865

News Notice.

A party of fifty-two citizens started from Abiquiu on a scout to the Navajo country of the 19th of June, and after having passed over a greater part of the country encountered about two hundred Navajo and Apache warriors near the San Francisco Mountains on the 8th of July. Two fights ensued, one of which lasted three hours and the other an hour and a half. Nine Indians were killed by the citizens, and one Mexican of some ten years of age was captured; eighty-five Indian horses, and about one hundred sheep were taken from the Indians. In the fight two of the citizens were wounded pretty severely. The third day after the second fight, when the citizens were divided, the Indians surprised the herders (twenty-two in number) and retook all of their stock excepting some fifty or sixty sheep which had been killed for subsistence of the party. The latter, after having lost their captured property, found their provisions growing short, and thinking it useless to campaign without a force sufficiently strong to protect whatever property they might capture, returned home.

These occurrences took place about 250 miles from Fort Wingate and west of the Moqui villages.

The citizens of Cubero and Sebolleta intend to start on a campaign with a force of about one hundred strong.

We gather the above facts from a report made by Col. J. C. Shaw dated at Fort Wingate July 24, 1865.

It is to be inferred from the great distances which this combination of Apaches and Navajos had removed themselves from the settlement and Fort Wingate that they had no confidence in their ability to defend themselves, and that they intended to seek safety in the seclusion of their retreat. But the perseverance of the citizens of Abiquiu enabled them to find their hiding place and administer to them a sound drubbing, but they were not strong enough to secure the advantages they had obtained and which should have awarded their exertions.

Fruitland

by Mrs. R. T. F. Simpson

Name: Fruitland.

Population: Un-incorporated, and the census is not taken separately, but with that of the precinct in which it is located.

Altitude: 5200 feet.

Location: Twelve miles northwest of Farmington on U.S. Highway 550.

Transportation: On Farmington-Gallup Canon Ball Bust line. No railway.

Hotels: None.

Tourist camps: None.

History: Luther C. Burnham was one of the earliest settlers of Fruitland. He left Utah with a small colony of Mormons in the winter of 1877-78 and journeyed to "Savoya" now called "Ramah," New Mexico, traveling with oxen, in covered wagons and taking three months to make the trip. There were horses in the caravan, too, but their speed was controlled by the slower moving animals, for they dared not allow the horses to go on ahead, as this would split the caravan into two sections, weakening it, and the ever present fear of attacking Indians kept the party close together.

Wherever they made camp, the covered wagons were the outer boundary of a great circle, within which there was greater safety, and here, as by magic, a little settlement was established within a few minutes, developing the fine community spirit necessary to the group to maintain in attempting the crossing of that great uninhabited desert country.

Frequently, it was several days before the camp was broken, and this time was spent in making bread and preparing other food to be used while on the road, to do laundry work, sewing and mending, caring for the sick at times, as well as to rest both man and beast; and there was harness-mending and horseshoeing and blacksmithing to be done.

When they arrived at the crossing of "The Big Colorado" river, the ice was none too thick, so it was decided to have the women and children walk across, which was done in safety, and thus lightened much of the load; the men drove the wagons across, but one of the oxen was too heavy for the thin ice, which broke, and the ox was drowned in spite of every effort to save it. It was greatly missed and mourned. To their horror, small-pox was raging in the settlement when they arrived in Ramah after their long journey, but this trouble was met with the courage and fortitude that characterizes the pioneer and the early missionary.

In his work among the Indians, Mr. Burnham was obliged to travel over the greater part of New Mexico, and during this time was greatly impressed with the beauty of the Fruitland mesa. Later he moved here, where he was made the first Mormon Bishop at the territory called "Burnhams' Ward," and was Bishop for seventeen years. He chose this locality because of the very evident fertility of the soil, where the grass grew tall and in great abundance, which was in striking contrast to the barrenness of the near-by desert.

During the very early period in Fruitland, as a protection from the hostile Indians and the ever present dread of extermination by them, nearly all the settlers lived in a long adobe, L-shaped building of some twelve rooms or sections, built by Mrs. Mary Bigler. Quite near was the sturdy log-house of Mr. Walter Stevens. This log house was also used as a church till the first church was built by the community under the able direction of Mr. Albert Farnsworth, Counselor to Bishop Burnham. This little fort-like place was located in or very near the center of what is now the well established and prosperous settlement of Fruitland.

In a short time Bishop Burnham bought a farm down by the river, from a man named Hart, where now lives Mr. Jos Hatch, whose father was an early settler also, and here he built a good three roomed house under the shelter of a group of large cottonwood trees. It was near the river, so he built a levee a little above them to protect the house from a rise in the river, but in spite of every effort to save it during the flood of 1883, "old man river" came into his door, and melted down the adobe walls just as Mr. Burnham and his family with their house-hold goods escaped to higher ground, viewing in deep distress the destruction of their great efforts to found a home in this locality.

However, he remained here, and Fruitland was always his home where he was held in worthy respect and great esteem and where the many members of his large family grew up to be among the most substantial citizens of the district. Luther C. Burnham was born Nov. 28, 1835; died May 21,1914.

Source: Farmington Office U.S.G.S, Person Information. Interviews with daughters of Luther C. Burnham, Mrs. J. M. Palmer & Mrs. Maria B. Winder.

Reminiscences of Mr. Joe Prewitt

by Mrs. R. T. F. Simpson

Mr. Prewitt came to Durango, Colorado in 1881, and in May, 1882 he came to Farmington, which was his home for several years. At that time Farmington contained only about ten buildings, and all of them were made of adobe, with dirt roofs. "Not a shingle in the town. Well," he said, "it was just as well, and in some instances, better; for frequently, there would be a group of cowboys sitting in a saloon, and just for amusement they would shoot through the roof with their six-shooters, which would have made a regular sieve of a shingled roof, but with a dirt roof it did but little harm, for the bullet could be seen to raise a little streak of dirt a few inches in the air; then the dirt in the roof would just settle back and the hole closed up.

"Some of the old buildings are still in pretty good shape, especially the old Markley Building, where I was located when I first went to Farmington. The two old school houses were both adobe, but are now both encased in a sheathing of lumber. The second school house was really a church which was dedicated on Christmas Day in 1883. The building was used for all kinds of meetings—except dances. There was a man named George Meedham, who was Presiding Elder of the Methodist Church, who opened a "School For Higher Education" in the building, but it did not continue.

"The first fruit crop was harvested in 1883, but there was not more than a bushel or two of it all told. But the crop was soon greatly increased, and before many years the fruit from the San Juan Valley was shipped by the trainload across land and sea, and has made for itself a wide reputation for good fruit with fine flavor. At this early day Farmington had no shade trees, but today the town can boast of many beauties and they add much to the attractiveness of the homes there.

"Frank Allen's 'Grand Hotel' was just three rooms and west and north of Allen's place. Schuyler Smith had a farm (later bought by Blake) which was broad and flat and unfenced, and often on Sundays, when the cow-boys of the town were out for a bit of fun, they raced their ponies across this flat and on through the town, shooting their guns into the air with a whoop, stirring up both dust and noise.

"Occasionally Indians indulged in the same pastime, till one day in the winter of '84, it had been fenced in by 'Dobe Jack' who lived on the place. The fence, which they did not see in time to stop, was hit full force and all piled up in a heap, both Indians and horses, and that was the last of the Indians racing through the town.

"The Navajo frequently brought in a wild turkey or a saddle of venison, which they gladly sold for fifty cents.

"In front of the present 'Avery Hotel' to the south and west of it, was (and is) an acre or so of good flat ground, which had been sowed to winter wheat. In the spring it was fresh and green-looking and a good feeding ground for wild geese which frequently furnished the inhabitants with a very palatable dinner of roast wild goose.

"Making the trip to Durango at that time was quite an undertaking. The Animas River was crossed nine times, and there being only one bridge, it had to be forded just eight times. There was no road; it was but a trail where someone else had driven, avoiding as best he could the roughest places, and winding around trees and big boulders, and you had to keep going to make it in two days. If it was muddy it took three or four days, and you couldn't make it in two days. If it was muddy it took three or four days and you couldn't make it at all if the snow was deep, while now we make it in about an hour in any kind of weather. They had regular stopping places on the road where we could get meals, but the best place of all was at the home of Mrs. Kountz, who served such good meals that we made every effort to get there at meal time. The memory of them is still very vivid. She lived in an adobe house, just between the bridge and a large garage as you enter the town going north to

Aztec, still standing, but showing the age of its years.

"The mail arrived from Durango, by going first to Ft. Lewis, then to the 'Johnnie Pond Ranch' on the La Plata, where the stage stayed overnight, then to Pendleton, N.M., the Post Office on the La Plata, in the store of Dan Rhoads, Postmaster, on to Aztec, N.M. and across to Bloomfield, which was quite a town, and then down to Farmington. We got the mail twice a week except when the water was high.

"During the 'Stockton War' in the early eighties, and after 'Barker' had been killed, as well as Port Stockton, there occurred the killing of two men, one named Pyatt and one named George Brown, Pyatt being on the Stockton side and Brown on the other side. The shooting took place at a New Years dance when the two men met outside of the dance hall; both men shot and both men were killed, each killed the other as they were both dead shots.

"The first store in the town was 'Miller's,' and the second was 'Cheeney's,' in the old Markley Building, which was built by Cheeney, as well as the older Palmer house, just north of the present Palmer home, and both were bought by Mr. Markley when he arrived.

"I was employed by Markley, and later went into business with him. The demand for produce was good in those days, and when sold, brought good prices. Potatoes, 10¢ per pound. Hay $140.00 per ton at times. Everything hauled from Chama. There was more water in the old San Juan in those days than there is now, and in the high waters during the spring the river took its toll and many drowned. On August 5th, 1881, the first regular train on the new Denver and Rio Grande Railroad rolled into Durango, and Farmington helped to celebrate the event, which was done in a big way, as it meant so much to both towns.

"This was the beginning of the end of the 'old days.'

"Yes, this was, but they were, in some ways, superior days. For people then were honest and brave, and would go to any length to do the right thing. We never locked our doors—not even during a six weeks absence at a time. No stealing—stealing would not have been tolerated. People were always willing to extend their hospitality to the traveler. Even the Indians would do the same. I remember when my brother and I were lost on the reservation. Some Indians took us in to a two-room hogan, and made us comfortable for the night with plenty of comforts and blankets and sheepskins to sleep on. They were generous too, with food (no matter how hard it was for them to get), but it was better not to look too closely when they were preparing it. I have found that the Indians will treat you well, provided you go half way and treat them rightly."

Source of Information: Mr. Joe Prewitt, Durango, Colorado. Personal interview.

Interview with Mrs. William C. Heacock

by Janet Smith

Mrs. Heacock laughed when I said I had heard that her husband had been a famous judge in the old days in Albuquerque. Notorious had been the word that first occurred to me but I had of course rejected it.

She didn't think that she could tell me stories about her husband's career so well because she had never paid much attention to his business. She had been busy raising her family. She remembered well enough the shack she had lived in—you couldn't call it a house—and lucky to get that, for there weren't any real houses in Albuquerque in those days. The shack had been on South Second Street where the Crystal Beer Garden now stands. It was a dusty spot and she had wanted her husband to buy a little land near Robinson Park where there were a few trees and a pump. She would have been satisfied with a one room house and tent there, she said, but her husband said a house built on that spot would sink into the quicksand in no time. "He had no eye for business," she said. "He knew just one thing—the law."

She remembered too the board sidewalks and how the planks would bob up first on one end and then on the other see-saw-like as she pushed her baby carriage over them. There were half a dozen saloons to every block and the cowboys would loll in the doorways and against the walls competitively spitting amber juice. "When I think of it now . . . " she said, "but it seemed natural enough to me then!"

One night, about 1890 she thought, she was just clearing away the supper table when she heard shots outside. She ran to the door to see what was happening, when her husband called her back. The safest thing to do at such times was to lie down on the floor. The drunken cowboys generally had no desire to kill anyone, but it was safer to keep out of the way of their bullets. On one occasion a cowboy had killed a child. He was drunk and looking for black cats to shoot at. He was horrified when he realized what he had done, but they hung him. They had to make an example of someone in order to make Albuquerque safe for the children. Mr. Heacock had prosecuted the case, and was so upset when the man was hung that he refused thereafter to serve except as a defense lawyer.

Another time Billy the Kid had come to the door to get her husband to help him out of some kind of a scrape. Mrs. Heacock answered the door. She said he looked like any nice young lad to her. Afterward everyone was talking about him, and she was glad she'd seen him, but she didn't ever believe any of that talk about his being a bad character. They were after him, and he had to protect himself, didn't he?

I asked Mrs. Heacock if the story about her husband's fining the dead man for carrying concealed weapons was true. She laughed and said it was true all right, but she couldn't remember "just how it went."

This is the story as it was told to me, somewhat embellished with time perhaps, but a good story, and according to Mrs. Heacock based on fact.

Judge William C. Heacock and his cronies were playing three card monte in the back room of a saloon. The cards were up against the Judge that evening and along about one in the morning he found himself without funds to continue his game. As was customary with the Judge in such critical situations, he called his deputies who were drinking at the bar in the next room.

"Get me a drunk," he ordered, "a drunk with money in his pockets who is guilty of disorderly conduct."

The deputies departed on their familiar mission, and the Judge retired to the Court Room on the upper floor, where he prepared to hold a session of night court. A town like Albuquerque needed a night court to keep it in order.

Before long the deputies returned, carrying a limp man between them.

"What the Hell?" said the Judge. "What's that you got?"

"Your Honor," replied one of the deputies, as he straightened up from placing his burden on the floor, "we found him in the back room of the Blue Indigo."

"Can he stand trial or is he dead drunk?" asked the Judge.

"He's not drunk, but he's dead all right. He croaked himself over there in the Blue Indigo. The proprietor insisted that we get him out of there."

The Judge was annoyed. "Didn't the fool ever hear of an inquest?" he asked. He had sent for a lucrative drunk, not a drooling suicide.

He turned solemnly to his deputies. "This court is a court of justice," he said. "The right of habeas corpus must not be ignored. The prisoner must be given a speedy and fair trial. This court is ready to hear evidence. What is the charge?"

"Your Honor," spoke one of the deputies. "The charge has not been yet determined."

"This court will hear no case without a charge. Did you search the prisoner?"

"There was a letter to some dame—"began the deputy.

"Any money?"

The deputy counted $27.32.

"Any weapons?"

They took a gun from his hip pocket.

"Has the prisoner anything to say before the sentence is imposed upon him?"

Judge Heacock cocked his ear expectantly toward the prone prisoner. "In view of the unresponsiveness of the prisoner which this court interprets as contempt, and in view of the unlawful possession of a lethal weapon, this court imposes a fine of $20.00 costs," pronounced the Judge.

"You might as well leave him there till morning," said the Judge as he pocketed the money. The monte game was continued on the floor below.

Mrs. Heacock says they used to do funny things in Albuquerque in those days. And many of them were done in the name of justice. She remembers the time when a well dressed stranger arrived on the train from the East. He took a hack to the hotel on First Street and was just paying the hack driver, when two big deputies arrested and took him to court for being a suspicious character. "Because he was too well dressed and they needed money for the city that day," she added.

And then there is the story of how Judge Heacock sent Elfego Baca to his own jail for a month. Mrs. Heacock laughed about that one too.

The story is told in Kyle Crichton's book "Law and Order Ltd."

Judge Heacock's deputies were out searching for a drunk for the night court. When they tried to arrest Jesus Romero, who was a friend of Elfego Baca's, Mr. Baca objected to the extent of whanging one of the policemen over the head with a huge silver watch. The injured man was one of Albuquerque's favorite policemen, and when the crowd saw him lying unconscious, they assisted the other deputy in escorting Mr. Baca to the night court. Romero was completely forgotten.

"Disorderly conduct" was the charge, which Mr. Baca denied with some heat. But the night sergeant had discovered $18.19 in his pocket.

"Thirty days or ten dollars and costs," said the Judge.

But they couldn't pull that stuff on Mr. Baca. He took the thirty days, and a deputy accompanied him to the jail in Old Town where unbeknown to the Judge, Mr. Baca had recently been appointed jailer. The name of E. Baca was signed in the record, and the jailer, Mr. Elfego Baca, received the regular $.75 a day for the feeding of the prisoner. At the end of the month, Mr. Baca was $22.50 the richer for his encounter with the Albuquerque night court.

Perhaps it is only fair to add a bit concerning the more serious side of Judge Heacock's career. He graduated from Annapolis in the days when graduating classes were very small, studied law at Philadelphia, and at one time surveyed the harbor at Rio de Janeiro. Mrs. Heacock said that he had many offers to leave Albuquerque for positions in all parts of the country. But life as he was able to live it in New Mexico evidently suited him best.

Cesaria Gallegos

by Annette H. Thorp

There was no respect for the old any more, and she was muy vieja, "very old." She did not like the way young people behaved nowadays. When she was young, children always said, Si Señora, or No Señora. Now if you speak to them, they answer, Si, No or what do you want, said Cesaria Gallegos, who lives with her son Antonio and his wife.

She has nine grandchildren—four married—, and twelve great-grandchildren. Cesaria does not know how old she is, but she thinks she must be close to a hundred. She is bent, and walks with a cane. Her brown face is wrinkled, and she has very little hair. What there is of it is grey, and still streaked with black. She had on a black dress green with age, a grey calico apron, and a faded blue handkerchief tied on her head.

She cannot see very well any more; on cloudy days it is bad, and she stays home. But when the sun shines, she goes to church. Oh yes, she walks muy dispacio, "very slow."

Her son is good to her, and his wife cooks her food. But it is not like the food they used to eat. When she was a young woman, she made her own tortillas de maiz azul, "blue corn." She had a metate, and ground them fresh every day. There is no food como la Mexicana, "like the Mexican." Frijoles, and chili con carne seca, "dried meat." Jerked or dried meat is made as follows. Fresh beef or mutton is cut thin, sprinkled with salt, and hung in the sun to dry. When wanted, it is placed in the oven, and heated. While hot it is pounded on a metate stone until soft. Then mixed with chili.

Her mother's name was Dolores Lopez, and her Father's Vincente Ortega. They lived in Agua Fria, where she was born.

When she was a little girl, they use to go to the hills and gather pinions. One year they got so many, her father took them to Albuquerque, and sold them. He brought back mucho comida, "lots of food," and a barrel of vino Mexicano, "native wine." When she was—maybe fourteen—she married Antonio Gallegos, and came to town to live. She had two children. A girl who died of smallpox when small, and a boy with whom she now lives. Oh yes, she could have married again, but did not want to be bothered with any more children. So she remained single, and did washing and ironing for a living. Those were the days when there was a lot of money.

There are no remedios, "remedies" like the Mexican remedies. Why, one time she was walking downtown, and a car was backing out of a side street—she didn't see it, nor the driver her—and knocked her down. She was not hurt, but the man was scared, he picked her up, and wanted to know for sure if she was not hurt. When he found out she was alright, he gave her five dollars, and took her home. In the evening when her son came, she showed him the money, and told him about the car hitting her. He got very angry, and told her she should not have taken the money. But should have sent him to jail, rather than paying a big sum of money. No, her way was the best. She got five dollars, and maybe the other way she would not have got anything. Porque el todo lo quiere, todo lo pierde. "He who wants it all, loses it all."

But the next day her leg pained her, where she struck the cement. No, she was not worried. She boiled some ojas de rosa de castilla, "wild rose leaves," and bathed her knee, and the pain left her in three days.

Oh yes, she had worked very hard when she was young, and if her eyes were not so bad, she could still work. But there was one day in the week she never washed, and that was Friday. Because on that day Nuestro Senor died, "our Lord." And it was sacred. And she didn't want to come back to this world again, after she died, to do penance, like the woman her mother told her about.

Her mother had told her what her grandmother had told her. That there was once a woman who always washed on Fridays. No other day would she pick. But every Friday she went to the river and built a fire under her caldera, "boiler," and washed. Her friends use to tell her not to pick Fridays, but to wash on some other day. But she would not listen to them. And when she died, the people could hear crying every Friday down by the river. And some had even seen her, gathering palitos, "chips" for the fire. Her soul came back every Friday to do penance.

District Four: Stories of Old Time Happenings

"He took only time enough to ascertain who they were and his worst fears were confirmed: The band of horsemen were Apaches led by the renegade Apache Kid, the scar shining vividly in the brilliant sunlight."

From "Stories of Old Time Happenings In and Around Deming, New Mexico as told by Walter Lusk" by John M. Trujillo

Old Days in San Marcial in Socorro County

by Manuel Berg

Mrs. Watson: "Here's an example of the kind of law and justice we had around San Marcial in Socorro County in the early eighties. Both Pat Carmody and a fellow named Wiggins were in the regular army and located at Fort Craig. Fort Craig was five miles south of San Marcial. When they were discharged from the army they both married native girls and set up their homes at old San Marcial which was once known as Milligan. Years passed and Pat Carmody became quite prosperous and a leading merchant in town and he also had several farms. Wiggins hadn't been so successful but both men raised large families. By this time, in 1881 or 1882, the fort had been turned over to negro soldiers and Wiggins' daughter married a negro who had lately been discharged from the army. Pat Carmody became incensed at this marriage (you see he and Wiggins came from the same county in Ireland and he felt insulted at Wiggins' girl marrying a nigger) and since the nigger owed him money he took him to the Alcalde and had him peoned and had both the negro and his wife to work in Pat Carmody's chile patch.

"Now the peonage law had recently been repealed or something and Wiggins knew this so he went to the county seat at Socorro and swore out a warrant against Pat because it was illegal to arrest anyone under the peonage law. Pat was notified by some of his friends about what Wiggins had done and on the night of Wiggins' return from Socorro, Pat and a group of his friends raided Wiggins' house and strung Wiggins up a tree about half-way between old and new San Marcial, at a little settlement called Midway.

"Then Pat was arrested for the murder of Wiggins. He was indicted by the grand jury and sentenced to be hung. Friends of old Pat went to the jail that night and dug him out and furnished him means to get to Old Mexico. He located at Palomas, Mexico and his family joined him there. A daughter was born to them there and she is now living in Albuquerque. She married a Mexican by the name of Saavedra. He also has a son living in Socorro County now and the son's a Republican war-horse there. Around 1894 or '95 Pat got a pardon from the governor and he returned to San Marcial. Everybody had expected him to die a sudden death but he died in his bed. When he came back he was a broken man, he'd lost all his money and property and lived out his life on a government pension because he had been in the civil-war."

Mrs. J. S. Watson, 120 South Broadway Avenue, Albuquerque, New Mexico. NOTE: The husband of Mrs. Watson was at one time sheriff of Socorro County. Her father was a judge and also a sheriff in this region.

(About 150 words)

Clay W. Vaden, Field Writer,
Project #65-1700-J,
Quemado, New Mexico.

VALVERDE BATTLEFIELD

The battle of Valverde (Green valley) was fought in February 1862 between General Sibley, Texan Confederate General, with an army of about 2500 men marched northward for the major operation in New Mexico. At Valverde, seven miles north of Fort Craig, 4 miles east of San Marcial, he met General Canby with about 3,800 men from the Fort. In a desperate battle which lasted all day the Confederates were victorious. Pat Higgins, Senior says the two commanders in this battle were brothers-in law and "No part of the Federal army stopped until safely within the walls of Fort Craig." Colonel Kit Carson, the great pathfinder and scout commanded the first regiment of New Mexico volunteers who participated creditably. Sibley left his wounded at Socorro, captured Albuquerque without resistance, and marched on Santa Fe. A copper cannon which was buried on Salado River was found in 1925 by Mike Sarracino who still has it at Polvadera, New Mexico.

Valverde Battlefield, Clay W. Vaden, April 18, 1936,
NMFWP, WPA #232, NMSRCA

Old Timers Stories: Elizabeth Fountain Armendariz

by Marie Carter

Mrs. Armendariz, who lives in the family home of her parents at Old Mesilla, ushered me into a room of curios, explaining:

"This is the Gasden Museum collection which belonged to my father, the late Albert J. Fountain Junior. I follow in his footsteps, for collecting curios is my hobby. The Santos, or Saints, in this case are very old," she said, pointing to a large glass case of statues, ranging from one to three feet in height. Unlocking the case doors she took out a Santo and placed it in my hands. "That one is a hundred years old, and was found in a cave."

The Santo was a painted canvas stretched over a delicate frame-work of wood.

"Observe the paint," she said, "faded yet still beautiful, and the old Santo's features so easy to define. The Santo on the table is shrouded in mystery; I promised the donor not to tell from whence it came."

"Were you born in Old Mesilla?" I inquired.

"Yes," she replied, "and I have been a teacher in the Mesilla school for the past fifteen years. I want you to examine these articles; they were given to my grandparents by Juan Maria Justiniani, or the Hermit of the Organ Mountains, a Cartuchian monk. This little brass bell is the same one he always carried, tied to the handle of his cane. These brown rosary beads, which he gave to my grandmother, are made from the leaves of flowers. This black rosary he gave my grandfather. Note the artistic rose design hand-carved by the Hermit."

"And these?" I inquired, pointing to some odd-looking books.

"Were written by the Hermit," she replied. "The brown book is written in Spanish, and its cover is crude cowhide. The other book is written in Italian, and is covered with sheepskin.

The Hermit used to walk from the Organ Mountains to Mesilla to preach to the people. Here is another rosary much larger than the other two; it came from the Grotto of Our Lady of Lorades (France), and he wore it around his waist. This ring with the spikes in it he used for inflicting punishment upon himself. It was his way of doing penance.

"The Hermit was a very religious man. The natives feared him because they believed that he could read their minds; also predict their future. On one of his visits to our community, I have been told, he did something very odd. He happened to be talking to the resident priest when two men approached, one leading a mare. The priest introduced them to the Hermit. He shook hands with one of the men but when the man with the mare proffered his hand the Hermit ignored it, saying:

"'I cannot shake this man's hand; not until he restores that stolen mare to its master.'

"'Is that mare stolen property?' demanded the angry priest.

"The guilty Mexican bowed his head in shame as he responded in a low voice: 'Sí, señor.'

***

"The Hermit, Juan Maria Justiniani, was an Italian aristocrat, born at Sizzario, Lombardy, Italy. Some say that the Virgin appeared to him and told him to go westward, and that he followed her advice, while the others contended that he was expelled from Mexico. At the age of 20 he made a promise to travel to all the mountains of the world, to teach and to preach to the ignorant. At first he lived in a cave at Las Vegas, and then he move to a cave in the Organs.

"That," she said, pointing to a picture of a tall, white-bearded monk wearing the brown hooded cape of his order and leaning on a cane to which a small brass bell, the one she had shown me, was attached, "is the Hermit. My father painted him from memory. Whenever the natives wish to find something real bad, they pray to the Hermit to help them. For 49 years he lived the life of a hermit, dying at the age of 69, April 17, 1868. His grave is in the Catholic Cemetery, here, in Old Mesilla.

"It seems that the Hermit predicted his own death. He was in the habit of lighting a bonfire every night to say his rosary.

"'Tonight,' he told Father Baca of Las Cruces, 'there will be no fire.'

"And when the bright flames, to which the people of Mesilla had grown accustomed, failed to appear in the eastern sky, they knew even before they found him that the Hermit of the Organs was dead."

Mrs. Elizabeth Fountain Armendariz, (Mrs. Aureliano Armendariz), granddaughter of Colonel Albert J. Fountain, commander of the Grand Army of the Republic June 30, 1891. Mrs. Armendariz was born in Old Mesilla, New Mexico, Feb. 4, 1897; teacher in Mesilla school for fifteen years; she is an artist, musician and curio collector; has a painting painted by her father and taken from the original photograph of Mary Todd, wife of Abraham Lincoln. The original photograph is dated 1859, N.Y. On the lower part of the painting is the word "Consagrado," which means consecrated.

Old Timers Stories: Volney Potter

by Marie Carter

When I called on Volney Potter at La Mesa, he told me some interesting facts about his family and the old house in which they live.

"La Mesa, like the adjoining town of San Miguel," he said, "has not undergone any great change since I was a boy. With the exception of a few modern houses and stores it looks about the same. My parents moved here from Weir, Kansas. I shall never forget the day our family of five got off the train at Anthony. My cousin, R. C. Bailey, met us, and the kindly station agent, Royal Jackman, was amused because I stuck so close to my dad. He never dreamed that beneath my jacket my heart was racing madly with expectation. I am sure that sister Ana, who is now Mrs. Charley Davis of Anthony, guessed what was passing through my youthful mind, for she smiled as she gave my hand a reassuring squeeze.

"My father, who was a great reader, had told me many a thrilling story about the Southwest; hence the moment I landed I was prepared, keyed up and waiting, for the startling events he had narrated to start popping around me with the snap of a cap pistol. Every moment I expected yet feared to see the cruel face of an Indian slowly rise above some of the mesquite bushes at the side of the road, suddenly brandish a tomahawk, send forth a wild yell and leap upon us. To this day I am unable to define my feelings when the expected Indian failed to materialize. But on a whole I believe I was both disappointed and relieved.

"Then unexpectedly I received a genuine thrill. The Rio Grande as I remember it got pretty rough in the old days. It was wider than it is now and the current was strong and swift. But, then, that was prior to the building of the Elephant Butte Dam. On this particular day—the day we arrived in Anthony—I overheard the station agent remark that the river was unusually high. When we got into R. C. Bailey's skiff it began to rock from side to side, and when he took the oars and began to row us across my sensation of fear was almost unbearable. No one, not even Ana, guessed that it was all I could do to keep from leaping overboard.

"We first went to Chamberino where we remained for awhile and then moved to La Mesa. I was real happy when father bought a ranch for I was at the age when boys have visions of themselves costumed as cowboys with nothing to do but ride horses, but my boyish dreams were quickly shattered for my first experience with horses was limited to the work team hitched to the plow which I followed. We all worked hard that first year, but father had been a mining man all his life and knew very little about farming. At the end of the year we were in debt and forced to turn over everything we had raised to Charley Miller at Anthony, and yet, we lacked eight hundred dollars of having made a living.

"This old house is one of the show places of the valley. It is two hundred years old. I bought it from Holiaro Moreno, whose father was one of our early day sheriffs. Holiaro was over eighty when he sold me this house. His father and grandfather lived here before him, died and were buried in the back yard. Incidentally the largest and most beautiful roses we possess are those growing above their graves.

"We have tried to preserve every bit of the architecture in its original form. Look at these doors and these window frames, the joints are connected with wooden pegs—not a nail anywhere. The doors are heavy oak and hand carved. For a long time there were only three buildings in La Mesa, of course that was before my time, the Catholic Mission down the street, the Dusseler house on the other side of town and this one.

"Note the ceilings in this house; they are rare and seldom found in the so called 'pioneer homes.' Most of the old Spanish and Indian houses have the brush ceilings but very few have the genuine latillas like this one. They are made from trees about three inches in diameter, peeled and hand polished. Then they are fitted close together in a herring-bone design. The large beams crossing the latillas are viegas.

"There was no lack of timber in the early days. The fact of the matter is this whole valley was bosque or woodland. Perhaps that accounts for the building of a fire-place in every room. They are small but must have been built by an expert for they draw perfectly. I have been told that some of our furniture, which is over a hundred years old, was made in Zacatecas and brought through Mesilla by ox team over the Santa Fe-Chihuahua Trail. We have preserved the original water spouts on the roof of this house and quite a number of viegas on the roof of the shed in the patio. That old ox yoke above the gate was given to my wife's father by Geronimo the Apache chief.

"La Mesa was once a favorite camping place for the roving tribes of Indians. That is the reason the old timers built such substantial houses. These walls, as you can see, are three times the thickness of an ordinary adobe wall. In the early days the front part of this house didn't have any doors or windows and the only entrance was a trap door on the roof. Hence it made an excellent fort for protection against the Indians.

"Holiaro's grandfather Moreno was a man who believed in being prepared; so he had portholes made in his private fort and stocked it with plenty of food, firearms, and ammunition. The rope ladder leading to the roof could be used by the inmates of the house then pulled up and concealed. After getting the members of his household safely inside, the cunning old Spaniard would follow them and lock the trap door, which was a clever arrangement running the full length of the roof, defying detection by the keenest-eyed Indian on the warpath.

"One evening, it was just about sunset, so Holiaro told me. Moreno was warned that the Indians were going to make a raid on his place. Moreno immediately summons his family and servants, telling them to make haste and enter the fort for the Indians would soon be upon them. Finally the moon came up. Some of the servants stationed at the portholes reported that they saw shadowy forms skulking behind the trees across the road. Presently another outlook reported that the skulking forms were Indians, of that he was quite positive, for they had built a fire and as was their custom formed a circle around it. He then reported that they seemed to be holding a council.

"The council held by the Indians must have been of short duration for following the servant's report the Indians sent forth a blood-curdling whoop and charged Moreno's fort. Six rifles in the hands of six Spaniards exploded through the portholes, and six braves hit the dust. The remaining Indians looked at their dead brothers in amazement and returned to the fire. Moreno figured that their next move would be the hurling of fire brands to set fire to the house and burn the inmates. And all the time more Indians kept coming and increasing the circle around the fire. Moreno knew that the Indians were so superstitious that the least thing with a supernatural trend would have more power to drive them away than a thousand armed men.

"Along about midnight the Indians piled more mesquite on the fire and started to dance around it singing the weird uncanny notes of the death song working themselves into that frenzy which I have been told preceded a massacre. Suddenly some of them slowed down in the dance to stare at something on the roof of the fort, others followed suit, then pandemonium broke lose. With screams of terror they fled in a body, and no wonder! The cause of their fright was a ghost so tall that it seemed to meet the sky, with eyes as black as coal and as big as saucers. After the Indians left, old Moreno, who had been lying on the flat of his back juggling a ten foot viega wrapped in a sheet, let it fall to the roof of the fort with a thud."

Informant: Volney Potter (wife: Clara Mundy Potter). Interview: June 10, 1937.

Early Historical Events in New Mexico: Political Riot at Mesilla

by John E. McClue

𝕬 visitor today to the peaceful little village of Mesilla could hardly conceive that its streets were the scene of one of the bloodiest tragedies that ever marred the history of the Territory.

Today Mesilla is noted for its orchards and vineyards. Its streets are well laid out and lined with large shade trees. In addition to fruits and wine, considerable hay and grain is raised, the district being abundantly supplied with water by means of irrigation ditches from the Rio Grande River, and by deep wells. This old historic town is located in Dona Ana County, in the southern part of the state, bordering Old Mexico with only the Rio Grande separating. Mesilla is about two miles west of Las Cruces, now the county seat.

In 1880, Mesilla was the county seat, and headquarters of the United States Land Office and the 3rd Judicial District Court.

In 1871, the Republican and Democratic parties were thoroughly organized in Dona Ana County, the Republicans under the leadership of Colonel W. L. Rynerson and John Lemon, the Democrats being led by Pablo Melendez and Mariano Barela. The last two named were candidates for Probate Judge and Sheriff, respectively.

From the opening of the campaign, intense party feeling had prevailed, and there was a personal bitter feeling. Both political parties appeared ready for serious trouble, and seemingly eager to invite it.

It had been announced that on Sunday, August 27, 1871, the Democrats would hold a mass meeting in the plaza at Mesilla. Then followed an announcement by the Republicans that they would also hold a meeting at Mesilla on that day.

This caused a general expression of fear among the best citizens. There was danger of serious trouble, if the two meetings were held. And as a result of this strong belief the businessmen got together in the interest of peace. It was agreed that the Democrats should have the plaza, as had been originally planned, that the Republicans would meet in front of the residence of John Lemon. These arrangements were carried out.

Both meetings ended with what appeared to be satisfactory results, and many who had attended went home, the general impression being that all danger of trouble had passed.

But the agitators were not satisfied. Someone suggested that the day be closed by forming a procession and marching around the plaza. The person or the side that made the suggestion was never known. But in the end both sides decided on a procession, and the two parades marched in opposite directions around the plaza, during which time cheap whisky flowed freely.

The processions met almost half way around the square. Thereupon a man by the name of Kelley yelled insulting remarks at John Lemon. The two engaged in an angry political discussion. In the excitement, Apolonio Barela fired his pistol in the air, either accidentally or purposely.

Immediately Kelley struck Lemon a fierce blow on the head with a heavy pick handle which he had been carrying. He knocked Lemon to the ground. The next instant someone shot Kelley, mortally wounding him. The person who shot Kelley was instantly shot through the heart by some unknown person.

Then the fighting became general and for a time it sounded like the sharp rattle of musketry. The plaza was crowded with men, women, and children, and it was a miracle that many more were not killed before they rushed away from the plaza.

The fighting commenced about half past three in the afternoon. There were two companies of the Eighth United States Cavalry stationed at Fort Seldon, and shortly after the outbreak, a Federal officer then at Mesilla dispatched a messenger, asking for aid of the troops to restore order. About ten o'clock that night, a command of sixty cavalrymen arrived in front of the residence of Colonel Jones, who lived just at the outskirts of Mesilla. A small detachment moved into the plaza, where it was joined by a few citizens of both political parties, who had joined in a request for the troops. At this time, the rest of the troops entered the plaza, where they camped that night. The following day, the main body of soldiers withdrew and Major Kelley was left in charge with a detachment of twenty men. An additional detachment of fifteen men under Lieutenant Godwin was established at Las Cruces. These detachments remained in the vicinity about two weeks and prevented another outbreak.

In this riot at Mesilla, nine men were killed, and between forty and fifty were wounded. In fact it was not possible to accurately determine the number injured, as many were taken to their homes immediately.

At that time, there was no Judge of the 3rd Judicial District, and it is said that the country was "wild and wooly." The last Judge appointed had held one term of Court, and gone home. After this Mesilla affray, a few citizens got together and wrote to Judge Hezekiah S. Johnson of the 2nd Judicial District, asking him to come down and hold an investigation. He came, stayed three days, but made up his mind that it would be dangerous to do any investigating. He returned to his home, without taking any action, and the matter was never investigated. Nobody was ever punished by law for any act done the day of the riot. There were a few persons arrested that night, but they were immediately released by the arresting officer.

Following this riot, numbers of people abandoned their homes in the Mesilla Valley, moving to other New Mexico counties, while some went to Old Mexico, where they succeeded in securing a land grant, and established an American Colony.

Bibliography: *A History of New Mexico, Its Resources and People*, Pacific States Pub. Co., Los Angeles, Chicago, & New York (1907). Vol. 2.

Author's Notes:

1) The 2nd Judicial District was composed of Bernalillo and Sandoval Counties, with District Headquarters at Albuquerque.
2) Judge Hezikiah S. Johnson, the Judge of the 2nd District at that time, lived in Albuquerque.

News Item.

The New Mexican
Santa Fe, N. M. Nov. 10 - 1865

The New Mexico Press says while the District Court was in session
at Limatar, in the county of Socorro, the Indians said to be Navajos,
stole two thousand head of sheep from within a mile and a half of
the courthouse. They were pursued by the citizens and the sheep recovered with the exception of about two hundred and fifty. Indians
also attacked the wood train of Jose Jaramillo and Antonio Jose Chaves,
in Valencia county near the Puerco, drove off thirty two head of
oxen and killed two men.

The same paper states that four Indians from the pueblo of Isleta
were killed by Navajos near the Puerco, on the 30th ult.

Dec. 22. Navajos stole about fifteen thousand head of sheep at
Galisteo on Wednesday last week, and killed five herders. These are
only a few of the outrages that are constantly being committed by
this tribe, falsely represented to the government as subdued. (note)
Undoubtly this is a gross exaggeration. Fiften thousand sheep would
have been divided into six or seven bands and would have been scattered
over a large area.

The New Mexican, Santa Fe, N.M. November 10, 1865,
NMFWP, WPA #92a, NMSRCA

Pioneer Story: Years Ago . . .

by Betty Reich

Years ago there was a cattle ranch at Silver Springs, about thirty-five or forty miles from Deming, called the Double 'Dobe. They never left less than three cowboys at this ranch because of the danger of Indian raids.

One day when there were only three cowboys there and apparently no Indians within miles, one of the cowboys went to the spring, one went to the corrals and one went in the house. The Indians raided the ranch without warning, killing the cowboy at the spring and the corral immediately. The Indians captured the remaining cowboy in the house and tortured him by placing him on a cooking stove in which a fire was built, tying his hands and feet under the stove. When his body was found it was baked and had been terribly mutilated.

***

A few miles east of Deming are the Florida Mountains—a landmark which is visible for miles. In pioneer days two brothers and Yates, from Missouri, lived in the gap between Little Florida and Big Florida. Mrs. Yates had been in Deming as trouble from the Indians was expected. When the danger of Indians was thought to be past, her husband came for her and they started home. On the way, they were attacked by Geronimo and a band of Chiricahua Apaches from the San Carlos reservation. Mr. Yates was shot in the back and killed. The Indians attempted to capture Mrs. Yates alive. When her body was found most of her clothes had been torn from it. Her shoes had been cut from her feet. She had been killed by being struck in the head with a tomahawk. The Indians went on to the ranch of Shy Yates (the other brother) where they shot his son—he dying later from his wounds. A courier came into Deming and notified the people of this tragedy. Men from the town went on horseback, heavily armed, to recover the bodies.

Source of Information: Mrs. E. Pennington, Deming, New Mexico.

In the Early '80's

by Betty Reich

In the early '80's there were Apache teepees standing in a spot in the Florida Mountains (about ten miles southeast of Deming) called the park. This was a very narrow place and precipitous on each side so that it was safe from attack.

These teepees were made of yucca poles and the skins of animals. The Apache men rode horses, but the women walked and pulled "drags" which were made of poles bound together by thongs made from skins of animals. On these were carried the supplies, plunder, and the Apache children.

The smoke of the Apache was often seen around Deming, but the little town was never attacked. The Apache liked to raid the outlying settlement where resistance was slight. However, many times it was only the children that slept at night because the people of the town were fearful of an Indian raid.

When the railroad was built to Deming in 1881 the workers that were building the road were guarded to keep them from being murdered by roaming Apaches.

After the railroad came, when there was an Indian scare the women and children were put in box cars and sent to a place of safety.

Source of Information: Mrs. E. E. Pennington, Deming, New Mexico. Mrs. Pennington came to Deming in 1883 when it was a city of tents, saloons, houses of prostitution and gambling dens.

Cook's Spring

by Betty Reich

In early days Cook's Spring yielded the only supply of water between the Rio Grande and the Mimbres River.

This spring had long been a favorite camping ground of the Indians. Cochise and his Chiricahua warriors came from northern Sonora and Mangas Colorado and his Mimbreno Apaches from the Mimbres and Santa Rita Mountains.

From 1858 to 1861 the Butterfield Overland Mail was in operation over the trail which led past the spring. The Indians were held in check by presents of blankets and food during the three years that the mail company's coaches traveled this trail. In the winter of 1861-62 this peaceful condition of affairs came to an end.

There is a story told that a young West Point officer named Barkett sent for Cochise and demanded the return of a Mexican boy who had been lost. Cochise and his half dozen warriors denied knowledge of the boy's whereabouts and so Barkett ordered their arrest. Cochise slit the canvas of the tent and escaped—his warriors were held. A soldier named Wallace volunteered to go to the Apache camp and investigate. He sent back word to Barkett that in his opinion, the Indians had not stolen the boy, but that he, Wallace, was being held as hostage until the warriors who had accompanied Cochise should be released. Barkett promptly hanged the captive Apaches, whereupon Cochise hanged Wallace.

When El Paso fell into the hands of the Confederates, seven young men, Union sympathizers, succeeded in escaping from town in a Butterfield Overland Mail stage coach loaded with equipment from the mail company's office. They headed westward with the intention of going to California and joining the troops. At Cook's Spring they were stopped by Cochise and his Apaches. Using the stagecoach as a barricade the seven young men withstood the siege for twenty-four hours. When five of them had been killed the remaining two wrote a note explaining what had happened and declaring their intention of escape that night. Several days later a passing freighter found the blood stained note and buried the seven bodies.

The stagecoach massacre took place on Thursday, July 12, 1861. The names of four of the boys were: Emmett Mills, 19 year old brother of Brigadier General Mills, Joe Poacher, John Poutel and John Wilson.

Cochise is said to have admitted that forty of his braves had been killed and is reported to have said that with a hundred warriors as brave as those seven youths he could have driven all Americans west of the Mississippi back to their homes where they belonged.

Letter to Mr. Etheridge

by C.A. Thompson

Anthony, New Mexico
October 3, 1940
Dear Mr. Etheridge:

Referring to the naming of Las Cruces for a group of men who were massacred close to that town by Indians: I have known for over 50 years that such was the reason for the naming of Las Cruces but tales of who were the victims for whom they were erected was a matter of different and varying names or people, as well as where they came from until lately after the newspapers of Las Cruces published a tale or two about the party. One stated that the expedition was El Paso del Norte bound north to Santa Fe and included some Sisters of Charity as well as a Bishop of the Catholic church: south of Las Cruces was named Bishops Cap for the above reason. All this when Las Cruces was putting up three memorial crosses north of the city and held quite a celebration of this.

I met Don Santiago Giron, an old resident of Dona Ana, and I asked him to tell me what if anything he knew of the parties killed many years ago. He says that his father and grandfather were both alive at the time; he thinks he was but is not sure but he is sure that when he was about 8 years old he accompanied his father to Las Cruces with a load of wood and distinctly remembered the crosses first erected, one to each body as is an old Mexican custom, and says that they were right on the edge of the valley about a half mile directly west of where the present memorial crosses were put up. He says his father and grandfather told him the party was made up of quite a number of men from the northern part of New Mexico with carts drawn by oxen. It seems they were most all from small towns who had thrown in together to make the perilous trip to Paso del Norte for supplies. That they were commonly known as "Villeros," which means villagers, due to their living in villas or villages such was even Santa Fe at the time and other places or settlements on down the river. He is of the opinion that the party was over 40 men. They passed thru Dona Ana with their screaming carts with wooden axles and massive wooden wheels, and made camp at a well known place just north of Las Cruces known as "La Cuesta de Don Francisco," meaning the slope of Mr. Frank, a heavy hill down into an arroyo which debauched into the riverbed a short distance west of the road and where back waters of the Rio Grande came up and formed a pond where the stock could be watered and camp made. Either the same evening or early the next morning a band of Apaches rode down on them and shot down nearly all the teamsters. Some of them however escaped and fled back to Dona Ana where they told a rather peculiar story of the massacre. They said that while the party was well armed, on seeing the rush of Apaches, yelling and shooting as they came, the Villeros fall into each others' arms, begging for forgiveness for whatever they might have done during the trip or in their home towns and not a shot was fired!

Right here I want to mention a, to me, curious thing: the carts I have described built entirely of wood, were known as "Carretas Cristinos" or Christian Carts. Those with iron braced axles and iron covered wheels were known as "Carretas San Antoneños" or San Antonio Carts. Both of these carts I am well acquainted with though both types are now museum pieces. The wooden ones were usually greased with tallow at intervals and in spite of that screeched and squealed. When the drivers ran out of tallow, which was not unusual, they anointed the wheels with nopal or prickly pear cactus which gave off a slimy fluid.

Don Santiago is certain of the makeup of the poor devils who died unresistingly and I don't think there is any foundation whatever for the other story of the party having been made up of Sisters of Charity and a Bishop. My information is that the peak known as Bishop's Cap, on account of its shape, was so named by a Mr. Chas Herron who settled at Vado, 8 miles north of here, in 1882 or 1883. The name of this peak in the vernacular of the old timers among the natives is "La Vieja." This is not all the names they give it but the rest is a bit too nasty to include.

Don Santiago is the authority for the statement that Dona Ana, the town, was founded in 1840 and that the celebration held at Las Cruces in erecting the new crosses was also the hundredth anniversary of Dona Ana. Don Santiago's memory is fine and he enters into so many details that I believe he is exactly right on the tale of the massacre. He also volunteered the statement that the last known raid of Apaches in this part of the state was lead by Victorio, at which time, in 1879, two uncles of Don Santiago were killed at what is known as "Las Uvas" or "Mountain-Grapes Mountain" almost due west of Dona Ana. He tells with great detail how the news was brought to his mother as she ground corn on her metate and how he remembers she and her sister crying so bitterly when the news was brought to them. He is also the authority for the statement that Chief Victorio was a captive Mexican from the Casas Grandes section of Mexico. Raised by the Apaches from early childhood, he became more bloodthirsty and cruel than his captors. He also says that Manuel Costales, the bandit of El Vado de San Diego (Fort of St. James), known in song and story, was also a captive Mexican from Chihuahua, raised by the Apaches who he also surpassed in murder and robbery. I enclose a copy of a memo I wrote for one of our High School students on Costales, which may be of interest to you though not history, just an ancient Mexican or Spanish custom.

Who was the Frank Fletcher for whom the camping ground was named on the massacre is of interest to me. L.A. Cardwell, District Court Clerk of Las Cruces, who has delivered in the old records of this county, says that he has seen mention of this man in the transfer of lands very early in times past. I suggest that you write Mr. Cardwell about these old records if you have not already done so. He is like myself, a dilettante in ancient lore of the valley and also an archaeologist to some extent.

Don Santiago also says that Lordsburg was first named Tuston; Cliff, Arizona was known as San Francisco; that Silver City was first known as San Vicente among the old timers and changed to Silver City by the Americans.

That the Roblero Mountains west of Dona Ana were named for a soldier or officer of Spain who established Ft. Roblero to protect that traffic up and down the Mesilla Valley and that it was on the site of what was later Ft. Selden, founded and maintained by the U.S. prior to and after the Civil War.

I hope that this scattering letter covers some points of interest to you in your work.

Sincerely,

C. A. Thompson.

Other Incidents of the Southwest

by Col Totty

In September of 1883 a group of men including Henry Grey, Tom Glenn, Bob Ounby, and myself with others were sent up the Frisco River above Clifton, Arizona to bring back a string of horses.

Due to difficulties we were forced to stay up there, ten days before starting back. The first night on the way back we spent at the Old Siggin's Place on Big Dry. The next morning after the horses had grazed awhile we resumed our journey with Henry Grey leading. When we came to the Point of Rocks we found the old storekeeper of Cooney dead.

His body was still warm. He was on his way to Silver City with his wares, and the Indians killed him, and took what they wanted.

There wasn't anything we could do, but take the body back to Cooney or report the killing to the soldiers at White House, which we did. Henry and I returned with the soldiers to the body. This was just one of the numerous killings by the Indians. The soldiers trailed the Indians for a good many days, never getting close to them.

In those days the white man had no desire to come in contact with the Indians even though he carried a gun, and the Indian a bow and arrow, for the Indian was master of sound, and could overcome his enemy the Paleface with his cunning ways and bow and arrow.

During the time when the Indians were so cruel it became a custom when a call came, "that the Indians are coming," all women and children were to run to the old depot for protection, as that was the safest place in Lordsburg.

It seemed to me that Mother and Grandmother Glass were the slowest things to dress and run, that I ever saw.

Mother would always have to put on her dress and place white collars and cuffs on it, then carefully pin her watch and chain on her left shoulder, and slick down her hair.

A call came that the Indians were near. Mother took her usual old sweet time dressing, and Grandmother never even got up.

I kept going in and saying, "Grandmother, do get up, the Indians are coming and we've got to run." Grandmother wouldn't get up and said, "I'm through running from those darn old Indians, they can come and get me, I'm going to sleep."

Dad had hired a Chinaman from the coast to come and do our cooking and work around the house, he was just like one of the family and he had been called to go with us.

The Chinaman came to the door grunting and shouting, "Whassa Matter? Whassa Matter?" Not speaking very plainly he sounded rather like an Indian.

You should have seen grandmother getting out of bed; she nearly hit the ceiling, and did she dress, she didn't have any fussing or fuming about it.

From then on when you mentioned Indians to grandmother she left everything else behind and got out of the house.

There was Mr. and Mrs. Yorke who lived out from Lordsburg with their family of four girls and one boy. The girls now are Mrs. Foot, Mrs. Terrell, Mrs. Gay, and Mrs. Henderson.

Mr. Yorke was in the habit of leaving Mrs. Yorke and the children at home alone while he and his cowboys gathered the cattle.

One time when he had taken the cowboys and left, Mrs. Yorke saw some Indians coming, but before they got there some former cowboys of Mrs. Yorke's came up and asked to stay awhile. There were three Indians. The two boys went behind the house and told Mrs. Yorke and the children to stay in the house and have the children come to the back door and let them know where the Indians hid.

The first Indian came down and hid behind a cactus in front of the house. It didn't take the cowboys long to get him as he only had a bow and arrow. The other two came on horseback with guns, but the cowboys being faster and better marksmen with guns got the other two also. Mr. Yorke some time later strayed from his men while gathering cattle and was killed by the Indians. Mr. Yorke was buried at his ranch near New York station.

Mrs. Yorke is still alive and she resides with her daughter, Mrs. Foot, in Los Angeles. Mrs. Foot for many years has been connected with the Los Angeles Examiner staff.

A granddaughter, Beulah Burch, is connected with the Silver City Hospital.

Informants: B. B. Ounby, Nora Ounby, Lordsburg, New Mexico.

Early Days around Deming

by Frances E. Totty

In the spring of 1883 we left Little Rock, Arkansas and came to Las Vegas where we only stayed a short time. My husband came to Las Vegas in January and when he sent for me in the spring he wrote and said "For God sake bring some table clothes, for all they know out here is oil cloth and I had rather run my hand over a snake than feel of them." I brought only a few pieces of silver and dishes and these table clothes.

We had been in Las Vegas only a short time, and decided that the climate was not going to do us any good as we were both lungers. My husband decided to come to Deming and as he was a newspaper man he brought out the Headlight, and later, the Deming Tribune and Headlight Democrat and combined them all three into one paper.

The Indians under Geronimo had been causing the settlers a lot of trouble stealing horses and killing people that were not around town. The people of Deming united and began to drill to wipe out the Indians as they were tired of the depredations and raids. General Cooke never did have a chance to catch the Indians as his men rode large cavalry horses and the small pintos of the Indians soon left the soldiers behind, and if they were pushed too hard the warriors took the hill afoot.

The people had been training and drilling for around ten months when they decided it was time to take things in their hands and wipe out the Indians. Word reached Washington of their preparations, and General Cooke was called to Washington and General Miles sent out to take his place. General Miles had Geronimo in less than two months. It took several special guards besides the soldiers to keep the people from mobbing the Apaches as they were being taken to Fort Sill.

When my husband came to Deming he said that he thought

Las Vegas was the end of civilization, but God help this country.

When we arrived here he had rented us a room with a lean-to for thirty dollars a month, and we had to carry water three blocks.

I have some pictures taken of the Indians on the war path with their bodies painted and the trousers that the government had given them, cut off above the knees. In the day time we would watch them on the mountains with the field glasses and at night we could see their fire.

When my husband left the house he always locked me and the children in and told us not to go out. It wasn't only the Indians that he was afraid of, but as there were always fights on the street he was always afraid that we would be hurt. One night the people in town became tired of the crowd that was always shooting up the town and killed seven and left them lying on the steps of the station.

By the year of 1885 it was safe for a woman to go anywhere. I have ridden the range more than one day hunting cattle and our horse. I owned one of the two Arabian horses in this country, and was not afraid to go anywhere. I had a friend that I rode with a lot and we would go to anyone's ranch and stop and take a meal and go on our way.

People were living in all kinds of makeshift houses when we came in here. One family up on the hill was living under a piece of oil cloth stretched over two poles with a hole cut in the oil cloth to put the stove pipe through. This family lived in this place for over a year.

Source of Information: Mrs. Ed Pennington, age 84.

PIONEER STORIES

Letter from L. W. Collins to his wife Mrs. M. E. Collins, Deming, N. M. Mr. Collins, at the time, was a contractor building the Santa Fe Railroad---Lake Valley Branch.

                                        Lake Valley,
                                        Jan. 12-'84.

Mollie:

This night finds me in a rail road camp four miles from Lake. I have all my teams and wages are low, I pay drivers 25 dollars per month and pay $4.50 per week board so I am clearing only about ten dollars per day. I think I will sell out next week and if do I will come home and don't I will come any how. Shaw is driving a scraper team for me so I can leave the teams with him and come home a few days. We see the stars at both ends of the day that is we are at work before the stars quits shining and we are there when they shine in the evening. On Thursday we had a fearful snow storm and there is snow on the ground yet. I of times wake and think of you and the children and wonder if Zona and Jo Ike are cold knowing you have more than you can keep covered, tell our little children to be good children. I will come home as soon as I can to see them. Those cold days and nights seems like weeks to me for I know I ought to be at home so kiss the children good night for me and I will close as I have been driving a scraper team today and my light is very dim and no fire. So good-bye Mollie darling, as ever,

                            Your devoted husband,
Mollie divide grub with Smith.
                                    L. W. Collins.

"Pioneer Stories: Letter from L. W. Collins," Betty Reich, August 2, 1936, NMFWP, WPA #213, NMSRCA

Grant County Cattle War

As Told by John Oglesby of Pinos Altos

by Mrs. W. C. Totty

John Oglesby of Pinos Altos settled back to tell a long story, one of bloodshed and a fight of every fellow for his rights.

Talking of Grant County, we used to see some rather exciting and thrilling times here. The poker tables were piled high with gold nuggets and dust, and the faro tables didn't play for small stakes as today, but for large sums in gold. When a person wanted anything from the store, it wasn't the question of the price, but did the store have the desired product.

Every man wherever he was had one or two pistols strapped on his person with a good rifle on his saddle. Even though today we are looked on as tough, in those days self-preservation was the main thought of each man.

It wasn't unusual for two or three to be killed at one killing as in those days gunpowder was the law, but at that, Chloride Flats or present Silver City was a peaceful place compared to many other western cities.

When anyone from the east came to Chloride Flats, he realized he was in the west. There was a cattle war, which could be said to be between the big ranch owners, the squatters, rustlers, and small cattlemen. Every faction was fighting the other. It has been claimed by many that the cattle barons, T. G. Catron and Tom Lyons, the largest ranch holders in the country, were trying to drive out the squatters and small ranchmen; while the Lyons' side say they were fighting the rustlers and badmen of the country.

Tom Lyons, who used to come to Silver City in a fine coach drawn by the best of horses, always entered town surrounded by a bodyguard of men armed to the teeth as a king would go into the public to look over his country.

Tom Lyons has said he was not at war with anyone, but his

men were having some trouble with rustlers.

The D. D. Bar Cattle Company, which also included the Diamond Bar Cattle Company, was owned and operated by D. B. Catron and Tom Lyons. This company owned or had possession of all the good grazing land and all the important watersheds in this district.

The squatters and small cattlemen were coming into the district, and at the same time the rustlers decided to take over the country and let blame fall on the small cattle company, but at the same time ravage his herds. It has been said the rustlers and squatters were in cahoots, which from all probability is false, for something became of their herds as well as the cattle baron's.

The fight properly started when Dave Campbell, a badman from Pleasant Hill, Mo., killed James Moore, a foreman employed by the D. D. Cattle Company at the East Fork of the Gila.

I was working for the D. D. Cattle Company and when Moore was killed I was sent to the East Fork to take his place with the instructions from Catron to get Campbell. A gun was sent to me from Pleasant Hill, Mo., for the purpose.

When I got to my headquarters I sent word to Campbell. "I have no grudge against you and do not want any trouble with you at any time. I was sent here to take care of cattle for the Company, and I intend to do so to the best of my ability regardless of the consequences." Campbell came to my headquarters and spent a day. We parted friends. He later married a sister of Carey Nation and settled at Tularosa and is considered a good citizen. It has been rumored even though Tom Lyons said he didn't have anything to do with the war, he hired such gunmen such as Mike Trailer to do his killings.

Mike Trailer, an outlaw, was killed by a fourteen-year-old boy on Duck Creek. Trailer, it is said, went to the store to kill the owner and as there wasn't anyone in the store he went to the corral to see if he could find the owner of the store. There he found this fourteen-year-old youngster.

Trailer said to the youth, "I want some tobacco." The youth replied: "Just a minute, I must finish here." With a G---D---, and a few other words of profanity, Trailer demanded the tobacco.

"Can't you see I'm busy?" "Yes, I see; so am I, now get going." Trailer proceeded to take his quirt and whip the youth from the corrals to the store.

As the boy entered the door of the store he picked up a 30-40 standing by the door, and taking Trailer unaware, shot him. This was the end of another badman of the Southwest by a mere youth who probably had never shot anything more than a rabbit.

The youngster went to Cliff and gave himself up. He was tried the day he arrived in Cliff and found "not guilty." A purse of around two hundred dollars was made up and presented to the boy. With the regards of the people he was thanked for the good he had done the Southwest and told to go on his way with the instructions that he could claim one notch on his gun at so early an age: let it be his last.

The quickest at the trigger weren't always the ones to survive the longest. They were the ones who usually went first, for as a rule there were usually several waiting for the fast man on the draw, for he was a man who was feared.

Many highly respected citizens today, as the Hall family, were completely driven from the country, either by the large cattleman or the rustlers. The people would see their homes ruined or some member of the family completely disappear. The Halls left Grant County and settled at Deming where Laura Hall still resides. Laura Hall's brother Jim was killed, after leaving Grant County, by some member of the Greer Gang at Double Adobe.

Greer, an outlaw, was taken from jail at Deming by his gang. A posse was formed at once and set chase after the outlaws. The outlaws were overtaken at Double Adobe where a battle took place. During the conflict with outlaws, Hall and several other prominent men were killed. These men's bodies were returned to Deming by a slow, painful method. The remaining men had to carry the bodies, partly by horseback, and over other places by foot. These valiant men who had given their lives in an effort to make the Southwest a better place to live, were taken to a decent place of burial. These men were trying to rid the Southwest of outlaws and rustlers.

Hall and others whom we know were law-abiding citizens were driven from Grant County by who? Laura Hall will say "Tom Lyons." Is she mistaken? Could it have been the rustlers who sent the threats to leave? We know they drove off the cattle, leaving the owner holding the empty bag.

Tom Lyons killed a fellow by the name of McMagus over a personal matter about Lyons' wife. He in turn was killed by whom? Felix Jones did time for the killing, but did he kill Lyons? There seems to be some doubt by the old-timers about this matter. Lyons was told by an old Negro of the family the day he left for El Paso: "Massa, evil is gonna overcome you, please don't go for a ride with anyone for you will never return, for the cards say so!" Lyons was thus forewarned of his doom by a faithful servant whom he didn't see fit to listen to. He journeyed on to El Paso and took the fatal ride his faithful servant warned him about, and never returned.

I tell you there were some exciting times during the late '70s and early '80s. If Tom Johnson, a foreman, were alive, he could tell you of those bloody days on the Gila. We who are alive don't like to think and talk of those days. They are a memory to be blotted from our mind.

Mrs. Lyons is still alive and has one of the most picturesque homes that can be imagined. It is all furnished with antique hand-carved furniture. She alone lives with her memories. Maybe some day we will be able to determine who was fighting who and why, for certain. Was all this bloodshed caused by the rustlers, a bunch of outlaws who made law-biding citizens kill one another? That's your task.

Source: Story related by John Oglesby of Pinos Altos.

Early Days in Silver City and Grant County

by Frances E. Totty

"I left Tennessee in 1880 and came to New Mexico in 1881 arriving at Old Town for my first stop in Grant County. Señor Pena was running the store there at the time. I will never forget the fact that he served buttermilk with our meal, and I thought that it was the best milk that I ever drank.

"I settled in the Sappo and Mimbres district living on the Mimbres most of the time. I was living on the Mimbres when a Mr. Hayes was killed over near Lake Valley by the Indians. Mr. Moore, my nearest neighbor, wished to go over to his place at Lake Valley and wanted me to go with him after Mr. Hayes was killed. We were nearing Mule Springs when I noticed a moccasin track. I said, 'Look, there are tracks.'"

"Mr. Moore replied, 'Oh, they probably belong to some Mexican.'

"I soon cried, 'Look, look, the large tracks of the Indian.' Moore said, 'Let's go. Jesus Christ, is that fellow in this part of the country?' He began to kick and spur his horse and we were really leaving that part of the country. In all of the recent raids there was an unusually large track and when this track was seen it was generally known that some cruelty and destruction had been done in the vicinity and everyone had a horror of meeting the warrior and wanted to get away from the place that he was likely to be found around. We soon caught up with a chink and told him that the Indians were behind us and he said, 'Me no see Indians,' but he soon had his horse in a run also when we told him of the large track.

"We went on home and near night a fellow came by and told us the Indians were near and we were to go to the Brown place. We went over to the place and spent the night and the next morning returned home to find that the Indians had taken a large stone and thrown it through the door and had gone into the house and taken all of the best blankets, and we had a long frying pan which they took and left us a short-handled one. They took our violin and laid it on the floor with the bow across the center.

"The Indians were never as bad as they were pictured. I will admit there were times that none of us wished to see them, Nana, Geronimo, or any of the others, but as a rule the uprising started over some mistreatment that the Indians received."

Source: Louis S. Goforth.

The Murder of Judge and Mrs. McComas

by Mrs. W. C. Totty

In 1883, James Porter Ounby ran a hotel in Lordsburg, where David McComas, son of Judge McComas, lived while he worked at a nearby mine called the Pyramid.

One morning he came in from work at the mine and told Nora Ounby that he had received a letter from his father, Judge McComas, and he and his stepmother were coming over to see him from Silver City, and he had no way of warning him that the Indians were between Lordsburg and Silver City.

He sat all day on the hotel porch watching the Indians at night signal to one another across the flats. They would build huge fires, and then with blankets smothering the fires, signal to one another.

The next morning the stage driver reported the murder of Judge and Mrs. McComas. B. B. Ounby and George Parks were sent out to bring the bodies into Lordsburg for burial, but they were too late, for the people from Silver City had removed them to Silver City. The McComases were killed near Nights Ranch.

Lieutenant McDonald from Ft. Bayard and his company of soldiers followed the Indians by day, but always the Indians outwitted them. Judge McComas and wife had with them their four-year-old son, Charlie. The soldiers thought perhaps the Indians would kill him and throw him by the wayside, but no trace of the child was ever found.

The son David never straightened out after the terrible death of his father and he died some two years later. Another son who lived in Los Angeles was later made district judge. His wife threw acid in his face causing his death. There were two McComas girls by a first marriage, who were still living in Hollywood, as reported by old-timers of the Lordsburg vicinity.

The morning after the murder, people in Lordsburg saw the

Indians come down across the Lordsburg trail, cross the railroad at Lisben, go on across what is now known as the John Muir Ranch, and from there go into the Coyote Mountains. They evidently split in three groups in the Coyote Mountains. One company of soldiers trailed them from seven or eight days over that range of mountains. They were followed to the Old Mexico line, but were never caught up with, nor was the son, Charlie, ever heard of.

In later years there were numerous raids in and near the town of Cananea, Old Mexico, done by the Indians, and it is reported that they were led by a white man. It is the belief of the people in general that the leader was none other than Charlie McComas, who was raised by the Indians and who became their leader. However, there isn't any proof of the fact. Even though the boy could have been proven to be McComas, he could have never been brought back to civilization to live happily.

Informant: Nora Ounby.

Incidents of the Early '80s

As Told by W. Weatherby and Maurice Coates

by Frances E. Totty

Many of the things I am telling you are not first hand experience but were told to me by older settlers and I have saved notes and can be able to tell you as they were told to me. I have intended to write these out, but have not ever taken the time, and I also have data that I have saved about the district that will help verify my stories.

After the raids and degradation of Victorio, everything was quiet for several years. Then to the horror of the country, in May 1885, Geronimo was heard of in the country. Captain Cook, foreman for the W. S. Ranch, first saw them rounding up a herd of horses on the ranch. On the eighteenth of May, word was brought in that Nat Luse and Cal Orwig had been killed. I, Maurice Coates, was the foreman at the Cooney mine. The owner Jo E. Sheridan called me, and we organized a rescue party. We went out after the bodies and as we came to where the vicinity of the bodies were known to be we came up on a detachment of soldiers camped by the river. We asked them about the Indians and they didn't know anything about them and didn't seem to care if they carried off the country. The soldiers sure didn't do us any good. When we got to the place that the mutilated bodies of the two men were we were all so aroused that I think we wanted to go back and whip the soldiers, for the bodies had laid out in the sun until they were pitiful. The soldiers had loitered by the side of the river and the bodies of two men were less than a mile of them and they would not go out and bring them into town, or camp either. We took the bodies into Alma for burial. On May the 22 we found the body of Lyons, an Englishman, badly mutilated and decomposed. This body was buried on the W. S. Ranch and the grave can still be seen from the highway. Also the graves of the two W. S. Ranch foremen killed by the Indians.

The Apaches soon stopped their raids for a few months and weren't seen anymore until October when they were heard of in the Cliff country. Some soldiers were sent under Overton, from Fort Bayard, to stop the driving off of the cattle and horses, and as always before there wasn't anything done but loafing. Overton said it was only the word of children and old women that the cattle were being driven off and would not move from camp. Clark, an old timer, cussed out Overton . . . . Mike Fleming, William Bates, Arthur and Billie Clark, Jesse Dickinson, and an Englishman, followed the Indians to the Red Rock district, but got there too late as they had already killed Dutch John on Blue Creek.

The stage coach traveled by night as it was unsafe to go by day, and as the Apaches were superstitious about fighting at night it was fairly safe to make the run after sundown. A Mr. Lauderbaugh carried the mail and drove the stage. On one run he lost the mail pouch which he missed when he got to Plessanton at 1 a.m. He had with him a Shoshone Indian whom the Mormons had raised, called Indian Jack. He was told he would be well paid if he would return for the pouch. He hesitated, and pointed to the Mogollons and said, "They'll fix me if they catch me. If I get one of them, God how I will roast him. I'll go." At the break of day he returned with the lost pouch. When asked if he stayed with the road he replied, "Only one way, but coming back I took the ridges and all of the short cuts I knew or could find."

The women of the district were all as brave as the men. They took the Indians as something to be expected. There was one woman that was a woman from the mountain country that met the stage and said to Al Lauderbaugh on one morning, "Al, I reckon that you are going into town," and handed him a ten dollar bill. She told him to buy her three little children a hat apiece. The Indian signs and post offices were all around, but Mrs. Bush didn't seem to be the least worried; her husband was up in the hill hunting the cattle.

Mr. Lauderbaugh was fired upon during his return trip with the hats, but luckily he escaped uninjured. The Indians fired upon him at Little Dry and all the way across the mesa. He for many years wore as a watch charm a bullet he took out of the stage after the fight was over.

It wasn't uncommon then to hear each day of some one being killed, their cattle driven off, and their cabin burned; but the end came with the killing at Soldier Hill, about one mile south of the Old Meader Ranch on Big Dry. J. McKinney, who was serving as guide for Lt. Cabal, told how they were ambushed there. When they were crossing Cactus Flats, so called from the many cactus, they found two bodies, being Clark and McKinney. These men had been hauling ore concentrates. The men were killed and their ore sacks ripped open and the contents scattered all over the ground. They followed the Indians on and at eight miles from the head of Mogollon Creek where two men named Lillian and Pryer had started a ranch they found their bodies and also the Indians which they fired upon, killing nine of the Apaches. The soldiers were low on supplies and decided to return to Alma for supplies.

While at Alma a courier came through with a message and the group started going south with ten additional Navajo scouts and camped at the Siggins ranch the first night out. The next morning when starting out not a Navajo was in sight. The courier went back to Fort Bayard and the men started around Soldier Hill, the men singing "Good-by My Lover Good-by" when we were fired upon. My horse was killed. Dr. Maddox was killed and several others, and several injured. Ever since, this hill has been called Soldiers Hill. The Navajo scouts appeared soon after the fight was over. This fight seemed to be all the Indians were waiting for to return to the San Carlos reservation.

They returned to the reservation to be fed by the people and rest after causing the settlers so much trouble.

Source: W. Weatherby, age 79 and Maurice Coates, age 84.

Killing of Charlie Bachelor and Other Incidents

by Frances E. Totty

I was raised in Old Mesilla, New Mexico. There was only one other white family in the town, we all spoke the Spanish or rather the tongue of the people in Mesilla at the time which was nothing but an Indian language mixed with Spanish.

When we left Mesilla we went to Fort Seldon fourteen or fifteen miles up the Rio Grande river from Mesilla. While at the Fort we ran the ferry across the river. John Chisom has brought many a herd across the ferry at this point. John Chisom was always the worst dressed man on this crew. He as a general rule was dressed in old worn-out overalls that not a one of his men would have worn. He looked as some ragged tramp that had bummed into the country, but was one of the prominent men of New Mexico as well as one of the wealthiest. Mr. Chisom was a man hospitable to everyone that came his way whether he be an outlaw or the most prominent man of the country; all were treated alike and were welcome to his ranch.

We left Fort Seldon and came to Burrow Springs in the spring of 1878. We settled there and opened an inn, as this was the only water between Gila and Silver City. Everyone came to the springs to spend the night as it was a place that the Indians seemed to stay away from for they knew that the people were expecting them at all times and a guard were always on the watch.

One day Charlie Bachelor came into the camp with the stage and seemed to be nervous, he seemed to sense that there was trouble in the vicinity, and after eating decided to change his schedule in order that he cross the Ash Creek, a little northwest of Duncan, Arizona, after night. In order to cross the creek after night he stayed at the springs until three o'clock in the afternoon. When he left he requested that someone go with him as there weren't any extra men at the springs and Charlie didn't have a man or passenger along so he had to go on the way alone.

When he was about three or four miles from the springs, the Indians were hidden and opened fire on his team, shooting his white mule and crippling him. The next shot wounded Charlie in the thigh and arm, but he kept pushing his team on. Finally the Indians, thinking he was going to get away, ran out and surrounded the stage and caused Charlie to turn it over in a small wash where reeds had grown up. This was an ideal place for the man to save himself, but in his fright he rushed out of the hole and up to the side of the hill thereby making himself a target for two Indians that were on the side of the hill. The Indians put two 45-70 bullets through a deck of cards that Charlie had in his shirt pocket when they killed him. There were five Apaches in the party and when they began to shoot, their horses that they were riding escaped. The braves went down to the stage and raided it. They got a keg of whiskey and went a little farther on and got the keg open and proceeded to get good and drunk.

Just about dusk five horses came up the springs and we put them in the corral. In a short time a negro soldier came into camp and we told him of the five horses in the corral and he remarked that Indians had been seen in the district and that he was going to guard the corral. It was my night to stand guard and I usually stayed in the shade of the houses on a moonlight night. I was sitting by the side of the house when I saw a shadow moving out by the corral. Thinking that it might be the negro, I didn't shoot. Then I saw another shadow appear; I knew it was the Indians, but as I raised up to shoot I saw the barrel of the gun of the negro sticking up in the air after he shot, and jumped and called "Them were Indians I see'd them." I never wanted to kill anyone so bad in my life for he missed the Indians and caused them to get away before I had a shot at them and he was too scared to shoot anything. When he got to where I was his face was as white as mine and his eyes were popping out of his head as if he had seen a ghost. The Indians didn't come back to the springs, and in a few days the horses were all claimed by their owners that were cattle men in the vicinity.

The morning after the Indians came into the camp to steal

the horses, Jesus Duran came across the body of Charlie Bachelor and the stage and brought the mail on into town and notified the authorities. Jim Wood, a scout, led the soldiers to the place where the Indians killed Charlie, but they wouldn't follow the trail. Instead they turned back to the old trail, when they could have soon captured all five of the warriors as they had been drinking all night and were still close to the place where they killed Charlie. I tell you we old timers of '79 sure didn't have much use for the soldiers for they did us more harm than good; they were all afraid of the Indians and the Indians knew that they were far more skillful in the fighting of the frontier than the soldiers and usually laughed at the modes the soldiers used. The Indians were sure that they didn't try to massacre a gathering of frontier men though. The day Judge McComas was killed and I shot the Indian in the shoulder the same band of Apaches stole all of the horses of Lyons and Campbell.

We went over on the Middle Gila, the present Red Rock, to gather corn for George Cook. My job was to ride around the field and keep the cattle out of the field as there weren't any fences at that time. I was riding one night when the wind happened to blow my way and I received a scent that told me the Indians were in the wood by the field. I had every sensitive sense of smell and to this fact I can attribute the fact that I am alive today for it has saved me more than once: when I smelled the Indians I turned back, and went to the side of the house for I was afraid to tell the men that I smelled Indians for they would give me the horse laugh. When morning came the Indians had stolen all the horses including the work horses.

The Indians soon learned that I could tell when they were around and I didn't have any trouble with them.

Source: Ceaser Brook.

Rough Diamond

by Mrs. Frances Totty

On November 15, 1882 a party of boys were sitting around the stove in Conkling's billiard parlor conversing, when the front door opened and something, that was probably once a man, came swaggering into the room.

Without a word or a look to any of the little party he threw himself into a chair in their midst. A look of mutual disgust passed from one to the other, and the new comer was in a fair position to be bounced irretrievably or thrown bodily from the room, but the door opened again and all thought of the disgusting stranger was thrown to the wind.

A little, pale-faced woman, scarcely more than twenty-five years of age, came walking into the room. She led a little child three or four years old, and upon the features of the child could be traced the same evidences of sorrow and want that were reflected in the face of the mother.

Approaching the boys, she began: "Gentlemen, this is the first time in my life that I have ever been compelled to beg. My husband died in San Francisco on the 14th and as his illness has been long and the little money we had saved to buy us a home has been swallowed up entirely, his death left myself and little daughter almost penniless. We had but recently come from the east and life looked all sunshine. Now we are friendless and only wish money enough to take us to Cleveland, Ohio, where my father, who although he's not rich himself, will see that we do not starve."

This was the little woman's story, and as the boys wiped the tears from their eyes with one hand, the other went to the bottom of their pockets for odd change. The barkeeper gave five, the yardman three, the letter carrier three, the dentist five, the compositor two, and four others a dollar each.

The twenty-two dollars were handed over and through her

tears the little lady was trying to express her thanks.

Just at this juncture the nonentity, who had been the subject of our disgust before, and who had been asleep during the telling of the story and the collection, straightened himself with an awkward flourish of his long bony hand and said: "I say, little lady, I didn't catch on to all of that there story. Been keeping late hours fur the last week or so. Feel kinder broke up."

The gang looked at each other and just as they were about ready to throw him through the skylight the lady came forward and although she showed that she did not like his looks, began telling her story again. She had not gone far when the long bony hand again appeared in the air, waving her to silence.

"Never mind, mums, that'll do. You and the little kid is in need. That's nuff fur me." Opening out his vest and ramming his arm almost through it, he brought out a roll that made the boys open their eyes. Taking the first bill from the top he handed it to her, and laying back in the chair half asleep, he mumbled almost to himself, "Never mind, bout rest of story. That's nuff. I had an old mother onst what would rise up in her grave and call me mighty hard names if she ever heard me refuse to help a woman that was in want." With this he placed his feet on the stove fender and was fast asleep.

The bill was a fifty, and the old lady went on her way rejoicing. The boys scratched their heads, shook hands and quietly dispersed; not a word passed between them, but many a brain went home puzzled.

Informant: Dick (Lying) Clark.

Bear Moore

by Mrs. W. C. Totty

"Oh! John, come here at once. There is a man that looks terrible."

I went to the door and imagine my astonishment when I saw an old friend John Moore.

"Hello, John, won't you come in the house?"

"No, John, I'm not fit for the women to look at. I just wondered if you wouldn't let me have a little grub."

"Sure thing old fellow but come on in, and have some coffee."

At the mention of coffee somehow Mr. Moore just couldn't resist.

Mr. Moore's face was nearly all torn away, and his clothes were very muchly torn. I was very curious to know the trouble, but as Western hospitality called for no questions asked, I knew I'd never know what happened unless Mr. Moore decided to tell his story.

"John, I know you are wondering what could have happened to me."

"Well, I'll admit I'm a little bit curious."

"John, I've been trapping all winter and Old club-foot just kept carrying off all my traps. You know that bear was a devil if there ever was one."

"Was, you mean is, John."

"No, John, he isn't now for I killed the old cuss."

"What!"

"Yes, John, Old club-foot won't kill any more calves and cows for the ranchers now. He sure has caused a world of misery in this part of the country. Wonder how many people that old bear has killed. I know that he is the one that killed that woman and child at that camp in the canyon northwest of Pinos Altos. I went over to the camp and that place look like a cyclone had struck the place. The tracks showed club-foot had been the cyclone. You know that bear must have lost his foot while a cub."

"Yes, John, that bear was one to run from, when alone."

"Well, John, I got tired of running from that devil, and I knew the only way to ever get him was to trail him to his den. I once thought I would get a hunting party, but you know Old club-foot was smart. Of the dozens of hunting parties that have gone out to end his mischief, not a party ever saw that old bear.

"I trailed that bear for several days and one morning as I came around a boulder there stood Old club-foot in the opening of a cave. That bear raised up on his haunches and made ready for a battle. You know that cuss was a brave old fellow, and he could fight!

"I raised my gun and said, 'Well, you devil, say your prayers, for you have caused me all the worry that you will ever cause.'

"Bang! But Old club-foot still stood there and I saw my gun flying through the air like a match. That darn bear had reached out with a paw and knocked my gun away, and hadn't even been struck by the shot.

"Well, John, I said my prayer then for I only had my hunting knife left for protection. That bear came lumbering to where I was, and I didn't move, so he walked around me, and politely looked me over. Then I made the mistake of moving, and that old cuss just reached out and cuffed me one. Dizzy, my God, I saw millions of stars. Someway I got hold of a club and by darting around and using the club for protection I managed to make club-foot good and mad. I knew if that bear ever got hold of me I was a goner. I dodged and stepped aside until I was worn out and so tired I knew the end was near.

"Old club-foot acted as a cat playing with a mouse; finally I sunk down on my knees and club-foot grabbed me for a death hug in those arms of vise.

"I drew my hunting knife, and with every drop of strength I had left in my body, I lunged my hand into his mouth and down his throat, then everything went black.

"When I came to that bear was laying down beside me, as dead as could be. I was stiff and sore so I could hardly move. I managed to get my knife out of the bear's throat, and I skinned him, and I wish you would look at these two pockets full of arrows, and bullets, you know he sure must have been an old critter. I have been out there in those hills for a month trying to get my face well, there were wounds all over my body, but I know I'm some scarecrow, and the funny thing about the fight, I don't remember when I received one scratch. I wonder if that old cuss in his last moment didn't tear my face up, after I passed out."

Bear Moore stayed at my house several days, and rested up, but poor fellow never went around people after his fight with the bear, he was so self-conscious of the condition of his face. I must admit it was the most horrible thing I ever saw. His face was half gone, and having healed without any medical treatment it was badly drawn, and the scars looked horrible.

Mr. Moore was called Bear Moore until his death; children would run from him if they saw him. He cut himself off from the human race, but he sure did this part of the country a favor when he killed club-foot.

Mr. Moore was a very independent person, he always paid for everything he received. In the early days even a stranger outlaw or respected citizen was never asked to pay for anything, but Bear Moore would never accept this western hospitality.

Informant: John Oglesby, Pinos Altos.

The Kidnapping of a Rancher's Daughter

As Told by Mrs. Tom Johnson

by Mrs. F. Totty

When I came to Silver City on April 2, 1889 we came in a covered wagon. Our first night, in Grant Co, we stopped first at Hudsons Hot Springs now called Faywood Hot Springs.

The next day we drifted to Warm Hot Springs at that time the home of a wealthy Spanish Rancher. We stopped at his water hole for the night.

The next morning my husband (Tom Johnson), was watering the horses when he heard a large confusion. Tom said, "I'm going to the house to find out the trouble."

On going to the house the rancher said: "My daughter had been kidnapped by one of my cowboys. My men are all Mexicans, and I can't trust them to go after her. I'll pay you, pay you well to go after her, and furnish your horse, saddle, food, gun, and your pick of men." Tom said, "Push them out here, I'm ready to go." Tom took the buckskin, horse and supplies furnished by the rancher, and chose two of his best men, and left in search of the girl.

As the rancher's orders were to bring the girl back regardless of the consequences to others Tom pushed his horse for two days without thought to the horse.

Whenever Tom and his men overtook the men and girls he ordered them to "Halt." The cowboy with his companion opened fire on Mr. Johnson and his boys, using the girl as a shield. Tom scouted around to the other side of the campfire, and took the boys by surprise, and got the girl to take back to her parents. The men were never heard of again or never left their camp site.

Tom returned the girl to Warm Hot Springs as the rancher said to do, and he asked no questions.

The Spanish Rancher offered to pay him for the trip, but he wouldn't accept any pay, but when we left we found twenty dollars in our supplies that we know he put there.

Informant: Mrs. Tom Johnson.

Stories of Old Time Happenings In and Around Deming, New Mexico

by John M. Trujillo

Mr. Walter Lusk, colorful old time pioneer and resident of Deming, New Mexico was born in Fort Gibson, Oklahoma. He came to New Mexico in 1890. Since coming to New Mexico he has roamed the Southwest as a cow puncher, horse breaker and all around cattleman. Mr. Lusk has a record and is known from coast to coast as one of the best horse breakers in the Western Country and there is many a cattle man from the Gulf of Mexico to the Pacific Coast that can testify as to his prowess in the saddle in roping wild steers.

For many years Mr. Lusk has worked as an all around cowhand in Uncle Steve Birchfield's cattle ranch, situated four miles from the Mexican Border on the east side of the Florida Mountains. Mr. Lusk has also worked with practically every cattle outfit in the Southwest including the Diamond A. Ranch. Mr. Lusk is now sixty four years old and still remembers many incidents that once happened in this once wild country. His life has been one colorful adventure after another and his reminiscences are typical of stories usually found only in Western fiction, but which are facts and events that have really happened in his life. For instance, Mr. Lusk vividly remembers when the Apache Kid once shot at him.

The Apache Kid was a tall rawboned slim half breed Indian with a vivid scarlet scar running across his right cheek. He spoke Spanish, Indian, and English and was once the terror of this western country. He never traveled alone, but always he had packs of from seven to twenty Apaches with him. One day Mr. Lusk started from Uncle Steve's ranch down into Bear Creek Canyon to get some horses. While he was in the canyon searching for the horses Mr. Lusk sighted what was apparently a cloud of dust; presently the cloud revealed itself into men on horseback. He took only time enough to ascertain who they were and his worst fears were confirmed. The band of horsemen were Apaches led by the renegade Apache Kid. The scar shining vividly in the brilliant sunlight. The Kid sighted Mr. Lusk and immediately started in pursuit, sending wild shots after his fleeing quarry; luckily, none of his shots took effect. Mr. Lusk, now thoroughly alarmed, was running for his life. He had covered quite a distance hiding and running from rock to rock when he spied one of his horses. To this day Mr. Lusk doesn't know how in a split second of time he jumped on the back of the frightened horse and escaped the doom that nearly overtook him. The Apache Kid, finally tiring of the sport, gave up the chase. Mr. Lusk believes now the Apache Kid merely shot at him to see him run and didn't intend any harm.

Situated on the south side of the Florida Mountains is a natural spring. This spring was named by the old settlers the Brass Kettle Springs due to its natural formation in the form of a brass kettle. The water is always running, it fills up the kettle from an underground vein. The water never runs out of the kettle, but the kettle is kept brimming full; the springs run into a canyon.

Near this spring in 1894 there occurred a battle between a regiment of colored soldiers from Fort Bayard and the Indians.

The country around Brass Kettle Springs was a favorite hunting ground of Mr. Lusk and Ed Slinger, a cowhand from the Birchfield ranch. On one of their numerous hunting trips they sighted the battle going on between the Indians and the soldiers. Mr. Lusk does not remember what cavalry the regiment of soldiers was, but more soldiers were killed in this battle than Indians; finally, the soldiers killed the Indian chief. This broke the morale of the remaining Indians and they fled. The old Indian chief is buried one quarter mile from Brass Kettle Springs. The soldiers are buried in the vicinity of the Springs also.

In this vicinity around the same years between 1894 and 1896—Mr. Lusk was then a young man and doesn't recall the exact year—an old prospector was camped four miles from Brass Kettle Springs. The old prospector had an old dilapidated covered wagon hauled by two big black mules. The Indians swooped down upon this poor old man, killed him and burned his wagon, including the mules which were tied to the wagon wheels. Mr. Lusk found his remains, the charred bodies of him and the mules, burned table ware, spoons, forks, knives, frying pans scattered around; of the wagon, only the iron in the wheels and of the body remained. The old prospector's skull was taken later into town and displayed in the various saloons in Deming at that time, among which were Mr. Hannigan's and Mr. Corbett's saloons. Mr. Lusk believes that to this day the petrified remains of the prospector and the mules' bones remain, a grim reminder of an awful tragedy of the early West.

Years later Walter Birchfield, son of Uncle Steve Birchfield, and Johnny Clemens had a battle right near Bear Creek Canyon on the Mexican border with about twenty Mexicans who were rustling cows into Mexico from the United States. Walter and Clemens stood their ground and shot it out with the Mexicans. Seventeen Mexicans were killed; the rest "turned tail." Walter loaded the heavy six shooters while Clemens fired. Walter was shot right through the knee. He had to have made a special heel for his shoe so he could walk. Mr. Walter Birchfield is now living in El Paso and to this day he still limps from that old wound.

In 1897 Mr. Lusk and other cattlemen went to Palomas, Mexico on cattle business. The Timoche Indians took the town of Palomas. They shot at two or three officers but nobody was hurt. The Indians took all the ammunition from the Custom House; then they went and took the groceries from the stores, but they paid for them in money. The next day there occurred a big battle at Boca Grande River. The Mexican government killed nearly all the Indians. Mr. Lusk and the other cattlemen climbed the mountains nearby and saw the battle progress through four days.

Mr. Lusk remembers many incidents in Deming in the early days of Deming. In those days they didn't have any picture houses as now, and gambling and racing constituted the main entertainment of the town.

Where Silver Avenue now stands it used to be a race track. Racing started about two weeks before the Fourth of July and continued till two weeks afterwards. Races were conducted on a

298

betting basis on the best horse. Mr. Lusk had a prize winning horse in those days and many a time he came through with flying colors.

Mr. Lusk still has a bridle that that horse used to wear. The bridle was handmade in Midland, Texas by Bob Casey of solid steel with a ten cent piece on each side of the bridle. The bridle was made in 1897. Mr. Lusk also has a quirt made of rawhide with Spanish Knots on the handle. This quirt rode with him on his many adventures in this colorful country.

Source of Information: As told by Walter Lusk.

Early History of Monticello

by Clay W. Vaden

In 1856 the Spaniards in this section of the Southwest taught the Indian tribes farming, building of simple huts with adobe, and even the difference between a man and a horse or any other brute, as a preliminary work toward their more difficult task of civilizing and later Christianizing them.

The Apache Chief, Indio Victorio and his son, "Washington," together with three daughters lived in La Canada Lamosa now known as Monticello. Other famous Indian chiefs who lived in this immediate vicinity were: Nana, Nagoloha, Mangas Coloradas, Esquirno, Chinago, Esqulfo, Parajito (Victorio's son-in-law), Carullas, and El Plumas.

In 1873 on the third of May, the various Indian tribes were greatly angered at General Hatcher's order for them to be moved from Ojo Caliente United States Government Fort, 12 miles north of Monticello, Sierra County to another Fort at San Carlos in what is now the state of Arizona.

The San Mateo and Black Range mountain area were favorite haunts of the Indians because of the big game to be found in abundance, and they resented very much having to leave their choice hunting ground.

Victorio and his band took matters into their own hands and went to the Fort to protect against being moved. On the way they met Cheffie Hill, an eighteen-year-old boy who was on his way to the commissary to buy some matches from Mr. Kelly who was in charge.

Chief Victorio and El Toribio Largo and Nagolcha asked the youth, "Where is George, el viejo?"

Cheffie answered, "He is in his adobe hut," and pointed it out to them.

When he returned with the matches he was surprised to find

the old man, his employer, in bed. He called to him several times and finally went to the bedside and lifted the covers and discovered that the old man had been murdered by the marauding Indians. George, el viejo, (the old man) was selected as the first victim because the Indians realized that he was one of the best scouts and sharp shooters in the white man's fort.

These same Indians killed five negroes that were hired to care for the officer's horses, and with a large band of their Indian braves terrorized the whites with their Indian raids and massacres.

As a means of greater protection the Spanish American families arranged for their homes to be built facing a plaza or court with only two entrances with massive gates placed at the Northeast and Southwest corners. The plaza was used as a natural fort in times of Indian dangers.

About the middle of September, 1880, the villagers received a message that Bishop Juan Bautista Lamy was expected to reach Sr. Chillis ranch near Fort Ojo Caliente. Knowing how treacherous some of the Indians were, a large party of men from Canada Lamosa rushed to meet their beloved Bishop. They got to the Fort just in time to save his life, for a large band of Indians bedecked in their war paint were dancing their war dance around the house where the Bishop was to have been entertained. Juan Pomenseno Trujillo, Pedro R. Montoya, Manuel Sanchez, and Jose L. Torres, "Pelecho," were among the oldest members of the rescuing party and when they gave the Indians the peace signal, Chief Victorio commanded his braves to abandon their blood-thirsty plans.

Grateful for his life having been saved in this manner, the Bishop vowed that he would establish a permanent Catholic Mission with a resident priest at Canada Lamosa, now Monticello, and this pledge was religiously kept and will be for all time to come.

In August 1881, the Indians and the residents of Canada Lamosa, together with the owners of the adjoining ranchitas fought quite a battle. Many Indians were killed and wounded and among the whites who were wounded were: Juan Pomenseno Trujillo, Sergeant Patterson, Bernabel Chavez, and Pedro R. Montoya. The scrimmage occurred about two miles from the Alfonso Bourguet ranch north of the present site of Monticello. Victorio and his tribe killed Jose Maria Sedillos, Pedro Vallegos, and though they retreated they ambushed and killed two young boys, Antonio Encinia, and Sisto Sedillos, who were only about twelve years of age. One beautiful Spanish senora, Placias Martinez, with a baby in her arms, was captured by the Indians and carried to their camp. When she became tired marching and carrying her baby, an Indian said, "Let me take the child," and grasping it by its little feet dashed its brains out.

Barnabel Chavez was herding Rafael Tafoya's goats on a hillside called Tenasco. The Indians surrounded him and were in the act of murdering him, as he was unarmed, when Francisco Montoya and his brother, Jose Montoya, who knew that the Indians had but recently killed four men, Julian---, Juan Trujillo, "Negor" Chavez, and Julio "El Mudo" (the dumb), arrived just in time to frighten the Indians away with their rifles.

About this same time, Manuel Chavez and another Spanish youth were on their way from Monticello to Nogal Canyon. At the San Jose canyon he and the other boy were captured by Victorio's Indian tribe. The Indians were planning to kill them when Victorio and Nagolcha arrived. Mr. Chavez called to his Indian friend, "Nagolcha, don't let these Indians kill us!"

Nagolcha told an Indian who was trying to make Sr. Chavez angry so that he would have an excuse to kill him, "You get away. Don't kill this white man."

Then another tribe of Indians came into view on the hilltop about 15 yards from them. Mr. Chavez recognized Victorio and called to him, "Victorio, don't let your Indians kill me and my companion."

Victorio talked in the Indian tongue to his braves and then said to Manuel Chavez, "No. Indians won't hurt a man from Canada Alamosa. But don't go any further. There are a lot of Apache Indians between you and Nogal Canyon. Now give my Indians all your cartridges and we will let you go free."

He refused to give away all his precious cartridges but handed over one to each of thirty Indian braves, keeping eleven for himself, thinking they might some day be very useful. But as fate would have it, an Indian squaw, Jusepe, came riding up at this moment and the Indians set up a clamor demanding that she be given a cartridge also, claiming that it would not be fair for him to keep an odd number so he was allowed to keep only ten cartridges.

Two days later this same tribe killed Mr. Matello Mirando who was the substitute mail carrier from San Jose Post. The Indians cut open the mail bags and scattered the torn and slashed bits of letters and papers until the hills were white like a stage snow storm had fallen.

Don Manuel Chavez, one of the oldest and most highly respected pioneer citizens of Monticello, New Mexico, although blind in his last years of life was a power in his home community, for he and his blind friend, Don Francisco Montoya, always give good advice to the younger generation who come to them to profit by their wisdom acquired by their years of varied experience. Two unique friends who visit these blind old gentlemen annually are two Indians from the Mescalero Reservation, Esquolfo and Chauano who, accompanied by a body guard of other Indians, make this long journey to secure some of their buried treasure in San Mateo Mountains and always leave new Indian carvings on the Indian Temple Cliff in picturesque Monticello Canyon.

Geronimo As a Hero

by Clay Vaden

Daughter of N.M. Pioneer Family Saved from Death by Geronimo, Has Happy Memory of Chief. Mrs. Al Shepard of Monticello Canyon Recalls Thrilling Events When Her Father Was Sergeant.

Having been saved from drowning by Chief Geronimo, Mrs. Al Sheppard of Monticello Canyon has a much more sympathetic appreciation of the old Apache Chief who is generally pictured by historians as a blood thirsty old savage, murdering men and women, pillaging and burning houses and kidnapping white children.

When a child, Mrs. Sheppard lived with her parents, Andrew and Cecilia Sheppard Kelley at Old Fort Ojo Caliente, 16 miles west of Monticello. She was born at the fort in 1882 and her father served as a quarter-master sergeant, manager of the commissary, postmaster, interpreter, and perfected a homestead claim nearby.

Saved by Geronimo

One spring day when she was a little more than two years old, Mrs. Sheppard relates, she was walking across a log footbridge crossing an arroyo which was running bank full with spring flood waters. She stopped to look at a horsehide staked in the water to soak so it could be cut into horsehide thongs, lost her balance and fell headlong into the swirling, muddy water.

Chief Geronimo, lounging in the doorway of a nearby adobe hut, witnessed the accident, ran down the trail to a place cut in the back where army mules were taken to water, plunged into the arroyo and grabbed the half drowned child as she was swept by in the current.

Thus Mrs. Sheppard maintains that she owes her life to the

old warrior. She recalls how the old chief pulled her from the water and carried her to her parents.

Historic Family

Life in the Kelley family is interwoven intimately in the history of the Southwest and the Sierra County in particular.

Mrs. Sheppard's mother came to the Southwest with her parents from Topeka, Kansas. She was graduated from Loretta Academy in Santa Fe, and was a musician.

Mrs. Kelley's life recorded some harrowing experiences in New Mexico. Only a short distance from the historic government fort, Mrs. Sheppard relates, stood the old Dodd Ranch, where women and children from miles around sought refuge in times of greatest danger during the Indian raids. The men folk assembled to stand guard because frequently the fort was virtually deserted when the soldiers were called to the trail of raiding savages.

Once under such conditions, Mrs. Kelley convinced her husband that the danger had passed, and late in the afternoon with their children they started for their own ranch.

About halfway between the fort and their homestead, a dozen Indians in full war regalia swooped down out of a small side canyon upon them, formed a ring around them and began a war dance punctuated with spine-chilling war whoops.

The dance came to a sudden and amazed termination when Rancher Andrew Kelley spoke to them in perfect Apache tongue. The leader gave a command for silence. The tribesmen squatted on the ground, and Mr. Kelley began a powwow with the young chief.

"The white men have taken our country, plan to make us go as prisoners to some distant reservation. We want this country along Monticello canyon, and the San Mateo mountains for our last hunting grounds," the young chief said, and at the same time demanded flour, coffee, bacon, and ammunition.

Sergeant Kelley promised them provisions but no ammunition, if they would come to the Kelley ranch at midnight. Eventually and after much conversation and bartering, Mrs.

Sheppard relates, the Indians accepted the proposal for food and permitted the Kelley family to go on home. Later the Indians arrived to claim their food.

Geronimo's Present

Mrs. Sheppard possesses a solid gold slide bracelet which she says Chief Geronimo gave Sergeant Kelley as a present for Mrs. Kelley. She says Geronimo represented that he got the bracelet in a raid along the Arizona-Mexico border.

Frank Kelley, who is Mrs. Al Sheppard's oldest brother, was taught by Geronimo to shoot with a bow and arrow.

Mrs. Sheppard now lives with her husband on the Los Alamos ranch in Monticello canyon on Elephant Butte lake shore. Other living members of the Kelley family who recall the stirring days of Indian warfare, are Mrs. Charles Anderson, of Kingston, Martin Kelley, captain in the U.S. army and stationed at Washington D.C., John C. Kelley, range boss for Ladder ranch in Sierra County, and Phillip Kelley, also employed at the home office of the Ladder ranch.

A True Indian Story, Stranger Than Fiction

by Clay W. Vaden

Pioneer heroes of early days of the Old West are fast dying out but today there lives in the picturesque little Spanish village of Placitas, New Mexico, a little old Spanish gentleman, Don Roque Ramos, whose life story sounds like an unusual, exciting romance.

He was born in 1852 in the state of Sonora, Mexico. When quite young, his oldest brother, Ursulo Ramos, who loved him better than his own life, persuaded their mother to let him take his young brother to live with him on a ranch some distance from their mother's home.

When twelve years of age, he was working on his brother's ranch with two men, a woman, and a little girl, Chonita, whom the husband and wife had adopted. Earlier in the day the husband had left the ranch house to go hunting. When they heard a shot, they thought the hunter had bagged some big game, but looking up they saw some Indians on the war path rushing toward them. Besides bows and arrows the warriors had some rifles. The man, woman, boy, and girl tried to run into the ranch house for safety but they had locked the door and in the excitement of the moment had great difficulty in opening it. While huddled in front of the door the Indians shot the poor woman thru and thru, and the bullet glanced and hit young Roque in his side but it did no great harm to him as the force of the bullet was spent. Finally, the young twelve year old boy succeeded in opening the door and the girl, Chonita, and he dragged the wounded woman inside and locked the door. The first shot they heard had killed the woman's husband.

The other Spaniard was taken captive by the Indians. He called for the door to be opened saying, "The Indians will not hurt you."

Young Roque replied, "How do we know they will not harm us when they have already shot this woman?" However, he remembered that his older brothers had always advised him to try kind treatment if he were ever captured by the Indians, so he opened the door. When he opened the door he saw the other man, Cosme ------, standing near the door. The Indians had stripped him of all his clothes and he was standing there stark naked with both his hands tied behind his back.

As soon as the door was open, the Indians stalked inside the house, finished killing the woman, took all the corn and other provisions and things they wanted, and took Roque and the little girl as captives. After this they started on their long homeward journey back to their reservation near Ojo Caliente, north of Monticello, N.M. (they had gone on one of their frequent raids down into Old Mexico). The two young captives were being driven ahead of the Indians. Hearing a terrible cry, young Roque looked back just in time to see the other Spaniard captive pierced thru and thru by a lance in the hands of one of the cruel Indians. The boy, very much frightened, started to run but was held by the Indians. The heartless Indians were on their way, leaving the Spaniard lying in the path gasping his dying breath.

Soon after this harrowing experience the older brother, Ursulo Ramos, returning with several other men to the ranch discovered what had happened as they could see the Indians and the two young captives.

The oldest brother begged to be allowed to follow and attack the Indians because he had previously promised his mother to take the very best care of his young brother and he said he would rather die than have to tell his mother about his young brother being captured by the Apache savages. The other Spaniards had to tie him until they could persuade him how useless and dangerous this would be, outnumbered as they were, for they feared the Indians would retaliate by killing the two young captives. The older brother hated to go and report the sad happenings to his mother for he loved his younger brother very dearly and all his lifetime blamed himself for what had happened.

For three years young Ramos was kept a captive with the Indians ruled over by their Apache Chief, Chiz, near Ojo Caliente.

During this time he tried his very best to get along peaceably with them but when they spoke to him in their own language and he could not understand they often beat him cruelly. One day while cutting timber his Indian guard gave him an order which he could not understand and the guard became so angry that he struck the young lad over the head with a spear. An inch scar is still to be seen on the right side of his head. Another Mexican boy captive that Roque recognized told him every time he tried to escape the Indians punished him severely, so the young boys did not make many attempts to escape. Whenever the Indians saw the two Mexican boys talking together they would separate them. Then, too, the little girl, Chonita, begged him not to escape unless he could take her with him.

At one time some other Spanish-Americans, some of Trujillo's forefathers were camped with the Indians. Meat was scarce in camp and a large bear was seen nearby. The Indians, however, were superstitious concerning bears. They had a legend to the effect that a bear has a close relationship to an Indian, so they would not kill a bear. One of the Indians forced the young captive boy, Roque, to fire at the bear (the first time he had ever shot a rifle). He succeeded in hitting the bear in the neck and the other Mexicans rushed into camp and finished killing the bear with pistols. The bear was very fat, so besides using part of the meat for food the Spaniards rendered up much lard. But the superstitious Indians refused to eat any of the bear meat and even separated camps from the Spaniards. They used young Roque Ramos to carry messages back and forth between the two camps.

Once, after robbing expedition or raid, the Indians were followed and attacked by some English speaking people and the Indians scattered and fled. The young captive was knocked down by one of the Indians but afraid to go to the white men as he could not speak English and was afraid they would think he was an Indian as he was dressed like one, and kill him. He hid in the brush until the white men left. Then he came out from his hiding place and found his way back to the Indians. After his voluntary return to them, the Indians trusted him and were kinder to him.

At the time he did finally make his escape he and the other two captives were separated so he never learned what became of the other Spanish boy or the little girl, Chonita. The Indians had a camp near what is now Perfecto Silva's ranch a few miles north of Monticello. At times the Indians were friendly with the Spanish settlers at Monticello and Placitas, and on these occasions the young captive had become acquainted with several of the Spaniards living in these villages. Seeing that the Indians were all getting drunk and preparing to go on one of their raids against the whites, the young boy decided to take advantage of their drunken condition and run away at night. He did so and ran to the ranch where an old Spaniard joined him and together they ran along the creek in Monticello canyon until they reached the home of Jesus Garcia at Placitas. Garcia took him on horseback to Paraje, a village below San Marcial which has now disappeared for in later years it was covered by the impounded waters of Elephant Butte Lake. Gregorio Sedillos, a wealthy Spaniard living there adopted Roque Ramos and Garcia returned to his home at Placitas that same night so the Indians would not suspect him of helping the boy to escape.

When less than 20 years of age young Ramos wrote to his relatives in Sonora, sending the letter by a friend to Tucson, Arizona, who met a man from Sonora who knew his brothers made a special trip to try and persuade Roque to return with him to Old Mexico and see his mother and the other members of their family, and remained here more than a year because he had promised his mother faithfully to bring his young brother back with him, but was unsuccessful.

Later the young boy who had escaped from the Indians bought a home in Placitas where he continues to live surrounded by many relatives—the Sedillos, Aragons, and others.

When about twenty years of age he married Miss Sacramenta Sedillos, the daughter of Senior Gregorio Sedillos, the man who adopted him. They had one son. The mother died when the son was seven years of age. His second marriage was to Miss Josefita Gutierez who is still living and they have a large family, five daughters and one son and about twenty-five grandchildren living.

A sister, Mrs. Maria Jesus Asebedo, who now lives in Harshu, Arizona, has visited him in recent years and an older brother still lives in Sonora.

For the last five years Senor Ramos' health has been failing and at times his tongue has been partially paralyzed but even with this slight handicap he can tell a story of real adventures that will grip the attention of the younger generation.

List of Illustrations

Bibliography of New Mexico Federal Writers' Project Documents

WPA—Works Progress Administration/NMFWP—New Mexico Federal Writers' Project

NMSRCA—New Mexico State Records Center and Archives

A Church as a Stable, W. M. Emery, August 14, 1936, NMFWP, WPA #227, NMSRCA

A Good Bluffer at the Toll Road, W. M. Emery, July 12, 1937, NMFWP, WPA #239, NMSRCA

A. J. Ballard: Buffalo Hunter 1875-1876, Georgia B. Redfield, March 8, 1937, NMFWP, WPA #185b, NMSRCA

A Last Steal—Pioneer Story, Mrs. Benton Mosley, September 14, 1936, NMFWP, WPA #191, NMSRCA

A Navajo Superstition Leads to the Killing of a Negro Slave, Dr. Louis Kennon, July 1865, NMFWP, WPA #92b, NMSRCA

A Pioneer Horse Race, J. Aveguel Maes, July 25, 1936, NMFWP, WPA #153, NMSRCA

A True Indian Story, Stranger Than Fiction, Clay W. Vaden, July 23, 1936, NMFWP, WPA #230, NMSRCA

Albuquerque in 1853, From the Personal Writings of Franz Huning, B. W. Kenney, April 18, 1939, NMFWP, WPA #179, NMSRCA

Albuquerque Pioneers: Merchants and citizens of the past era, B. W. Kenney, April 24, 1939, NMFWP, WPA #179, NMSRCA

Battles of the Civil War in Apache Canyon, Bright Lynn, September 1, 1938, NMFWP, WPA #93, NMSRCA

Bear Moore, Mrs. W. C. Totty, November 20, 1937, NMFWP, WPA #153, NMSRCA

Biographies of Mr. and Mrs. Thomas O. Boggs, Carrie L. Hodges, November 5, 1936, NMFWP, WPA #239, NMSRCA

Blizzard Happenings, Mrs. Benton Mosley, July 20, 1936, NMFWP, WPA #208, NMSRCA

Buffalo Hides, Kenneth Fordyce, February 5, 1937, NMFWP, WPA #188, NMSRCA

Buffalo Hunting in the Seventies, Georgia B. Redfield, March 1, 1937, WPA#185a, NMSRCA

Buster Degraftenreid as Buffalo Hunter, Mrs. Belle Kilgore, July 3, 1937, NMFWP, WPA #192, NMSRCA

C. D. Bonney: Old-Timer Interviewed, Georgia B. Redfield, no date, NMFWP, WPA #186a, NMSRCA

Camp Maddox, H. P. Collier, September 24, 1936, NMFWP, WPA #182, NMSRCA

Cesaria Gallegos, Annette H. Thorp, September 23, 1940, NMFWP, WPA #153, NMSRCA

"Chihuahua" District Roswell: The Hot Tamale Man, Georgia B. Redfield, December 27, 1936, NMFWP, WPA #187, NMSRCA

Cook's Spring, Betty Reich, January 25, 1937, NMFWP, WPA #86, NMSRCA

"Cump" Reed—On the Vermejo, Kenneth Fordyce, October 3, 1938, NMFWP, WPA #190b, NMSRCA

Early Days around Deming, Frances E. Totty, August 9, 1938, NMFWP, WPA #213, NMSRCA

Early Days in Silver City and Grant Co., Frances E. Totty, June 1, 1938, NMFWP, WPA #203, NMSRCA

Early Days in the Southwest, By Otho Allen, Billie the Kid, Frances E. Totty, February 25, 1938, NMFWP, WPA #212, NMSRCA

Early Historical Events in New Mexico: Political Riot at Mesilla, John E. McClue, May 24, 1938, NMFWP, WPA #196, NMSRCA

Early History of Monticello, Clay W. Vaden, July 16, 1936, NMFWP, WPA #182, NMSRCA

Early Settlements in Northeastern New Mexico, W. M. Emery, no date, NMFWP, WPA #205, NMSRCA

Early Settlers of Llano Quemado by George Torres, L. Raines, August 3, 1938, NMFWP, WPA #223a, NMSRCA

Extracts from "The Story of Early Clayton, New Mexico by Albert W. Sharp," D. D. Sharp, March 27, 1938, NMFWP, WPA #238, NMSRCA

Foster's Log House, Kenneth Fordyce, June 27, 1938, NMFWP, WPA #190b, NMSRCA

Fruitland, Mrs. R. T. F. Simpson, August 15, 1936, NMFWP, WPA #226, NMSRCA

Geronimo as a Hero, Clay Vaden, February 14, 1936, NMFWP, WPA #86, NMSRCA

Grant County Cattle War, Mrs. W. C. Totty, July 26, 1937, WPA# 202, NMSRCA

His First Bear, W. M. Emery, June 7, 1937, NMFWP, WPA #153, NMSRCA

History of Juan Tafoya (Marquez), A. A. Carter, May 12, 1936, NMFWP, WPA #242, NMSRCA

In the Early '80's, Betty Reich, July 17, 1937, NMFWP, WPA #213, NMSRCA

In the Year 1893, Rosario O. Hinjos, no date, NMFWP, WPA #233b, NMSRCA

Incidents of the Early '80s As Told by W. Weatherby and Maurice Coates, Frances E. Totty, July 20, 1938, NMFWP, WPA #203, NMSRCA

Interview with Mrs. William C. Heacock, Janet Smith, July 20, 1936, NMFWP, WPA #179, NMSRCA

Interview: William Cooley Urton, Georgia B. Redfield, September 14, 1936, NMFWP, WPA #186a, NMSRCA

Juan y el oso ladron (Juan and the Robber Bear), Lou Sage Batchen, May 21, 1941, NMFWP, WPA #224b, NMSRCA

José's Escape from the Indians, L. Raines, no date, NMFWP, WPA #153, NMSRCA

Killing of Charlie Bachelor and other Incidents, Frances E. Totty, June 5, 1938, NMFWP, WPA #197, NMSRCA

Letter from Franciscan Fathers, Rev. L. Holtkamp, September 30, 1940, NMFWP, WPA #223, NMSRCA

Letter to Mr. Etheridge, C.A. Thompson, October 18, 1940, NMFWP, WPA #196, NMSRCA

Mora, L. Raines, March 24, 1936, NMFWP, WPA #216, NMSRCA

Old Bank Building—Raton, Manville Chapman, May 13, 1936, NMFWP, WPA #190a, NMSRCA

Old Days in San Marcial In Socorro County, Manuel Berg, March 22, 1937, NMFWP, WPA #231, NMSRCA

Old Timers Stories: Captured, W. M. Emery, October 17, 1936, NMFWP, WPA #238, NMSRCA

Old Timers Stories: Indians, Firewater, a Night of Terror, W. M. Emery, October 12, 1936, NMFWP, WPA #238, NMSRCA

Old Timers Stories: Elizabeth Fountain Armendariz, Marie Carter, May 3, 1937, NMFWP, WPA #197, NMSRCA

Old Timers Stories: Volney Potter, Marie Carter, June 28, 1937, NMFWP, WPA #197, NMSRCA

Old Timers Who Saw Coffin and Knew Pall Bearers Say Billie the Kid Is Dead. Albuquerque Journal, June 23, 1938, NMFWP, WPA #211, NMSRCA

"On the Vermejo in '74," Kenneth Fordyce, February 27, 1937, NMFWP, WPA #189, NMSRCA

Other Incidents of the Southwest, Col. Totty, no date, NMFWP, WPA #86, NMSRCA

Pioneer: Daily Robbery, Kenneth Fordyce, March 26, 1936, NMFWP, WPA #188, NMSRCA

Pioneer Stories: Letter from L. W. Collins, Betty Reich, August 2, 1936, NMFWP, WPA #213, NMSRCA

Pioneer Story: Daniel Carabajal, Edith L. Crawford, January 23, 1939, NMFWP, WPA #210, NMSRCA

Pioneer Story: Dick's Hat, Katherine Ragsdale, August 3, 1936, NMFWP, WPA #200, NMSRCA

Pioneer Story: Elerdo Chavez, Edith L. Crawford, July 7, 1938, NMFWP, WPA #210, NMSRCA

Pioneer Story: Henry Lutz, Edith L. Crawford, March 14, 1938, NMFWP, WPA #179, NMSRCA

Pioneer Story: Jose Apodaca, Edith L. Crawford, May 1, 1939, NMFWP, WPA #210, NMSRCA

Pioneer Story: Mary Lee Queen, Edith L. Crawford, June 13, 1938, NMFWP, WPA #210, NMSRCA

Pioneer Story: Mrs. Annie E. Lesnett, Edith L. Crawford, September 7, 1938, NMFWP, WPA #210, NMSRCA

Pioneer Story: Mrs. Mary E. Burleson, Edith L. Crawford, February 19, 1938, NMFWP, WPA #189, NMSRCA

Pioneer Story: Nellie Reily, Edith L. Crawford, May 16, 1938, NMFWP, WPA #210, NMSRCA

Pioneer Story: Years Ago . . . Betty Reich, June 24, 1936, NMFWP, WPA #213, NMSRCA

Pioneer: The Day of Petitions, Kenneth Fordyce, March 26, 193-, NMFWP, WPA #188, NMSRCA

Plains Man Whips His Wife Seventeen Miles, Mrs. Benton Mosley, August 10, 1936, NMFWP, WPA #208, NMSRCA

Pursued by Wolves, Kenneth Fordyce, February 19, 1937, NMFWP, WPA #153, NMSRCA

Reminiscences of Mr. Joe Prewitt, Mrs. R. T. F. Simpson, October 14, 1936, NMFWP, WPA #225, NMSRCA

Rough Diamond, Mrs. Frances Totty, September 10, 1937, NMFWP, WPA #153, NMSRCA

Rumaldo Martinez: Indians on the Martinez Ranch, Kenneth Fordyce, August 29, 1938, NMFWP, WPA #239, NMSRCA

Santa Fe Weekly Gazette—Aug. 12, 1865, NMFWP, WPA #92a, NMSRCA

School Days in Old Taos, James Burns, October 24, 1936, NMFWP, WPA #233a, NMSRCA

Societies—Severity Corruption, Reyes Martinez, April 12, 1938, NMFWP, WPA #89 NMSRCA

Spanish Pioneer: Kidnapped, J. C. Roybal's Story, L. Raines, August 31, 1936, NMFWP, WPA #220, NMSRCA

Spanish Pioneer: The Captive Shepherd Boy, Robert Lucero's Story, L. Raines, August 31, 1936, NMFWP, WPA #153, NMSRCA

Spanish Pioneer: Mañana, L. Raines, March 24, 1936, NMFWP, WPA #216, NMSRCA

Stories of Old Time Happenings In and Around Deming As told by Walter Lusk, John M. Trujillo, no date, NMFWP, WPA #213, NMSRCA

Tales of Old-Timers: Harry Coddington, Mrs. Eleanor DeLong, December 14, 1936, NMFWP, WPA #214, NMSRCA

The Blizzard of 1889, W. M. Emery, July 6, 1936, NMFWP, WPA #239, NMSRCA

The Burial of Old Jose As Told by Christiana Baros, Mrs. Lou Sage Batchen, January 9, 1939, NMFWP, WPA #224a, NMSRCA

The Death Sentence, Reyes N. Martinez, August 3, 1936, NMFWP, WPA #236, NMSRCA

The Fulfillment of a Longed For Wish, Reyes N. Martinez, April 2, 1937, NMFWP, WPA #234, NMSRCA

The Horse Trader As told by Juan M. Romero, Lester Raines, July 25, 1936, NMFWP, WPA #234, NMSRCA

The Kidnapping of a Rancher's Daughter, Mrs. F. Totty, NMFWP, WPA #153, NMSRCA

The Magician, Kenneth Fordyce, June 20, 1938, NMFWP, WPA #188, NMSRCA

The Murder of Judge and Mrs. McComas, Mrs. W. C. Totty, no date, WPA#203, NMSRCA

The Navajos As told by Sarah Garcia, L. Raines, August 31, 1936, WPA#61, NMSRCA

The New Mexican, November 10, 1865, NMFWP, WPA #92a, NMSRCA

The Old Windmill, Las Vegas Plaza, Lester Raines, May 13, 1936, NMFWP, WPA #227, NMSRCA

The Peace Plot As told by Patricio Gallegos, Mrs. Lou Sage Batchen, November 29, 1938, NMFWP, WPA #224a, NMSRCA

The Round Mountain Fight, W. L. Patterson, July 20, 1936, NMFWP, WPA #217, NMSRCA

The Snow Bride As told by Rumaldita Gurule, Mrs. Lou Sage Batchen, January 9, 1939, NMFWP, WPA #224a, NMSRCA

Turley's Mill—A Frontier Barony, B. W. Kenney, January 30, 1939, NMFWP WPA #235, NMSRCA

"Uncle" Bill Jones and George Pickett (of Last Chance Canyon and Sitting Bull Falls, southwest of Carlsbad), Allen B. Cooke, August 12, 1936, NMFWP, WPA #200, NMSRCA

Valverde Battlefield, Clay W. Vaden, April 18, 1936, NMFWP, WPA #232,
    NMSRCA
Wetherell's Death, Bright Lynn, December 13, 1938, NMFWP, WPA #92b,
    NMSRCA

Names Index

CPSIA information can be obtained
at www.ICGtesting.com
Printed in the USA
LVHW111605290922
729617LV00018B/153